rejuvenile

rejuvenile

KICKBALL, CARTOONS, CUPCAKES, AND THE REINVENTION OF THE AMERICAN GROWN-UP

Christopher Noxon

THREE RIVERS PRESS • NEW YORK

Grateful acknowledgment is made to the following for permission to reprint previously
published material:

Pearson Education, Inc.: Excerpt from *We Come and Go* by William S. Gray,
Dorothy Baruch, and Elizabeth Rider Montgomery. Copyright © 1940 by Scott,
Foresman and Company. Reprinted by permission of Pearson Education, Inc.

Simon & Schuster Adult Publishing Group: Excerpt from *The Partly Cloudy Patriot* by
Sarah Vowell. Copyright © 2002 by Sarah Vowell. Reprinted by permission of Simon &
Schuster Adult Publishing Group.

Library of Congress Cataloging-in-Publication Data
Noxon, Christopher.
        Rejuvenile: kickball, cartoons, cupcakes, and the reinvention
of the American grownup / Christopher Noxon.—1st ed.
Includes bibliographical references and index.
        1. Inner child.   I. Title.
BF698.35.I55N69   2006
305.240973—dc22   2006003859

ISBN 978-1-4000-8089-2

Printed in the United States of America

Design by Barbara Sturman

10   9   8   7   6   5   4   3   2   1

First Paperback Edition

To my playmates,
Charlie, Eliza, and Oscar

contents

ADULTS ARE JUST
OBSOLETE CHILDREN AND
THE HELL WITH THEM.

— Dr. Seuss

rejuvenile

WHOLE NEW STAGES ARE SPRINGING
UP AT SEVERAL POINTS ALONG
THE ROUTE OF ADULT LIFE, LIKE
BRIGHT NEW CITIES, POSING MANY
NEW OPPORTUNITIES AND
DISCONTINUITIES THAT SIMPLY HAVE
NOT BEEN PART OF THE MAPS IN
OUR MINDS.

—Gail Sheehy, *New Passages*

introduction

ONCE UPON A TIME, boys and girls grew up, set out on their own, and, somewhere along the way, matured. They got serious. They set aside childish things.

Or so the story goes. Today, the process of maturity is rarely so straightforward. To be sure, many people pass the usual milestones and comfortably take their place as respectable, responsible adults. But such upstanding citizens are getting lonelier all the time. Most of us reach adulthood feeling entirely out of sync with what sociologists call age norms. And a few of us are waging all-out assaults against long-standing notions of young and old, mature and immature, novice and pro.

rejuvenile

Captains of industry now appear on the cover of *Business Week* with Super Soaker water pistols and Sea-Monkey executive sets. College students with lunchbox purses and Muppet berets walk arm-and-arm with moms sporting rock star tattoos and sparkly T-shirts poached from the Junior Miss section. Middle-aged professionals download pop song ringtones and punctuate correspondence with language swiped straight from the schoolyard. ("You da man!" says the insurance adjuster. "Duh!" agrees the building inspector.) Crowds flock to Las Vegas to catch Cirque du Soleil's latest extravaganza, watch pirates clash sabers in front of Treasure Island hotel, or hop on one of several casino roller coasters. Twentysomething nightclubbers in London wear school uniforms and dance to songs they dimly remember from their teen years, then finish the night with cupcakes and bowls of macaroni and cheese. In Manhattan crowds cram bars for all-adult spelling bees or drop $100 for tickets to *Avenue Q*, a show about maxed-out credit cards and career disappointments performed by googly-eyed puppets. Senior citizens team up for extreme-sports excursions and Disney World vacations.

It's hard to imagine adults in previous eras so unashamedly indulging their inner children. But these are not the adults of twenty years ago. They constitute a new breed of adult, identified by a determination to remain playful, energetic, and flexible in the face of adult responsibilities. Whether buying cars marketed to consumers half their age, dressing in baby-doll fashions, or bonding over games like Twister or stickball, this new band of grown-ups refuses to give up things they never stopped loving, or revels in things they were denied or never got around to as children. Most have busy lives and adult responsibilities. Many have children of their own. They are not stunted adolescents. They are something new: rejuveniles.

Evidence of the presence and influence of rejuveniles is all around. The Cartoon Network boasts bigger overall ratings among viewers aged eighteen to thirty-four than CNN, Fox News, or any cable news channel. Half of the visitors to Disney World are childless adults, making the Magic Kingdom the number-one adult vacation destination in the world. Department stores stock fuzzy pajamas with attached feet in adult sizes. The website Classmates.com reports that 60 million people have signed up to reunite with long-lost school pals. ("There's something about signing on to Classmates.com that makes you feel sixteen again," reported *60 Minutes*.) The Entertainment Software Association reports that the average age of video game players is twenty-nine, up from eighteen in 1990. Hello Kitty's mouthless cartoon face now graces toasters, taxicabs, and vibrators.

Such pop culture ephemera reflect seismic social change. Adults are now putting off marriage longer than ever (the average age of women at their first marriage was 25.3 in 2003, a historic high; for men it was 26.9); they are waiting longer to become parents (middle and upper classes are deferring childbirth ten to twenty years later than their parents); and living with their parents far longer than ever (38 percent of single adults aged twenty to thirty-four live with their parents). Meanwhile, the few remaining rites of passage that historically set adults on a new course in life are fading or losing their meaning altogether. For some, this erosion of clear boundaries has created confusion and uncertainty. But for rejuveniles, it means a sudden lifting of sanctions that would otherwise discourage a sudden impulse to collect Japanese manga, indulge a love of Scooby-Doo, or develop a Necco Wafer habit.

This book describes the new breed of adult and explains the rejuvenile's role in shaping and reflecting our age. I identify the demographic forces that fostered the rejuvenile, survey the pastimes rejuveniles have built their lives around, and look back at a remarkably similar outbreak of kidcentric enthusiasm one hundred years ago. I talk with adults who live with their parents, parents determined to reexperience childhood via their offspring, and grown-ups who dress and play and party like they did in high school. And I take a hard look at Walt Disney, the most influential rejuvenile of the twentieth century, the person most responsible for the blurring of adult and child sensibilities. By loitering in a territory established as the exclusive dominion of children, rejuveniles are challenging a rarely examined assumption: that one's age should dictate one's activities, social group, and mind-set. Adults we meet in the following pages are blithely shredding those scripts to confetti, giggling as the pieces float to the ground.

The Tricky Business of Rejuvenile Classification

I should specify right at the start precisely what I mean by this new word: *rejuvenile* describes people who cultivate tastes and mind-sets traditionally associated with those younger than themselves. It can be used as an adjective ("Those sneakers are so rejuvenile"), a noun ("Pee Wee Herman's brand of rejuvenalia is more subversive than Raffi's"), or, infrequently, a verb ("Most adults are busy rejuveniling," filmmaker Randy Barbato remarked on National Public Radio shortly after I coined the word in an article in the *New York Times*). Existing phrases that describe aspects of the phenomenon include *Peter-pandemonium,* which describes the resurgent popularity of retro brands among the coveted 18–34 demographic, *kidult,* defined by an Italian toy company as "adults who take care of their kid inside," and *Twixter,* a buzzword coined by *Time* magazine to describe unsettled adults who "hop from job to job and date to date, having fun but seemingly going nowhere." Even the *Concise Oxford Dictionary* has weighed in, defining *adultescent* as "a middle-aged person whose clothes, interests, and activities are typically associated with youth culture."

It should be clear that this is not simply a Gen X phenomenon. While the ranks of the rejuvenile are heavy with adults hanging on to juvenile pursuits into their thirties and forties, evidence of what British sociologist Frank Furedi calls "a self-conscious regression" is plentiful among adults in midlife and beyond and even among teenagers. Rejuveniles are young and old, male and female, American, European, and Japanese. That said, in talking to the toy collectors, candy connoisseurs, and other playful characters who match the rejuvenile profile, I couldn't help noticing certain demographic similarities. Most are from the urban upper classes—free time and disposable income being important components in the rejuvenile lifestyle. Those in creative fields and high technology are more likely to display rejuvenile tendencies. There appear to be more male than female rejuveniles. And while it's tempting to dismiss the rejuvenile phenomenon as yet another indulgence of well-off white folks, there are plenty of counterexamples—witness the curious enthusiasm for Tweety Bird among Latino immigrants, or the mind-boggling rejuvenalia on display in Japan.

Once I had a name for them, rejuveniles seemed to pop up everywhere. One of my wife's coworkers bragged about celebrating her thirtieth birthday at Chuck E. Cheese and often spent Saturday nights with her girlfriends dressed in frilly nightgowns watching Disney movies. One day at the playground I found myself sharing a teeter-totter with a grinning mom while our kids sat nearby casually sucking on sippy cups. Then there was the night my wife and I went to a dinner party where we spent the bulk of the evening playing board games and talking about how psyched we were for the *Willy Wonka* remake.

It should also be clear that not all rejuveniles are alike; rejuvenile behavior is measured in degrees. The Lexus-driving, straitlaced executive who keeps a stash of vintage baseball cards is a rejuvenile, but he's a whole lot less rejuvenile than, say, Mr. Rogers. Further muddying the task of rejuvenile classification is the fact that the rejuvenile impulse is often mixed up with other entirely unrelated compulsions. Collectors who hoard Barbie dolls or Matchbox cars, workaholics who blow off steam riding $3,000 mountain bikes, lackadaisical commitment-phobes who fend off adulthood skipping between jobs and skirting intimacy—all these characters are in part rejuvenile, but each is compelled by his or her own particular blend of fuzzy ideals, lofty rationales, and unexamined neuroses—the sum total of which may have little to do with an adult appreciation for the mind-set and culture of kids.

Of course, rejuveniles aren't alone in mangling traditional age norms. As they double back along the developmental pathway, rejuveniles can't help but notice a rush in the opposite direction. These days, actual children can't seem to ditch childish things fast enough—my eight-year-old niece, for one, canceled our weekly appointment to watch *The Powerpuff Girls* on the grounds that the show was "for babies." (I protested, arguing that if she was right, I should be wearing a diaper. She agreed that maybe I should.) Market research confirms that children used to identify themselves as kids until the age of twelve but are now more likely to advance out of kiddie culture at eight or nine. It's as if there's a limited amount of room in the domain of childhood—and rejuveniles have taken it upon themselves to reclaim territory left vacant by all the rapidly advancing kids.

There's more to it than that, obviously. Among the forces at work in the rapid erosion of childhood are overscheduling parents, overcompetitive schools, and the insidious advance of Tween marketing (out with the rugged playclothes and plush dolls; in with the micro-miniskirts and pricey gadgets!). While kids often flounder in the fast-moving current toward maturity, adults heading the other direction have a far easier time. Unlike prematurely mature children, most rejuveniles have at least a tentative grasp on the demands of independence and responsibility. Notwithstanding the occasional sad case who amasses action figures while nagging his mom for gas money, rejuveniles generally take pride in controlling their own destinies. They can move comfortably in the world of practical realities, but they also enjoy reaching back into childhood without being treated like a baby or being stripped of the ability to make their own decisions. They've grown up enough to finally appreciate the pleasures of being a kid.

In Which the Author Cops to His Own Rejuvenile Tendencies

Growing up, I always had a pretty clear idea of what it would be like to be an adult. My adult self was always, it seems, gripping something—a steering wheel, a coffee mug, a carving knife. Unlike the twitchy, loudmouthed kid I was, my adult self was confident, serious, commanding. I reached conclusions, made decisions, took charge. I wasn't sure when I'd take possession of all those great props and wondrous powers, but I liked to think that one day soon my turn would come and I'd be pulled aside, presented with a leather-bound rule book, and sent out to get on with the serious business of adulthood.

The book failed to materialize on my eighteenth birthday, or on my twenty-first, or at any of the events that supposedly signal the onset of adulthood. I had somehow managed to finish school, get married, and start a career without ever feeling particularly grown up. I couldn't deny the rapidly mounting evidence that I wasn't a kid anymore—a receding hairline, a slowing metabolism, a wife, two children, and a late-model minivan. But amid all this, I found myself drawn to ostensibly childish things. At twenty-five, I rediscovered kickball, joining a group of other adults in a local park on Sunday afternoons to play a game we all learned as schoolkids. At thirty, I loafed around the house in Converse All Star sneakers and an Oscar the Grouch T-shirt. At thirty-five, I read books about a wizard named Harry and watched a cartoon about a sea sponge named SquarePants.

Even parenthood didn't put an end to my childlike ways. If anything, caring for small children gave me license to try things the adulthood rule book would surely list as felonies— tag-playing, paint-splattering, Popsicle-eating. I was thus forced to recognize the plain but painful fact that playing with kids is not the same thing as being a kid. My children's experience stacking Legos or watching cartoons was plain and pure; mine was spiked with kitsch, a small swirl of rebellion, and a vague sense of shame. At thirty-five, shouldn't my interests have been more sensible—mutual funds, say, or lawn care? What was an otherwise well-adjusted and relatively responsible adult getting out of PlayStation, green Popsicles, or the Muppets? Shouldn't I have outgrown all this by now?

It was from that seed of doubt that this book took root. Talking first to friends and peers and then going out and doing two years of intensive research, I was first relieved—then genuinely shocked—to discover how many like-minded adults there were. People all over have simply stopped acting their age. I came to think of the border between adulthood and childhood as a Cold War checkpoint, once spotlit and armed, now unguarded and porous. Today there is simply no sanction against childlike enthusiasm, little shame in childish impulsiveness, no one to stop us from cultivating pleasures that adults of yesteryear were pressured to abandon the moment they entered the workforce. It's worth noting what we've lost in the process (fedoras were spiffy; civility is always nice), but there's no denying how much freedom adults have gained. The spectacle of fully grown adults behaving like toddlers or teens might seem comical, even undignified, but let's be honest: Traditional adulthood didn't do us many favors. As we'll soon see, what we now think of as adulthood is mostly a remnant of the Industrial Revolution, a set of standards established to encourage regularity, stability, steadfastness, and other virtues that aren't worth half as much now as one hundred years ago.

Why Now, Why Here, Why at All?

Meeting this motley assortment of adults who share similar tastes, enthusiasms, and insecurities, one question pops up again and again: why? Twenty years ago, a grown man who built a skateboarding ramp in his backyard or filled his office with superhero paraphernalia would be viewed as softheaded or not quite all there. Today, he's more likely to be celebrated as iconoclastic and hip. What happened in such a brief period to bust down the walls that once kept adult interlopers locked away from things loved by children?

Most obviously, the rejuvenile is a product of affluence and abundance. It's hard to nurture your inner child when you're struggling to keep food on the table. While a surplus of discretionary income has certainly given adults the means to more fully realize their aspirations, that doesn't explain why other, more mature pursuits—bridge, anyone?—have simultaneously fallen from favor. Rejuveniles themselves say their attraction to kiddie culture is at least in part a response to uncertain, anxious times—the terrorist attacks of 2001, followed by infectious disease scares, a convulsing stock market, war overseas, and natural calamities at home have generated a strain of free-floating anxiety that seems uniquely sated by childlike comforts. As explained by Cyma Zarghami, general manager of the children's network Nickelodeon, whose flagship cartoon SpongeBob SquarePants emerged after the 9-11 terrorist attacks as a totem of chaotic playfulness for kids and adults (a full 26 percent of SpongeBob's audience in 2003 was over eighteen), we are simply seeking comfort in jittery times: "Especially around 9-11 and the war, we're all attracted to someone who's ridiculously optimistic," says Zarghami. "I can't see how that's a bad thing."

Other more immediate demographic changes are shaping the rejuvenile character. At work, looser hierarchies have eased long-standing pressures to conform—witness row upon row of cubicles piled high with lunch boxes, action figures, and Beanie Babies. At home, changing gender roles have blurred traditional roles of authority, prompting many adults, both men and women, to identify with their kids in ways their parents would have found ridiculous. And perhaps most significantly, the fact that we're living as many as seven to eight years longer than adults fifty years ago has kept us in tune with our childlike sides longer than ever. As our life spans stretch out, whole new stages of development are emerging—those periods of adult life that Gail Sheehy calls "bright new cities." In the absence of uniform zoning laws, it's perhaps not so surprising that many of us have reconstructed the carnivals, playgrounds, and nurseries that provided the backdrop for our most vivid early memories.

Many rejuveniles offer a more straightforward explanation for their tastes: They just like this stuff. The culture of children, they tell you, brims with qualities—wonder, adventure, absurdity, make-believe—in short supply in the adult world. Those qualities may be associated with childhood, but they're essentially, even primitively, human. A century ago, Walter Crane, the illustrator of the first picture books, spoke of how the new medium gave him license to "revolt against the despotism of facts," a sentiment shared by many of today's rejuveniles. "Comics get past our adult critical defenses," explains Pulitzer Prize–winning cartoonist Art Spiegelman. "Like the best stuff in kid culture, they appeal to our lizard brains."

One of the most creative and dedicated rejuveniles I encountered while working on this book is Jake Austen, a thirty-five-year-old Chicago native whose life revolves around activities that grown-up men of past eras would find highly unusual: He's a stay-at-home dad, a freelance editor of children's books, a sometime puppeteer, and a producer of a local kids' TV show that might be described as a cross between *American Bandstand* and *Sesame Street*. Austen also happens to be the nation's foremost expert on Alvin and the Chipmunks, part of a genre of kids' music known affectionately as "rodent rock." The satisfaction he gets studying arcane corners of kiddie culture isn't about nostalgia, he insists. "I don't pretend to be a child," he says. "I like this stuff because it makes me laugh and feel good. A good thing that appeals to a child is universal, after all—it should appeal to everyone forever."

Sucked In by the Tractor Beam

Media professionals offer similar reasoning to explain why kiddie culture has gotten so cool among grown-ups. Ads for cartoons, plush toys, and even themed hotels appeal to adults with a familiar spiel: for kids from eight to eighty. Fun for the entire family. Age ain't nothing but a number. In Hollywood, where adults can command million-dollar salaries while dressing like sixth-graders on their way to a playdate, this sort of "we're all kids deep down" pitch has less to do with an embrace of human nature than simple economics. It's about casting the widest net possible, appealing to the youngest common denominator. That's the key to the success of *The Simpsons,* Harry Potter, *Star Wars, The Incredibles,* and on and on—they are, to borrow a bit of ad jargon, "bi-modal," entertainment that operates on multiple levels.

The ascendancy of such all-ages fare reflects rejuvenile tendencies, but it's also clear that it encourages them. The tone of the culture has changed, with flourishes of fluorescence appearing in places previously colored in subdued, muted hues. Adults who scoff at superhero movies, MTV, or the latest movie from Pixar risk coming off as snobbish, uptight, or—worst of all—out of touch. Some rejuveniles admit that their attraction to kid stuff is at least partially driven by a desire to stay young in a culture that equates being young with being cool and being old with being irrelevant. It's a troubling notion, one that all rejuveniles at some point or another must come to terms with—that a lifelong barrage of media attention aimed at youth has created a cultural tractor beam, drawing older consumers back into the target market. By so lavishly fixating on youth, the market presents those who are no longer young with a stark choice: Buy in or be forgotten.

The label "rejuvenile," then, isn't meant to be entirely celebratory, or for that matter pejorative. It's value-neutral. Rejuveniles are geniuses, mavericks, oddballs, and crackpots. They are people whose refusal to give up cherished qualities of childhood has bettered themselves and the world. But they can also be lost souls whose taste for childish things is creepy at best. Sex fetishists in jumbo diapers, flaky devotees of inner-child therapies, Michael Jackson—there's no shortage of fringe-dwelling, off-putting characters to populate the doomsday scenarios of social critics concerned about what they call "a crisis in maturity."

"Something has gone horribly wrong," writes psychologist Frank Pittman in his book *Grow Up!: How Taking Responsibility Can Make You a Happy Adult,* part of a curious self-help/sociological genre that argues that the cultural obsession with youth is to blame for a host of personal and social ills. "Our times are enamored with youth; we seek to escape the confusion of social change by lustily celebrating the freedom of adolescence while dreading the still, calm contentment of maturity and age." Pittman is one of a growing faction of social critics who see the rejuvenile impulse as destructive, regressive, and, quite possibly, a harbinger of the collapse of Western civilization. Commentators from what might be called the Harrumphing Codger School of Adulthood look back wistfully to a time when young people endured epic hardship (world wars, economic depression) and emerged as restrained and productive adults.

Among the most ardent Harrumphers is Canadian semiotician Marcel Danesi, whose book *Forever Young: The Teen-Aging of Modern Culture* rails against adult enthusiasm for slang, street fashions, and pop music. "For some reason since the 1960s, some rock musicians feel impelled to constantly rant and scream against anything that exists in society," he writes. Then there's poet Robert Bly, who warned in *The Sibling Society* that we've become a society of "half-adults built on technology and affluence" that risks sliding "into primitivism and those regressions that fascism is so fond of."

The alarm Bly and his compatriots raise is basically, I think, reactionary; something about the sight of college kids chilling out to *Teletubbies* or grandmas at Grateful Dead concerts offends them to the core. But they also raise a question of basic social order: If all the adults are busy tap-dancing, skateboarding, or otherwise unleashing their inner pipsqueak, who will be left to get things done, ponder complicated questions, and clean up the mess?

Many of the rejuveniles in this book share this concern, but most of us have a hard time working up much righteous indignation about the idea that we are a nation of Peter Pans squandering our most vital years behaving like children. We figure, with characteristic simplicity, that the world is big enough to contain all sorts of adults, some sober-minded and civilized, some not so much. And many have discovered that it's possible to be mature in many ways and immature in many others, that one can lead a happy and healthy life that includes charity *and* skateboarding, G-8 summit position papers *and* midnight cupcakes, long stretches of concentrated seriousness *and* mad fits of impulsiveness. Rejuveniles can be moral, political, religious, and also frivolous, impractical, and off-the-charts silly.

I do harbor my own doubts about the rejuvenile character (mostly about the difficulty of cultivating a childlike part of oneself without resorting to childishness, discussed in chapter 7), but there's not a lot of teeth-gnashing in the following pages. Instead, we meet an assortment of playful, conscientious, competent adults who are dedicated to the obligations they've incrementally taken on. For every hopelessly sheltered loner or self-centered flake, we encounter a dozen who have gained the practical skills and emotional resilience of adulthood without sacrificing the prizes of childhood—the spontaneity, the curiosity, the toys. To these rejuveniles, being a grown-up means being done growing. And if there's one thing rejuveniles fear, it's the notion of being done. The games, the play, the refusal to get serious and buckle down—what respectable adults see as indulgence, triviality, and pettiness, rejuveniles see as proof that they're still open to change, still searching, still in formation.

Whatever your conclusion—whether rejuveniles are ushering in a new era of freedom or leading a mass movement of irresponsibility—the fact is that rejuveniles are dramatically redefining what it means to be an adult. Their example is setting new norms, shifting expectations, and forcing everyone from marketers to social scientists to reexamine canonical rules of their business. And while some may dismiss the phenomenon as just another fad that will soon wear thin, there's a wealth of history to suggest that rejuveniles represent the crest of a cultural current that has been swelling since the dawn of the Industrial Age. As we'll soon see, rejuveniles are direct descendants of a disparate group of reformers, misfits, and eccentrics who led a familiar assault on dominant age norms a century ago.

ONE

roots of the rejuvenile

I DON'T WANT TO GO TO SCHOOL
AND LEARN SOLEMN THINGS. NO ONE
IS GOING TO CATCH ME, LADY, AND
MAKE ME A MAN. I WANT TO BE A
LITTLE BOY AND HAVE FUN.

—J. M. Barrie, *Peter Pan*

Before he was a cash cow for Walt Disney, an inspiration for Steven Spielberg, and an obsession for Michael Jackson, Peter Pan was simply a revelation. When J. M. Barrie's play *Peter Pan,* subtitled *The Boy Who Wouldn't Grow Up,* opened at the Duke of York Theater in 1904, it announced the arrival of something entirely new. The theatrical fashion of the time was for so-called problem plays, heart-wrenching melodramas that dealt with social ills and political complexities. Parting that gloom was Barrie's tale of a flying boy, his fairy sidekick, and their adventures in a faraway land where children remained children forever. Part farce, part pantomime, part inside joke, *Peter Pan* was a tale of pirates and fairies told in the sophisticated language of adults. Based on tall tales Barrie spun to amuse the five sons of a local barrister—his favorite being a rascal called George whom he met in Kensington Gardens when the boy was all of five—*Peter Pan* was the sort of cross-generational sensation that would become a model for mass entertainments of the next one hundred years.

First of the preteen heroes, Peter Pan attracted a rabid following of young matinee fans. But his real power was over a generation raised on fairy tales and nonsense rhymes and now anxiously adjusting to the social changes and gadgetry of a new century. On the night of the premiere, according to Barrie biographer Andrew Birkin, "the elite of London society, with few children among them, emulated Sentimental Tommy by 'flinging off the years and whistling childhood back.'" Wistful, lighthearted, and condemned by a chorus of critics who saw no good in such open celebration of childishness, *Peter Pan* was the first of the rejuvenile blockbusters.

Peter Pan was all the more resonant because it was the product of a celebrated public figure who shared his hero's deep ambivalence about adulthood. James Matthew Barrie was a small and moody Scotsman with a bushy mustache and no interest whatsoever in growing up in any conventional sense. Of this, he'd apparently always been sure. "Greatest horror—dream that I am married—wake up screaming," the eighteen-year-old wrote in his college diary. "Grow up and have to give up marbles—awful thought." While Barrie eventually did get married, to a comely stage actress named Mary Ansell, he made few other concessions to adulthood. When he wasn't locked away in his study, Barrie liked nothing more than practicing magic tricks, wrestling his giant St. Bernard, and most of all, playing with the sons of barrister Llewelyn Davies, whom he dressed as pirates, wrote stories for and about, and kept entertained with his vast knowledge of cricket, fishing, and Sir Walter Scott.

There has never been any evidence that Barrie's relationship with the Davies boys was anything but friendly, but their closeness has nonetheless prompted psychoanalytic suspicion and prurient interest ever since. Critics have scoured his biography for clues to explain Barrie's lifelong fight against traditional adulthood. Was he stunted by the death of his older brother, the doting of his indulgent mother, or the rejection of his loveless wife? All those things undoubtedly had a profound impact on Barrie, but one ultimately learns very little attempting to attach this misery or that to his rejuvenile tendencies. Barrie's legacy has less to do with his private sorrow than his articulation of childhood as a poetic and primitive life force that can linger long after its expected expiration. More than a fairy tale, *Peter Pan* announced the arrival of a new and enduring breed of adult.

The Invention of Adulthood

When I set out to learn about the roots of the rejuvenile, I didn't expect to find much. I figured a quick historical survey would turn up little scraps here and there—a few childish eccentrics in ancient Rome, maybe a popular children's game in Colonial America, perhaps a juvenile fashion craze from the 1920s. But early in my search for historical precedents, one thing became clear: This has all happened before. In seemingly every book I opened on social history, children's literature, or popular culture, I landed again and again on parallels from the same few decades. 1865: *Alice's Adventures in Wonderland* is embraced by children and adults. 1893: Grown-ups flock to the first amusement park at the World's Fair in Chicago. 1893: The first newspaper comic strip, featuring a one-toothed, bald-headed ragamuffin called the Yellow Kid, is published. 1907: The Scouting movement is founded by a self-described "boy-man." And at the very peak of that kidcentric period was the 1902 premiere of *Peter Pan,* which neatly summed up the myth of the eternal child.

For rejuveniles today, all roads lead back to *Peter Pan* and the turn of the twentieth century. The natural capacities of children, which for centuries had been viewed as weak and wayward, were over the course of these few years discovered as a primary source of inspiration and profit. It would be another century before the rejuvenile rebellion we know today, but resistance to what historian Woody Register calls "the enfeebling prudence, restraint and solemnity of growing up" began here, with the first flight of Pan and the dawn of the twentieth century.

The temptation today is to think of adulthood as a historic and natural fact. In a 2004 essay on "The Perpetual Adolescent," Joseph Epstein wrote that historically, adulthood was treated as the "lengthiest and most earnest part of life, where everything serious happened." To stray outside the defined boundaries of adulthood, he wrote, was "to go against what was natural and thereby to appear unseemly, to put one's world somehow out of joint, to be, let's face it, a touch, and perhaps more than a touch, grotesque." A quick survey of history, however, reveals that adulthood is neither as ingrained or ancient as Epstein and other Harrumphing Codgers assume. Before the Industrial Revolution, no one thought much about adulthood, and even less about childhood. In sixteenth-century Europe, for instance, "children shared the same games with adults, the same toys, the same fairy stories. They lived their lives together, never apart," notes historian J. H. Plumb.

This shouldn't suggest that people in olden times didn't distinguish between kids and grown-ups. Of course they did. The distinction forms the basis of rites of passage that are as old as human history, as well as some of more recent vintage. Amazonian initiation rites, Jewish Bar and Bat Mitzvahs, Muslim *Khtme Qur'ans,* Christian confirmations, American debutante balls—all serve the same basic function: to formally announce the end of childhood and the assumption of new duties and freedoms. It's a mistake, though, to confuse maturity with adulthood. The maturity celebrated in traditional rites of passage—assured variously by the onset of menstruation, the acquisition of literacy, or the ability to stalk and slit the throat of a large prairie mammal—is not the same thing as the idea of adulthood hatched a century ago by a coterie of Victorian clergymen and society ladies. Maturity is old. "Adulthood" is new.

The fact is that, for most of human history, age simply didn't matter much. Everyone from Aristotle to Dante had idly puzzled over the comparable merits of each stage of life, with an obviously middle-aged Aristotle arguing that middle age was best, since young people exhibited too much trust and old people too little. But such distinctions were mostly made by philosophers; for average people, age was more a matter of biology than identity.

Children got the hard end of this bargain. For more than two thousand years, from antiquity to the eighteenth century, children had little of the special status they now enjoy. Young people were mostly treated as deficient, imperfect creatures whose lives and interests were largely unimportant and certainly nothing any adult would want to emulate. There's some disagreement about precisely when adults first developed an awareness and feeling for childhood. French historian Philippe Aries's seminal 1961 book *Centuries of Childhood* held that childhood was "discovered" between the fifteenth and seventeenth centuries; other scholars have pointed to eighth-century monks who wrote admiringly of children's capacity for wisdom and honesty.

In any case, it's clear that today's obsession with the moral and physical development of children is relatively new. As recently as the eighteenth century, the word *childhood* was under-

stood to mean littleness, immaturity, irresponsibility, helpless-
ness, and irrationality—qualities that adults actively sought to
restrain in their offspring and suppress in themselves. Partially, this low status was a product of hard biological and social realities; life spans were relatively brief and rates of infant
mortality were so high that parents often had seven or eight
children in the hopes that one or two would survive. "People
could not allow themselves to become too attached to something they regarded as a probable loss," Aries wrote. Even
those children who survived the perils of nature sometimes
didn't survive their elders; infanticide was a routine and often
legal practice through the Middle Ages. The depiction of children in medieval paintings offers an eerie demonstration of
the perspective informing such atrocities—children appear as
genderless and shrunken, with the extended limbs and mature
features of people three times their size.

It's hard to figure which was worse: this sort of confused
disregard, or the equally common notion that children—
indeed, childhood itself—were inherently depraved. Seventeenth-
century Puritans called children "young vipers" and "filthy
bundles of original sin." French cleric Pierre de Berulle put it
succinctly, writing that childhood is "the most vile and abject
state of human nature, after that of death." The best a child
could hope for was to be born to a relatively enlightened parent like Renaissance essayist Michel de Montaigne, who extolled the entertainment value of children, saying they could be
valuable to adults "for our amusement, like monkeys."

It's no wonder then that adults felt no need to revisit a period either completely disregarded or derided as wretched at
the core. This conventional wisdom also helps explain why
children grew up so much more quickly in centuries past.
While it's now common for people to spend much of their

twenties and thirties anguishing over when (or if) they'll reach adulthood, for most of human history people were thrust into fully adult roles at a truly tender age. Children as young as six were hustled off to work in eighteenth-century England. A sixteen-year-old Caucasian boy who today would be lucky to find work as a fry cook had, as recently as 1750, all the rights and responsibilities of a full-grown man—he could enter contracts, enlist in the army, even work as a physician. Girls of the same period obviously had fewer choices but were similarly hustled into maturity; American common law of Colonial times held that girls were fit for marriage at the age of seven.

What historian Howard Chudacoff calls "age consciousness" blossomed in the 1800s, as people who grew up in an agrarian society moved into cities, took jobs in offices and factories, enrolled their children in public schools, and began to sample the products of a new mass media. In this new modern world, how old you were suddenly took on all sorts of new meanings. In premodern America, many people didn't even know how old they were; now birthday celebrations were treated as important holidays. At the same time, the idea of age-appropriate activity took hold, encouraging parents to enroll children in age-based grades in school and buy books and periodicals written specifically for children, adolescents, and young adults.

This emphasis on age formed one basis for new Victorian notions of etiquette in an era when propriety was endlessly analyzed and debated. Mainly, these new codes of conduct dealt with class distinctions and gender roles. But the nineteenth-century preoccupation with correct behavior also resulted in a novel organizing principle: adulthood. The word *adult* can be traced back to the 1500s but didn't gain currency until the

1700s. It quickly became synonymous with Victorian ideals of "character," such as obligation, integrity, manners, duty, service, honor, and, above all, self-control. While adulthood was a mark of moral virtue, it was also a product of economic necessity. You were an adult when you could provide for yourself and your family, when you met the job requirements for a new urban industrial economy.

And from the start, adulthood was conceived as a perilous, deadly serious business. "The only safety for man or woman is to do exactly right" was the advice to youngsters in the popular 1889 family magazine *Worthington Annual*. "The least deviation from the path of rectitude may lead to the direst disaster." Those who wished to avoid ruin were urged to conform to a set of standards meant to encourage civility, consideration, and charity, but which in retrospect appear about as natural and forgiving as the rib cage–crushing corsets of the era.

The spirit of adulthood is best appreciated by perusing a class of literature that was first embraced at the close of the nineteenth century: etiquette books. The first popular guides for manners appeared in the 1830s; by the turn of the century, etiquette was an American industry, with an average of six new titles appearing every year advising readers how to speak, dress, play, work, walk, eat—even think. Readers of all ages and classes could find codes of conduct in titles including *Manners for Men, How to Be a Lady, Behave: Papers on Children's Etiquette,* and *The Negro in Etiquette: A Novelty*. They ranged in heft and price from an 872-page tome known as *The Encyclopaedia of Business and Social Norms* to slim volumes that could be had at newsstands for a dime. Taken together, they represented how-to guides for would-be adults. The modern gentleman or lady, decreed these new arbiters of correct behavior, must constantly struggle to suppress habits of spontaneity, emotion, impulsiveness—in short, anything at all childish.

Self-control, formality, and seriousness were core values of the new adult character. A proper gentleman, advised the 1890 family magazine *Sunday Chatterbox,* "is not easily led astray by dreamy and speculative people . . . He very rarely, if ever, makes a fool of himself—this is a great thing to say of a man." Young women meanwhile were advised to associate only "with those who are truly serious . . . Nothing is more unbecoming than trifling, giggling, and talking nonsense to each other." Adults of both genders should keep a tight lid on any "undue emotion, whether of laughter, of anger, or of mortification," advised John Young in his 1883 book *Manners, Etiquette and Deportment.* "Keep yourself quiet and composed under all circumstances," he continued. At the dinner table, readers were cautioned to avoid jokes, anecdotes, or linguistic flights of fancy ("Puns are always regarded as vulgar," he sniffed).

Equally offensive was the spectacle of mature women dressed in "gay hats" and "gaudy silk gowns" better suited to girls, wrote Florence Hull Winterburn in her 1914 guide *Principles of Correct Dress.* Elder women of the day had been swept up, Winterburn clucked, in "an age of fast motors and flying machines and feverish craze for excitement," and had thus cast aside suitable brocades and satins in favor of "youthful" materials and styles. "What a loss of dignity!" she wrote. "What a pathetic admission she makes of dwarfed intelligence, deficient womanly qualities and little magnanimity of spirit! Not to know how to grow old gracefully is a grave fault, a serious misfortune, for the growing old is inevitable, in the eyes of the world, whatever the individual may think."

This prohibition on modes of speech and dress associated

with youth didn't end with adults. Children had their own separate code of conduct based largely on the suppression of natural energies of childhood. "We cannot give ourselves over entirely to the pleasure of having fun," Isabelle Thompson Smart wrote in the 1911 volume *What a Father Should Tell His Little Boy.* "Boys even at your age must begin to bear in mind the great purpose for which they are brought into the world, for you have often thought, I am sure, of the time when you would be a full-grown man."

This emphasis on childhood as a brief and mostly miserable period of preparation wasn't shared by all etiquette experts. In his 1883 manual, Young allowed that "children should not be prohibited from laughing and talking at the table." The rationale for this uncharacteristically liberal allowance was justified on physiological grounds: "Joyousness promotes the circulation of the blood, enlivens and invigorates it, and sends it to all parts of the system, carrying with it animation, vigor and life."

Birth of the Child Admiration Society

There had always been, of course, adults who found solace, diversion, and even divine inspiration in youth. Ancient Romans erected temples to the goddess of youth Juventas, grantor of growth and preservation. In the fifth century, Pope Leo the Great preached that childhood was "mistress of humility, rule of innocence, model of sweetness." In his poem "The Passionate Pilgrim," Shakespeare considered the merits of each stage of life and came down strongly in favor of youth: "Youth is nimble, age is lame/Youth is hot and bold, age is weak and cold/Youth is wild, and age is tame."

rejuvenile

But the forces of child admiration found their ultimate champion in Jean-Jacques Rousseau, the Romantic philosopher whose 1762 treatise *Émile* argued that childhood should be nurtured and celebrated rather than replaced with "civilized values" that were, in his view, mostly contemptible. While Rousseau's commitment to children was entirely abstract—he reportedly abandoned his own to orphanages—his philosophy was still vastly influential, filling a wellspring of idealism that became a primary source for Romantic poets, who were fond of depicting children as angelic creatures of deep wisdom and acute sensitivity.

It was left to popular authors and illustrators of the nineteenth century to venture through doors opened by the Romantics to describe what had so far been hidden from adult view—worlds of untold poetry, mystery, and nonsense. Even as the Victorian mavens of manners sought to snuff out childishness in children and adults, a growing movement of artists and writers was finding inspiration in the early years. Among the more popular proponents were illustrators of a new genre known as "toy books"—forerunners to today's picture books—who marshaled sophisticated graphic and printmaking techniques for the sole purpose of pleasing children. Walter Crane, who illustrated some forty toy books between 1865 and 1898, wrote that creating art for children had a profound impact on his craft and life. "In a sober and matter-of-fact age, toy books afford perhaps the only outlet for unrestricted flights of fancy open to the modern illustrator," Crane wrote.

A fellow agitator for the forces of childlike absurdity was Edward Lear, who surely ranks as a grand master of the rejuvenile movement. Lear, twenty-first in a family of twenty-two, found early recognition as an illustrator of exotic birds. While living on the estate of an English lord who had commissioned him to draw the animals in his private menagerie, Lear took out pen and paper to amuse his benefactor's young nieces and nephews. Lear's *Book of Nonsense,* filled with surreal line drawings and nonsense verses like "The Quangle-Wangle's Hat" and "The Dong with the Luminous Nose," became an unlikely bestseller in 1872, standing in stark contrast to the improving literature for children of the era. While other authors of children's books built their stories around moral values, Lear seemed interested only in merriment, a quality he found sorely lacking among his peers. "The uniform apathetic tone assumed by lofty society irks me dreadfully," he wrote in his diary. "Nothing I long for half so much as to giggle heartily and to hop on one leg down the great gallery—but I dare not."

While artists found newfound freedom exploring the imaginations of children, a different class of Victorians found inspiration in their day-to-day struggles. In 1862, Charles Dickens's *Oliver Twist* focused attention on the plight of poor street children. Mark Twain celebrated the heroism of boyhood in his bestseller *The Adventures of Tom Sawyer,* and then, in 1885, ditched the third-person literary voice entirely and gave in to the language of his adolescent hero in his follow-up *The Adventures of Huckleberry Finn.* The popularity of these stories launched a raft of youthful protagonists who represented the restless, irrepressible American spirit. Critics saw in Peter Pan the spirit of youth and liberty, who led children out of their antiquated Old World nursery into the Neverland of the New World.

Then there was Louisa May Alcott's *Little Women,* the thinly fictionalized 1868 account of the author's childhood in New England. Alcott's father, Bronson, the transcendentalist educator, had devoted much of his career to extolling the virtues of childhood, famously declaring, "Childhood hath saved me!" Louisa recast his philosophy as warm domestic drama, lovingly depicting topics that had long been far beneath the regard of sophisticated adults. Girls read Alcott to identify with heroic Jo. Adults read Alcott to be transported back to a childhood lost.

Dickens, Twain, and Alcott celebrated childhood, but they did so at a proper Victorian distance. To them, and indeed to most adults of the era, childhood was a blessed period that could only be briefly and bittersweetly recollected by adults. Oliver Twist goes from street foundling to adopted son. Jo grows up, channels her high spirits, and becomes a mother. Huck's raft is broken apart in the tide. The message was explicit: Childhood, which might be as adventurous as Huck's, as warm and sweet as Jo's, as rough-and-tumble as Oliver's, ultimately fades.

The Forefathers of Rejuvenalia

This hard fact proved vexing to three other celebrated authors of the era. Hans Christian Andersen, Charles Dodgson, and J. M. Barrie were all enormously popular authors whose lifelong struggles to stay immersed in the receding tides of childhood produced great books and various measures of melancholy and dysfunction. They differed in many respects: Andersen was an itinerant Danish poet whose stories were largely based on bitter childhood memories. Dodgson was a well-to-do mathematics professor and Anglican deacon with an unnerving fondness for little girls. Barrie was a married playwright and novelist who came alive in the company of boys. But the three men also had much in common: Each was a socially awkward and anxious adult who found refuge and inspiration in the company of children, though, interestingly, none had children of his own.

Born in a small town in Denmark in 1804, Andersen was eleven when his father, a cobbler who amused his children with a homemade puppet theater, died in the small room they shared at the back of the family shop. Andersen spent much of his youth in bitter poverty, trying his hand in the theater, ballet, and, finally, as a writer. After writing a forgettable work of scholarly nonfiction, he published a collection of stories including "The Little Mermaid," "The Ugly Duckling," and "The Princess and the Pea." He spent much of the rest of his life as a vagabond, living in rented rooms and hotels around Europe, releasing tepidly received attempts at serious literature and apologizing for his work for children. Painfully shy, Andersen never married and seems never to have come to grips with himself or his work.

More depressing still is the biography of Charles L. Dodgson, the English mathematics professor better known by his pen name, Lewis Carroll. One summer afternoon in 1862, Dodgson took the three young daughters of the don of his school, including an ethereally pretty ten-year-old called Alice, for a row on the Oxford River. "The day was hot and the children wanted to have a story told for them," according to an account by children's literature scholar Bettina Hurlimann. "So the young lecturer complied, his mind relaxing in the drowsy heat and his thoughts, which did not tire so easily, following paths of their own making." Those paths led down a rabbit hole and into a bizarre world of mad hatters, sage snails, and Unbirthday Parties, which the young Alice Liddell persuaded him to write and illustrate. The little manuscript he prepared was later expanded into the books *Alice's Adventures in Wonderland* and *Through the Looking Glass*. While Dodgson is credited with changing the direction of children's literature by favoring stream-of-consciousness narrative over traditional morals and lessons, there was a sly point to all his silliness. Aligning himself with a child struggling to make sense of an incomprehensible world, Dodgson communicated to all his readers, young and old, what many had suspected all along: Adults might claim to know the truth of things, but their "truth" is actually so much nonsense.

Dodgson himself never made peace with fellow adults. Afflicted with a lifelong speech impediment, Dodgson still managed to make the acquaintance of children wherever he found them: in parks, at railroad stations, in the homes of friends and colleagues. His campus office was filled with trinkets, toys, puzzles, and other doodads collected for the amusement of young visitors. "With his child friends, Dodgson could be at ease," wrote biographer Lisa Bassett. "His stammer usually disappeared, and he could give his humor and playfulness free rein." Toward the end of his life, he estimated that he had between two hundred and three hundred friendships with children, the vast majority of whom were girls between the ages of ten and twenty. Dodgson claimed that he was "out of his element altogether" with boys. Dodgson's attraction to girls aroused suspicion; Alice Liddell's mother ended their association when her daughter was still a child. Judging from his tortured diaries and the imploring letters he sent to parents of children he invited for visits that often lasted several days or more, Dodson's motives were not entirely pure. Whether or not the creator of Wonderland was a pedophile is still an open question.

J. M. Barrie's life was also shaded by heartache, disappointment, and sexual intrigue. After receiving worldwide acclaim for *Peter Pan,* Barrie continued to court the family that had served as a model for the Darling clan; he showered the Davies boys with gifts and adored their mother, Sylvia, causing some irritation both in his wife and in Sylvia's husband. In 1908 the arrangement fell apart when Arthur Llewelyn Davies died after a painful bout with facial sarcoma. Barrie's pledge to support his surviving wife and children, along with ongoing marital problems—"Love in its fullest sense could never be felt by him or experienced," his wife wrote later—prompted Mary to file for divorce. Two days after the divorce was granted, any possibility that Barrie might assume a permanent role of patriarch ended when Sylvia discovered that she too had cancer. She died the following year, leaving Barrie to care for the five boys. Peter Davies, the eldest of the five brothers and the model for Pan, grew up resenting Barrie and called *Peter Pan* "the terrible masterpiece" before burning correspondence between the writer and his adopted sons. In 1960, he jumped onto the rails of an approaching subway car. The British press reported it as "Peter Pan's Death Leap."

It's not the most inspiring story for rejuveniles looking for historical heroes. Indeed, it's tempting to view the biographies of all these childlike, childless Victorians as cautionary tales: *Bad things happen to grown-ups who don't forsake childish things.* If Barrie had quit cavorting with boys, if Dodgson had stopped writing love letters to young girls, if Andersen had put away the puppets and settled down—if all three had just buckled down and acted their age, surely their lives would have been happier, and at the very least, the adult embrace of childhood wouldn't carry such sinister associations today.

But who can say whether some other personal demon or

social pressure—here, the question of sexuality looms large—wasn't the true source of their misery? More important, if they had managed to grow up and keep their immature sides in check, they never would have created the works they did. And however tortured these men were, their stories radically redefined our conception of childhood and its value for adults. Previously, the dreamworlds of children were treated as curiosities, of interest mainly to mothers or nursemaids. But with the arrival of the Ugly Duckling and Alice and Peter, childhood took on mythic dimensions and the ideal of the inner child found an enduring place in modern Western culture.

Kiddie Culture Goes Commercial

Poets, playwrights, and artists of the nineteenth century discovered the magic world of childhood. When the natives of that magic world grew up, they made a discovery of their own: Childhood was also an industry.

At the dawn of the twentieth century, people were living longer, having fewer children, and devoting more of their time and money to the products of a new mass culture. Telephones, electric lights, moving pictures, and horseless carriages offered everyday proof of the might of a new consumer economy. The arrival of novelties like Kewpie dolls, the Ferris wheel, and Cracker Jack offered evidence that it was also a ruthlessly efficient generator of kiddie culture.

The commercialization of childhood had a profound impact not only on children but also on adults. No longer were things loved by children relegated to the nursery or nurtured by the occasional tweedy eccentric. Magazines, catalogs, and department stores hyped a new class of goods designed primarily for children, including clothing (pinafores, knicker-bockers, sailor suits), housewares (high chairs, school desks, and nursery furniture), and special foods (Jell-O, Campbell's soup). Meanwhile a new class of toys and games promoted the power of play and offered instant escape from the drudgeries of modern life. Most adults kept their focus on the concerns of adulthood; kids' stuff, it was understood, was strictly for kids. Still, there were occasions when the tantalizing promise implicit in these new goods proved too tempting for even the most respectable adult.

Bankers, manual laborers, and even a few senators were among those caught up in a craze that took off in 1889 like, according to one commentator, "a plague of locusts." Pigs in Clover was a handheld puzzle containing four marbles that rolled around a tiny maze. Most toys of the period were primitive, decorative, or reflective of the age-old Puritan suspicion of play. Previous bestsellers included a board game called the New Game of Virtue Rewarded and Vice Punished and another known as The Siege of the Stronghold of Satan by the Christian Army. Pigs in Clover (which took its name from a popular expression meaning happy, "clover" being a stand-in for "shit") was simple, silly, and highly addictive. Within two weeks of hitting the stores, toy factories were shipping eight thousand a day, and everyone from society ladies to congressmen were passing hours "driving the pigs." Upon its release in London, a newspaper ran a story on the "New American Device for the Propaganda of Insanity," describing it thusly: "Apparently an infant's plaything, it can take a strong man in its octopus-like tentacles and swirl him in the wildest abyss of insanity."

Other kiddie fads followed. As described by historian Charles Panati in his account of *Fads, Follies and Manias,* adults led a rush on Ping-Pong paddles, nets, and balls in 1903 as kitchen tables in homes across both sides of the Atlantic were cleared to make room for a game variously known as wick-wack, click-clack, whiff-waff, and flim-flam. A few years later Ouija boards became a fashionable party game. And in 1912, a line of elfin, androgynous dolls known as Kewpies became favorite gifts for children and adults alike. Such all-ages hits fueled a toy industry boom. By 1910, there were more than five hundred toy manufacturers in the U.S., with sales amounting to $40 million. Toys were the spoils of the new urban industrial economy, objects of pure fantasy and impracticality.

Adults who indulged their playful impulses, however, faced censure in a society that was still solidifying its sense of adulthood. A rapidly growing middle class bought more than 10 million "pedaling machines" in 1895, prompting alarm among critics who saw menace in the undignified spectacle of doctors, salesmen, and respectable ladies whizzing about on bicycles. "Claims were made that before the turn of the century, America would be a nation of physically exhausted illiterates," writes Panati. The problem was even taken up in Congress. Ultimately, though, another mode of transport did the job of getting grown-ups off their bikes, as automobiles gained favor and bicycles were relegated to gifts for children.

Even the teddy bear aroused the suspicion of Harrumphing Codgers of the day. The first teddy bear was stitched in 1903 by a toy store proprietor in Brooklyn as a tribute to President Theodore Roosevelt, who had made headlines when he refused to shoot a bear cub on a Mississippi hunting trip. A sign reading "Teddy's Bear" was hung in the store window over a plush brown doll with movable arms and button eyes. Soon America was gripped by a condition newspapers dubbed

"Bearmania." Women wore teddy bear scarf pins; gentlemen carried teddy bear briefcases. All of which was fine with the president himself, who had never fully advanced out of his own boyhood. ("You must always remember," a friend of Roosevelt's once remarked, "that the president is about six.") Still, the proliferation of stuffed animals among adults provoked some alarm. A Michigan priest, according to historian Marvin Kaye in his book *A Toy Is Born,* "denounced the teddy as an insidious weapon leading to the destruction of the instincts of motherhood and eventual racial suicide."

More proof that children's tastes could be mined for grown-up profits was printed in kaleidoscopic color in every major newspaper of the era. The first popular comic strip was published in 1893, during a fierce circulation war between Joseph Pulitzer and William Randolph Hearst. To lure readers to a new Sunday supplement, Pulitzer hired a technical draftsman and sometime cartoonist named R. F. Outcault to draw a strip called *Hogan's Alley.* Outcault brought a new juvenile spirit to a form that is as old as Paleolithic cave drawings, capturing the antics of a wisecracking gang of street kids led by The Yellow Kid. After the strip took off, Hearst offered Outcault a bigger salary and stole him away, announcing that he was launching his own supplement consisting of "eight pages of polychromatic effulgence that makes the rainbow look like a lead pipe." Soon the two rival papers were both running Yellow Kid cartoons and New York was blanketed in images of this strange barefoot ragamuffin who lived and played on streets teeming with hoboes and goats and littered with tin cans and old boots.

Outcault went on to create another seminal comic strip featuring Buster Brown, a scamp in a sailor cap who represented a far rosier, more domesticated vision of American childhood. Other comic artists celebrated children as free spirits and fearless truth tellers in strips including the *Katzenjammer Kids, Little Jimmy, the Kin-der-Kids,* and *Stubbs and Tipple.* But the single most sublime vision of childhood in the funny pages was *Little Nemo in Slumberland.* Looking more like the work of an art nouveau designer than an ink-stained comic, Windsor McKay's strip was devoted to the dreams of a kid from Brooklyn. In any strip he might encounter space creatures, clowns, cannibals, or queens, the fulfillment of each quest always cut short with a bump as the boy fell from bed and woke up to an ordinary life of parents and Sunday school. While kids were the primary audience for Sunday "funny papers," its stars transcended the world of children. The Yellow Kid appeared in ads for ladies' fans and cigarette packs; Buster Brown promoted everything from cigars to whiskey. Comic book stars represented mischief and chaos and everything that civilized society was not. Adults adored them.

Rise of the "Boy-Men"

Among the many new adult fans of comics was an anxious, cigar-chomping showman nicknamed "The Kid." Fred Thompson was a free-spending, hard-drinking bachelor and self-described "grown up boy at play" who recognized in the comics, and particularly *Little Nemo in Slumberland,* a story that deserved telling far beyond the funny pages. In 1908, Thompson helped mount a stage version of *Little Nemo,* pledging that the production was "not a 'baby play' to interest the nursery occupant only." The most expensive and extravagant Broadway production to date, it featured constellations of spinning pinwheels, an army of dancing teddy bears, and waves of flag-draped chorus girls, who at one point joined in the refrain: "Uncle Sam is once again a boy at play."

The extravagance was typical of Thompson, the most prominent of a new class of entrepreneurs who made fortunes creating amusements that appealed to children and adults in equal measure. Penny arcades hummed with games and prizes. Nickelodeons lured viewers with new features every day—two on Saturdays. Newsstands peddled Oliver Optic adventure stories and Horatio Alger novels. Then there was Thompson's specialty, a whole new sort of enterprise that materialized like nothing else the dreamworld of children for the consumption of adults: amusement parks.

Thompson was there at the beginning. At nineteen, he took a job as a janitor at the Chicago World's Fair, sweeping floors and emptying trash bins in a warehouse coated with plaster molds to resemble a neoclassical palace. A showcase for the supremacy of Western civilization, the 1893 Columbian International Exposition encompassed a square mile of neoclassical fountains, statues, columns, arches, and pavilions— the largest of which, the promoters bragged, could hold the entire standing army of Russia. Thompson found the main section, dubbed White City, impressive but dull. He was much more keen on the portion of the park known as the Midway Plaisance. In an attempt to boost sagging attendance and "enliven" the fair—to promote what architect Frederick Law Olmsted called "incidents of vital human gaiety"—planners hired a San Francisco showman to assemble a mile-long sideshow that mixed technological attractions with re-creations of "exotic" villages. A Turkish bazaar bustled next to a cluster of Indian tepees, which sat in the shadow of a hydrogen balloon, which floated alongside a gargantuan steel contraption known as the Ferris wheel. A riotous celebration of the spirit of child-hood, the Midway became the model of the modern theme park. Visitors ogled Algerian belly dancers, snacked on a new confection known as Cracker Jack, and sampled mass-produced bars of chocolate generated by a new German machine (so impressing a plucky young Pennsylvanian named Milton Snavely Hershey that he bought all the equipment on the spot). White City was a monument to civilization and maturity. The Midway was something else, a fantastic jumble of the primitive, the commercial, the childlike, and the childish. Crowds dutifully milled through White City. They mobbed the Midway. By the time it was done, paid admissions topped 21 million. The country—and Thompson—had developed a taste for the sort of garish spectacle that could turn a respectable adult into a wide-eyed child.

Thompson became an "exposition fiend." As described in Woody Register's brilliant biography, *The Kid of Coney Island,* Thompson joined the family construction business and began designing fair amusements. At the 1897 Tennessee exposition, he created a seventy-five-foot-tall steel teeter-totter known as the Giant Seesaw. Three years later, he upstaged the Spanish Renaissance exhibit halls at the Buffalo World's Fair with an audacious attraction called A Trip to the Moon. Visitors paid a dime to board a ferryboat-sized, cigar-shaped moonship suspended with wires from the ceiling of a warehouse filled with incandescent lights and blowing fans. After landing on a surface of lunar craters and papier-mâché toadstools, visitors were greeted by twittering midgets and dancing Moon Maidens, who offered platters piled high with chunks of green-tinted cheese.

Riding high from his success in Buffalo, Thompson set

out for a marshy strip of Coney Island to create a more permanent home for his amusements. In 1903, he and a partner opened a twenty-two-acre amusement park described as "the biggest playground on earth." Luna Park was a palace of exotic architecture and rides Thompson described as "elaborated child's play." There were trick chairs, tilting platforms, swooping slides, spinning barrels, and a new attraction known as the roller coaster. Adults dropped children off at the Luna Park nursery—children were welcomed but adults were the primary audience—and spent hours being jostled, disoriented, and utterly awed in a "palace of play" that mocked genteel notions of propriety and maturity. Crowds at Coney Island inspired entrepreneurs across the country. Soon amusement parks sprang up on the outskirts of big cities all over, from Paragon Park and Revere Beach in Boston to Manhattan Beach in Denver to the Chutes in San Francisco. By 1915, there were Luna Park copycats operating as far away as Berlin and Buenos Aires.

The thrill was short-lived. Built out of the same flimsy plaster compound used to construct the disposable palaces at the Chicago World's Fair, Luna Park was as fragile as it was dazzling. The first of a series of fires ripped through the park in 1912. Meanwhile, Thompson himself was losing his grip on his empire. In 1913 he hosted a surreal groundbreaking on the shores of San Francisco Bay for a park to be called Toyland Grown Up in which a lineup of spade-wielding children buried toys—which Thompson called "magical seeds"—before "fertilizing" them with dollops of ice cream and sprinkles of rock candy. Toyland was to be the purest expression of his "kid grown up" ideal, a park of towering tin soldiers, rubber duck ferryboats, and a five-story hotel modeled after Mother Hubbard's cupboard. His plans were scuttled, however, by investors concerned about Thompson's increasing overspending and alcoholism.

Thompson's brand of amusement was also under attack from social critics and reformers. After touring Coney Island, critic James Huneker proclaimed it "a disgrace to our civilization." "Once en masse," he wrote, "humanity sheds its civilization and becomes half child, half savage." Others lumped Coney Island in with the melodrama theaters, movie houses, dance halls, and other new forms of entertainment that encouraged loose morals and a surrender of intellect that might otherwise be engaged in addressing horrendous social conditions of the era.

Writer and activist Jane Addams had her purse stolen on the opening day of the Chicago World's Fair and seems never to have quite gotten over it. Such amusements, she believed, encouraged hooliganism and vice; childhood was better spent in supervised activities that cultivated rather than encouraged natural impulses. "Looping the loop amid shrieks of simulated terror" was fine, she wrote in her 1909 bestseller *The Spirit of Youth and the City Streets,* but "the city which permits them to be the acme of pleasure and recreation to its young people commits a grievous mistake." To Addams and other reformers of the era, it was the solemn duty of adults to protect—not indulge or profit from—youth.

This spirit of improvement informed a host of new programs and policies, from child labor laws and juvenile courts to after-school programs and public playgrounds. These improvements were mostly made by socially conscious adults alarmed by the wretched living conditions of urban children and the exploitation of young workers. The leaders of the "child saver" movement were by all accounts conscientious adults who bore little resemblance to the rejuveniles of today. Their success at improving the welfare of children had less to do with their seriousness, however, than with the larger culture's nostalgia for the glories of childhood. Adults wept over mournful ballads with titles including "The Little Lost Child," "For Sale: A Baby," and the 1903 hit "Toyland," which included the refrain

> *Toyland! Toyland! Little girl and boy land*
> *While you dwell within*
> *You are ever happy then.*

The same wistful sentimentality was given full rein in pamphlets promoting adult participation in a new organization devoted to celebrating the spirit of youth: the Boy Scouts. One pamphlet featured a painting titled *If I Were a Boy Again,* picturing a boy bounding out the front door of his house for a day of play, watched enviously by his slouching, defeated, house-bound dad. Fathers who became Scoutmasters would "renew their youth," the pamphlet promised, and discover their inner "boy-men."

The label "boy-man" was a badge of pride for Boy Scouts founder Lord Baden Powell, who started the Scouting Movement in 1907 to spread a message of self-reliance that the former British soldier developed while leading young volunteers in the Boer War. While Powell was an enthusiastic *Peter Pan* devotee (he saw the original production twice during its first month), his brand of rejuvenalia was of a different breed than that of Barrie. The boyhood Powell prized was synonymous with backwoods adventure, athletic contests, and youthful camaraderie; he was at his happiest leading a gang of boys in a Zulu war chant or sitting in the bleachers at his former boarding school, cheering on the lads. Recapturing the spirit of youth, Powell believed, was a discipline, one with supervised activities, chains of command, and orderly sets of rules (all of which were codified in *The Boy Scout Handbook*).

This particular strain of regimented rejuvenalia became one basis for what became known as "the play movement." Concern about "hooliganism" and inactivity among children recently freed from the workplace fed a drive to build playgrounds, parks, social centers, and public swimming pools. Children tossing balls in supervised games, the theory went, might not be studying Scripture, but at least they weren't throwing rocks at stray cats. Founders of the Playground Association of America, established in 1905, argued that play was not mere idleness but essential to the "moral development" of competent citizens. "Play seen from the inside, as the child sees it, is the most serious thing in life," wrote playground movement founder Joseph Lee in his 1915 treatise *Play in Education*. "It includes, indeed, the whole intention with which [nature] brought him forth, namely, to make a man of him."

While the play movement would seem to embody the rejuvenile spirit, the exact opposite is true. Stressing the importance of "directed" play and the value of structured games in preparing children for the vital tasks of adulthood, play reformers did two things: diminish the fun of play and erect heretofore nonexistent boundaries between playing children and supervising adults. Manuals like Jessie Bancroft's *Games for the Playground, Home, School and Gymnasium* described the rules and regulations of four hundred games, dictating age boundaries for each. After the age of eleven, for instance, children should no longer play tag, Bancroft wrote. Instead, they should be encouraged to join "strenuous team games that resembled primitive warfare."

Generations have undoubtedly benefited from the playgrounds and athletic fields that are the movement's legacy. But while we appreciate what we gained, we should also recognize what was lost. In one fell swoop, play was compartmentalized, institutionalized, and mostly sealed off from adults. It would be a century before another coterie of rejuveniles rebelled against the good intentions of play reformers, embracing child's play as something far more than a diversion from truancy or a tool to build character. Play, to the modern rejuvenile, is indeed the whole point of life.

TWO

the rejuvenile at play

YOUR PLAY NEEDS NO EXCUSE.
NEVER EXCUSE.

— William Shakespeare,
A Midsummer Night's Dream

In Washington, D.C., a group of friends get together for a beer and find themselves, as floundering, entry-level professionals are wont to do, complaining about the tedium of their jobs and reminiscing about how much more fun they had as kids. Cartoons are referenced, song titles are recalled, and soon conversation turns to the schoolyard sport of kickball. A few rounds later, they decide to organize a game at the foot of the Washington Monument, the first game in what becomes an international adult kickball league with corporate sponsors, official merchandise, and more than twenty thousand players.

In London, England, fifty women from as far away as Germany and Italy show up for a workshop devoted to the latest extreme sport: Parkour. Developed in the late eighties by a pair of bored French teenagers who videotaped themselves doing acrobatics in alleyways and office parks without benefit of equipment or formal training, Parkour has since earned a following among some highly unlikely sorts, including thrill-seeking women in their twenties and thirties. At the London workshop, they get tips on favorite Parkour tricks, including the cat leap, which involves hurling oneself over gaps as wide as seven feet, spinning around 360 degrees in flight, and touching down on sloped walls or rooftops.

In rural Massachusetts, a forty-five-year-old ad salesman lies awake all night after watching a documentary about a gang of California skateboarders. Recalling the drainage ditches and asphalt buffers he skated as a teenager, he resolves to build a skate ramp in the backyard of his brother's house for the benefit of his teenage nephews. A month later, the boys have taken only a few exploratory rides through the plywood pipe; their uncle, meanwhile, has a new board, a skinned knee, and a full-blown obsession.

One hundred years after reformers Joseph Lee and Jane Addams championed the power of play, rejuveniles have taken up their rallying cry in ways the original play activists would have found highly irregular. In fact, rejuveniles are as different from their forebears as Lee and Addams were from the Puritans who equated leisure with laziness and play with degeneracy ("The soul's play day is the Devil's work day," went the booming cry of nineteenth-century preachers). The first play activists prevailed by stressing the civilizing benefits of play, pointing out that structured playtime prevents delinquency and prepares children to assume adult roles. Play, their motto went, is the work of childhood.

Today's rejuveniles take the next leap, setting play loose from the nursery and schoolyard and making it available to any and all. They have their own motto: We don't stop playing because we grow old, we grow old because we stop playing. (Variously attributed to playwright George Bernard Shaw and pitcher Satchel Paige, this aphorism now appears as the official slogan of a Texas motorcycle club and a toy store not far from my house in L.A. that trades in such rejuvenile goodies as Einstein action figures, Hindu-god finger puppets, and windup walking vaginas.) Divided by geography, race, and class, rejuveniles are united by their shared devotion to play. And for the most die-hard rejuveniles, the more childlike the play, the better.

Duck Duck Goose, Jacks, Marbles, Capture the Flag—no childhood pastime or plaything is too simple or silly to escape rejuvenile reclamation. In small gatherings, amateur leagues, informal workplaces, and therapeutic groups, adults now find comfort, thrills, and even the occasional life lesson playing games that, by all traditional standards, they should have outgrown eons ago. The schoolyard favorites Four Square and Wiffle ball are enjoying a renaissance on college campuses. Jump rope is the specialty of a group of thirtysomething performers known as Double Duchess, whose members do acrobatic and theatrical jump-rope routines dressed in Catholic schoolgirl uniforms. Gym rats swear by the slimming power of the Hula-Hoop. Pac-Man is the inspiration for a real-world street game played by graduate students in New York, who use cell phones and global positioning devices in a three-dimensional re-creation of the arcade classic. Business executives in Japan settle high-stakes disputes with the help of Rock Paper Scissors, a schoolyard pastime heralded by the World RPS Society as "a game of wits, speed, dexterity and strategy" played at "world invitationals" by competitors who employ strategic sequences known by such names as the "crescendo" and the "scissor sandwich."

Often, familiar forms of child's play come wrapped in new packages that lend them a veneer of maturity. The boyhood game of Cowboys and Indians has been reinvented as paintball, perfect for a "team building" exercise with coworkers or a bonding afternoon with pals. Frisbee may be for kids, but Ultimate Frisbee is for sporty grown-ups. You may be too old for a sleepover with friends, but you're welcome at the Ultimate Pajama Party, a weekend of beauty demonstrations, chick flicks, and female bonding that draws big crowds of "grown up girls" across the U.S. and Canada.

Such child's play among adults often starts as a lark, a hoot, a small silly gesture that has more to do with a search for novelty than a resolve to modify norms of maturity. But inevitably the joke wears thin—which in the case of a game like tag can take less time than it takes to holler "olley olley oxen free." When that happens, the novelty-seekers drift away in search of something else—a pet iguana, a line-dancing class, a Kabbalah bracelet—that will feed their insatiable need to stand out. Typically, however, the play continues, thanks to those adults who simply can't find satisfaction in the exercise mills, yoga studios, or poker tournaments that are supposed to appeal to their more mature adult sensibilities. And as these stragglers absorb the kiddie play into their ordinary lives, what started as a childlike lark becomes part of their daily routine.

For many adults, child's play represents a sort of active nostalgia, a chance to reexperience some cherished sensation of youth, be it the squish of a spaldeen against a stoop, the churn generated by a roller coaster cresting a hill, or the intoxication felt by trick-or-treaters whose reason for being can be summed up in two words: get candy. Ask rejuveniles to explain why they still chase these prepubescent thrills in middle age and beyond, and more often than not they'll respond with a shrug and a simple comeback: Why not? It was fun as a kid and it's fun now. Some people like golf; I like tag.

That's hard to argue with, especially when by all appearances the adults playing tag are having a whole lot more fun than you're likely to see on your local golf course.

At Play with the Evangelists of All-Ages Tag

Kate Schurman discovered the fun of adult tag a few years out of college, working as the manager of a Kansas City law office. Kate was settling into an ordinary adult routine when she faced the ordinary adult issue of exercise. Having never paid much attention to maintaining her slim five-foot seven-inch build, Kate knew the time had come for her to start some kind of regular regimen—something most people begin taking seriously about the same time they find themselves having dinner party conversations about life insurance and patio furniture. But her heart sank the moment she pictured herself pounding out paces on a treadmill or contorting on a spongy yoga mat.

While Kate had never been particularly athletic, she did have vivid and happy memories of running around schoolyards, playgrounds, and parks as a kid. Which got her to wondering: Why do kids play and adults exercise? "I just wanted to run around and play like I used to," she says. "More than anything I wanted to play tag."

Most adults would stop there and dismiss the idea as a momentary fit of childishness. But Kate had never particularly minded if her interests were considered childish. As a teenager, she fell into a tight circle of friends who preferred playing with Barbies or swinging at the park than cruising the boulevard or sneaking off to house parties. As an adult, she started each day with Mr. Rogers. She made it a point to visit

Disney World twice a year, sometimes with family but also by herself, sharing company with other childless visitors. ("Last year was great—there was a podiatry convention at the Disney hotel, and let me tell you, those guys are *wild*.") Kate simply never went through the stage when things frilly or silly are rejected in favor of things that seem more mature. "Why should I give something up that makes me happy?" she says. "This stuff was fun as a kid and it's fun now. I guess I'm just stubborn."

So Kate went ahead with her idea of all-ages tag, announcing the establishment of what she jokingly called the Tag Institute to friends and relatives and posting ads in coffeehouses and the local paper. The initial response wasn't exactly enthusiastic. Most of the people she approached politely declined. Kate thought she'd have better luck when she mentioned tag to a friend who played in a local dodgeball game. "He was too cool for tag," she says. "The dodgeballers definitely have attitude."

Six people showed up the first night. Kate quickly discovered that no one actually knew how to *play* tag, beyond the fact that someone is *it* and he or she tries to tag someone else and make that person *it*. And what is *it*, anyway? Kids seem born understanding *it*, but the neutered, mysterious *it* begs questions among adults—Is *it* a person or a thing? Does *it* represent responsibility—and if so, what does it say that the game demands you immediately rush to unload it?

Chaos ensued as the fastest players scattered and others clustered together, unsure who was supposed to chase whom. Gradually, however, the players began to recall a few actual rules, establishing out-of-bounds and requiring that players raise their hands and count to five after they were tagged. As play continued, Schurman noted something else about the game she hadn't remembered from childhood: Certain players (the slow ones, the awkward ones, the misfits among the misfits) always seemed to end up being *it.* So she created a new rule: If you've been *it,* you can't be tagged again until everyone gets a turn. In much the same way adult kickballers and dodgeballers have modified the game to protect players from revisiting childhood humiliations, Schurman didn't want "anyone to feel they weren't good enough to play," she says.

Even with the feel-good, everyone-plays vibe, tag could get surprisingly rough. "There's a herd mentality about it," Kate says. "It's like watching the nature channel—all the people who aren't *it* stick together in this big group and then scatter when the animal goes in for the kill." Kate ended up on crutches for a few weeks after three players barreled into her during a game of partner tag. The repertoire soon expanded to include such varieties as octopus tag (tagged players sit on the ground and flail at free players), zombie tag (*it* is recast as a zombie, who turns anyone he or she touches into a fellow zombie), movie tag (players can save themselves the moment they are tagged by shouting out a film title), and caramel-corn tag (*it* links arms with his or her prey, forming a long chain of *it*s.)

One night an Australian backpacker showed up and taught the group a version of tag called Cougars and Horses in which *it* growls and leaps and free players whinny and gallop. This represented a major escalation—it's one thing for an adult to run around in a downtown park in full view of passersby, who would often stop, stare, and laugh, and not always in a supportive, "isn't-that-cute" way. Cougars and Horses upped the ante, requiring a level of unselfconsciousness that's difficult for most adults to recall, much less relive. But to

Kate's surprise, Cougars and Horses actually became a favorite in a group that soon swelled to include more than thirty regular players, including computer programmers, tattoo artists, doctors, soccer moms, college students, barflies, tourists, and an introverted twenty-eight-year-old radio producer who quickly became a "total tag evangelist."

"I was telling everyone I saw about it," says Dennis Conrow. "Playing a silly kids' game with other adults, acting like a buffoon, breaks down barriers . . . Playing tag with strangers is a chance to reaffirm faith in humankind."

Others reached similarly lofty conclusions. At fifty-two, Kate's mom, Susan, was among the oldest of the regular players. Like her daughter, Susan didn't have any reservations about playing a kids' game. She'd been a big believer in adult play since working as a therapist in a psychiatric ward where patients spent their days taking medication and undergoing therapy. It was, she observed, an almost entirely unplayful environment. Was it any wonder everyone was so unhappy? Couldn't all adults use a little more play? "To me, being able to play and give time and energy to that playful side of yourself is not about immaturity—it's about true maturity," she said.

Kate stresses that she and her fellow taggers do not believe that by playing they can somehow erase the realities of adulthood. Just because Kate's tastes and interests are more aligned with an eight-year-old than a twenty-four-year-old doesn't mean she wants to *be* eight. "The truth is that being eight sucks in a lot of ways," she says. "You have no control of your life. Everyone in the world, even strangers in the street, can tell you what to do. You have no say. But as an adult I can choose to play tag, then go home, pay my bills, make my dinner, and do whatever I want. There's so much freedom in being an adult. As much as I enjoy tag, I love being a grown-up."

The Brief but Thrilling Career of Kim Corbin, Professional Skipper

Fifteen hundred miles away in San Francisco, another idealistic young woman with a love of childhood play has also found a following of fellow rejuveniles. Kim Corbin became a believer in the benefits of child's play at the age of thirty. An Indiana native with a wide-open smile, Kim arrived in California in 1996 with a degree in elementary education and fuzzy plans for her future. She had a nice job in publishing and what she calls a "safe, easy, dull existence." That all began to change one Friday night when a particularly flamboyant friend, filled with good spirits while strolling through the Castro district, spontaneously broke into a skip. She gave chase, her feet falling into the shuffle-step pattern they hadn't followed for at least twenty years. Bounding down the street, making a spectacle of herself, Kim felt good. Something clicked. "I thought, this is so much fun," she says. "I thought, I haven't done this since I was a kid—why do we *ever* stop doing this?"

Kim didn't think much more about it until two years later, when a coworker mentioned that her daughter had recently asked her to skip. "Adults don't skip, dear," came the reply. Kim begged to differ. It was 1999 in San Francisco, so she did the natural thing: She set up a website dedicated to "an international grassroots movement" devoted to skipping. "Feel like a kid again!" read the banner headline on a page decorated with smiley faces and photos of adults bounding across blue skies. Skipping was much more than a silly cardio workout (though it was certainly good for that—Kim says she lost twenty-five pounds in her first two years skipping). It was also, she declared, a key to improving the world. "We believe that skipping is a simple, yet powerful way to make our communities happier and healthier places," she wrote on behalf of her so-far-imaginary movement. "And that world will be a much better place with more skippers on the streets."

To her astonishment, Kim's dream movement materialized, and more vividly than she ever imagined. Twice-weekly "group skips" in Golden Gate Park attracted a cadre of fellow skippers, many of whom arrived with funny hats or with signs meant to encourage passersby to join in: "Skip On!" "I'm Not Selling Anything—Skipping Is Free!" and "Skipping: It's a Natural High." After the local media picked up on the story, a crew from CNN turned up for a "Happy Hour Skip" through the city's financial district. Within a few weeks, features about the latest wacky fad from California appeared in *Time,* the *Boston Globe,* and the *Wall Street Journal.*

Kim's website became a magnet for kindred spirits as far away as Sri Lanka. In less than a year, more than fifteen hundred people had signed up for a skipping newsletter, including a cadre of "head skippers" who led "group skips" in sixty-five cities. In Queens, New York, forty-nine-year-old health food store manager Ashrita Furman designed his own heavy-soled skipping shoes and resolved to achieve skipping greatness. Having previously set world records in such endeavors as sack racing, pogo-sticking, and hopscotch, Furman earned his sixteenth mention in the *Guinness Book of World Records* for a five-hour, fifty-minute marathon-length skip. In Decatur, Georgia, the wife of a seventy-year-old owner of an industrial parts distribution company wrote that her husband had been a devoted skipper for more than forty-five years. "Charles skips in malls, hospital corridors, parking lots, and on sidewalks," she wrote. "He skips anywhere the silliness strikes him." In Miamisburg, Ohio, the fifty-one-year-old leader of a group called the Sacred Child Sanctuary celebrated skipping as a

rejuvenile

connection to that New Age ideal, the inner child. "Skipping is the physical expression of joy and 'kidness,'" she wrote. And in her own neighborhood, Kim found romance with a high school science teacher whose fondness for blowing bubbles inspired something of a companion crusade. "Blowing bubbles can change the world!" he declared on his website, iblowbubbles.com.

Sure she had found her life's calling, Kim quit her job and declared herself a "professional skipper." She wasn't entirely clear how she'd earn a living, but Kim figured that would take care of itself. There was talk from a fitness advocacy group about a $2.5 million cross-country RV trip and a book tentatively titled *Called to Skip*.

But like so many other wildly optimistic, profoundly impractical plans of the era, the skipping movement fizzled. Even calling it a movement may be overstating it—at the height of the media attention, a head skipper from Los Angeles urged his fellow skippers to keep their enthusiasm to themselves. "I hope to God it doesn't become a movement," he wrote. "Maybe I will actively pay people NOT to skip, so I can keep it small and authentic. Soon Nike will be putting out skipping shoes (Yikes!)." Outside the ranks, the backlash was even harsher. One San Francisco commentator, responding to the flood of perky publicity, called Kim "an annoying, pathetic, obsessive-compulsive moron." The skipping movement, he wrote, was "nothing more than an embarrassing and ridiculous attempt to get [Corbin] noticed." The book proposal failed to sell. The RV trip was scrapped. Romance with the bubbleman cooled.

After celebrating her thirty-fifth birthday and facing mounting debts and no stable job, Kim took a hard look at her passion. "I skipped myself to financial ruin," she says now.

Four years after devoting herself entirely to skipping, Kim stopped leading group skips and took a booking job with an adult education company.

But even in the midst of what she calls an "acute post-skip hangover," Kim is still wildly effusive about the power of childhood play. "Skipping reveals the true authentic self," she says. "I may be on the sidewalk on the way to the grocery store, but when I skip I'm an animal frolicking in the field. I'm a kid at play. It activates that part of yourself that your adult self ignores." Yes, her experience as a skipping ambassador led to some hardship and disappointment. But something unexpected came from promoting the virtues of childhood: Kim became a better adult. "Before skipping, everything was pretty easy for me," she says. "Skipping was a big leap. It taught me to follow my heart, no matter what happens. It was through that childlike spirit that I was forced to grow up. I thought when I started this that it was all going to be fun and easy, but of course that's not what life is. I had to learn about humility and patience and doubt and all this stuff that's not as much fun as riding the high."

A Brief Detour into Play Theory

For Kim, Kate, and all their fellow skippers and tag players, play is more than just recreation. It's their one true ambition, their main reason for living. "The opposite of play isn't work. It's depression. To play is to act out and be willful, exultant, and committed," says preeminent play theorist Brian Sutton-Smith, summing up a core rejuvenile value. For the rejuvenile, the usual forms of adult play are too often dull, repetitive, or competitive. In short, they're just not playful enough.

But what, precisely, *is* play? And what makes some play more playful than other play? Alongside love and happiness, *play* is among the trickiest words in the English language to define. Applied to the activities of everyone from babbling infants to grandmaster chess champions, play eludes rational explanation. It isn't even unique to our species. Cats, birds, even fish act in ways that can only be described as playful. No one knows for sure what the purpose of all this foolishness is—or if there is one. As early as the 1800s, scholars theorized that people and animals play to master essential skills like hunting and childrearing. And indeed, play is deeply preparatory, allowing us to try new activities and roles and absorb knowledge without much apparent effort. There's another crucial quality of play, however, that has nothing at all to do with its educational benefits. That ingredient, of course, is fun.

The first scholar to give fun its due was the Dutch anthropologist Johan Huizinga, whose 1938 book *Homo Ludens* challenged previous explanations of play. "To each and every one of the explanations," Huizinga wrote, "it might be well objected: 'so far so good, but what actually is the *fun* of playing?'" If all we're doing in play is discharging excess energy and practicing survival skills, we'd be better off hunkering down for rote mechanical exercises. But rote exercises, unlike play, aren't much fun. "In this intensity, this absorption, this power of maddening, lies the very essence, the primordial quality of play."

Essential to Huizinga's understanding of play was the idea of illusion—which, after all, comes from the Latin root *ludere,* meaning "to play." Huizinga argued that play is best understood not as preparation for anything but as a thing in itself. It is absorbing, unpredictable, and most important, it contains an element of make-believe. It transcends "real" life. It's this essential apartness—its independence from accepted rules and agreements—that makes it fun, and also makes it such an essential part of childhood.

Before we know how to walk or talk, we know how to play. As babies, we mimic sounds, bat objects hung before us, and laugh hysterically at peekaboo. This partly explains why our understanding of play is so often associated with children, and why rejuveniles are so drawn toward child's play. In his exhaustive review of the etymology of play, Huizinga notes that the most common word for play in ancient Greece meant, literally, "of or pertaining to the child." Even today, *Webster's Third New International Dictionary* defines play as "the spontaneous or organized recreational activity of children."

As we grow up, play progresses from roughhousing to pretending to creating to competing in contests with elaborate rules. It all happens naturally; play requires no training, no special setting, no specific equipment. We adults often forget this, even as we strive to keep up the appearance of fun. I'm reminded of a friend who visited Disneyland with her three-year-old son, who attached himself to her pant leg the moment he spotted the enormous rodent everyone seemed so interested in. He was much more drawn to the lids on the trash containers, which swung back and forth when he gave them a good whack. This natural-born expert in play spent his stay at Disneyland running from trash can to trash can. The moral: Play doesn't have to be presented as fun. It doesn't have to be done well—it just has to be fun.

The most gifted adults never lose sight of the essence of play. Huizinga identified what he called "the play element" as the foundation of romantic attachment, scientific discovery, religious ritual, indeed all advanced civilization. He proposed that the name "Homo Sapiens" (Man of Reason) be replaced with "Homo Ludens" (Man the Player), because "we are not so reasonable after all." "Play cannot be denied," he wrote. "You can deny, if you like, nearly all abstractions: justice, beauty, truth, goodness, mind, God. You can deny seriousness, but not play."

Other academic heavyweights have elevated play to similarly lofty heights, notably pioneering clinician and writer Erik Erikson, who lamented the adult habit of replacing active, spontaneous play with passive, predictable recreation. "Such a division makes life simpler," he wrote. "[It] permits adults to avoid the awesome suggestion that playfulness—and thus, indeterminate chance—may occur in the vital center of adult concerns." But for all his idealization of what Freud called *"die strahlende Intelligenz des Kindes"* (the radiant intelligence of children), Erikson seemed unsure whether adults could recapture some of that radiance through play. Grownups who set aside time for play are too often self-conscious, stilted, unnatural—they're "playing at playing," he wrote.

In recent years, the promise of adult play has inspired a new breed of academics, self-help authors, management gurus, and even politicians. Al and Tipper Gore devoted an entire chapter of their 2002 book *Joined at the Heart* to the proposition that "play pays," chronicling the fun they have horsing around with their kids, dressing up at Halloween, and pulling practical jokes (including the time Al pretended to shampoo with a bottle of Nair). Bemoaning the fact that "play is associated with childishness, and childishness has a distinctly trivial, even negative connotation in our goal-oriented society," the Gores argue that play is essential in building both family bonds and, perhaps more crucially in a rapidly changing society, flexibility. "Play is an aerobic workout for the human capacity to change," they wrote.

That argument finds full expression in the 1999 book *Beyond Love and Work: Why Adults Need to Play,* in which psychiatrist Leonore Terr urges stiff adults to loosen up. Terr urges adults to fiddle with puzzles and putty at work, be silly with their spouses, and otherwise make play a priority. Play doesn't have to take a childlike form—it can be found in any number of adult-approved activities, among them gardening, fishing, or wordplay—but Terr says the best place for play-deprived adults to start looking is their own childhoods. Thus the boy who couldn't get enough roughhousing as a nine-year-old is likely to grow up loving skateboarding or skydiving. "We step back down the developmental ladder, revisiting old rungs," she writes. Some developmental psychologists might diagnose this as unhealthy regression, but to Terr, it's simply a way to remain "in touch with our own beginnings."

Play has even inspired something of a social movement. Scottish author and activist Pat Kane based a 2004 manifesto titled *The Play Ethic* on the transformative power of adult play. Kane, a former pop musician turned "militant postmodernist," based the book partly on his work as a "play consultant," advising clients—including Tony Blair's cabinet office—how to make their workplaces more playful. Kane argues that the Protestant work ethic is a relic of the Industrial Age, that we'd all be better off if we reduced the number of hours we work (ideally, we should aim for a twenty- to twenty-five-hour workweek), and used our free time and new technologies to engage in creative, fulfilling play. In play, Kane says, we stretch our imaginations, try on new roles, and discover new capabilities—essential skills in an ever-changing economy. "The idea of play only being accessible to children is breaking down," he says. "To talk about play in adults doesn't infantilize them—it equips them for the twenty-first century."

63

Beyond the Desktop Bobblehead

Militant postmodernists like Kane aren't alone in preaching this gospel of play as key to twenty-first-century success. Play is now a prized commodity among innovation-minded managers, consultants, and even a few Fortune 500 CEOs. Even in an era of belt-tightening and total efficiency management, the notion that work and play are mutually exclusive is under direct attack by executives at Nokia, Southwest Airlines, PricewaterhouseCoopers, and dozens of other multinational firms that have in recent years developed strategies specifically designed to make their workplaces more playful.

These initiatives can be counterproductive or just plain cringe-worthy—I for one count a hamburger-eating contest sponsored by Viacom as one of the least pleasant experiences of my working life. But I realized I got off easy while reading about a Quaker Oats Convenience Foods employee retreat in "king of corporate funmanship" Matt Weinstein's 1996 book *Managing to Have Fun*. After a pep talk from a Quaker Oats division head, workers were hustled outside for a series of "Olympic-style events based on the different Quaker Oats product lines, like 'The Long-Distance Aunt Jemima Maple Syrup Squirting Contest,' 'The Aunt Jemima Pancake Flinging Marathon,' and 'Bobbing for Hotdogs' in a gigantic vat of Beanie Weenie–brand franks and beans."

Fortunately, one needn't dip one's head into a tub of meat to have fun at work. That's just an extreme example of the kind of silliness that managers now routinely encourage in the hopes that play can be harnessed to make workers more creative and productive (or at least cheerier). Employees at Kodak burn off steam in "humor rooms" stocked with toys, games, and Monty Python videocassettes. Job applicants looking for work at the Boston consulting firm ZEFER are asked to take a "Play-Doh test" to evaluate their creative abilities. Engineering professors at Stanford University host a conference billed as "a playdate of massive proportions" to show how play can inspire teamwork, spur creativity, and "make big dreams a reality." Restoration Hardware CEO Stephen Gordon has led employees at a company retreat in a water-balloon fight and a game of Red Rover.

Such efforts to make work more playful are mainly meant to alleviate stress and aid in staff retention; proponents cite the "Peter-Out Principle," which holds that workers will flee their jobs when they stop having fun. But play at work is also said to have a more immediate function, sparking productivity from employees worn down by the grind of business-as-usual. Executives in Lausanne, Switzerland, were among the first to test a protocol called Serious Play, which uses Legos to coax new ideas and lines of communication from hardened executives. Today Lego runs an international consulting firm that promises breakthroughs with the help of knobby plastic bricks. In Palo Alto, California, managers from all sectors of corporate America make pilgrimages to meet visionaries at IDEO, a design firm that generates new ideas through games with names like "deep dives," "bodystorming," and "unfocus groups."

"We've built a business around this principle of fun," Tom Kelly, general manager of IDEO, told the *Christian Science Monitor*. Kelly credits what he calls "productive play" with helping his company develop the first laptop computer, the Palm V, and the first stand-up toothpaste tube.

Indeed, for design firms, ad agencies, software developers, and the like, play is now built into the business plan. The ad agency Chiat Day's L.A. headquarters includes a boardroom table made of surfboards and a row of punching bags adorned with cartoons of upper management. Workers are encouraged to hang out long after work is over, clustering around cubicles for cocktails and conversation. "Our people know they'll have a chance in this big sandbox," partner Lee Clow told the *Wall Street Journal*. "It's designed to be a stimulating place, a fun place, an interactive place, a social place."

This inversion of traditional boss talk—it's not an office; it's a sandbox! It's not work; it's play!—might sound like the blue-sky happy talk of a corporate outcast, but it actually represents a common mode of management and a rare legacy of the late-nineties tech boom. Back then, the business press was filled with fawning profiles of the likes of Mark Cuban, the dot-com boy-man known to roller-skate down the halls of his corporate headquarters, and Steve Perlman, the WebTV founder who earned his stripes at Apple with a manifesto titled "Growing Up Without Growing Old." To these rejuvenile dream bosses, play was celebrated as an integral part of work, a tool for generating new ideas without worrying too much about what might go wrong.

Of course, when things did go wrong (see: bursting of dot-com bubble, collapse of countless business plans, trigger of decade-long recession), the embrace of play championed by New Economy moguls didn't seem quite so visionary. It suddenly seemed fitting that disgraced Enron exec Jeff Skilling organized motocross retreats while simultaneously duping employees and investors. All the foosball tables and desktop bobbleheads began to look like relics of a frivolous era, the burnt embers of an embarrassing flameout.

But a funny thing happened on the way to the New Austerity—the fun stuck around. The economy might have changed, but the workers didn't. They still couldn't suspend their playful impulses during the forty-hour-plus workweek. They still shuddered at the thought of themselves as corporate drones in a Dilbert universe. They still wanted, like no other class of employee before them, for work to be fun, creative, flexible, nurturing. They wanted it all.

Which explains why, long after the end of the end of the dot-com era, business is still brisk at Playfair, a thirty-year-old consultancy dedicated to the idea that "once we recall the feeling of jubilation that we once knew as children, we can even make *work* fun." And why CEOs continue to put their trust into a Virginia-based firm that, at the height of the dot-com era, adopted the red playground ball as its corporate logo and changed its name from Opus Event Marketing to, simply, Play. Today the firm is used by the likes of General Electric and Philip Morris to stage events and tweak corporate traditions — Play staffers have been known to force clients to brainstorm while lounging in queen-size beds and to deliver presentations while stomping on boardroom tabletops. They also take pride in their own playful workplace, where staffers gather every day for "morning storytime," dogs keep regular office hours, and employees invent their own titles; cofounder Andy Stefanovich is "In Charge of What's Next." Others call themselves "Voice of Reason," "Flying Buttress," and "Point Guard."

Courtney Farrell, whose title is "Number 17," says the people at Play make a distinction between the sort of deep, systematic play they foster and the forced, superficial playfulness of the dot-com era. "The play we're talking about isn't something separate from the work we're doing," Farrell says. "It's not like we're telling people to work really hard and then go outside and hit the company climbing wall. Play should be part of your work. It's nice to have fun, but play is deeper than that—it's about how you approach your work, the energy and spirit you bring to it. It's the attitude you had as a kid on the playground."

While consultancies like Play can encourage that attitude, certain CEOs require no coaching whatsoever in the merits of workplace play. I first heard about Richard Tuck while talking to adult amusement park fanatics—Richard is something of a star in these circles, claiming to have ridden every roller coaster in the United States and leading a long, costly campaign to memorialize the amusement park of his boyhood, a long-shuttered San Francisco attraction called Playland at the Beach. After a few phone conversations rhapsodizing over his love of the park and all things childlike—Richard is also a big fan of magic, circuses, and toys—Richard invited me to visit his personal shrine to Playland, a museum he built to display models of original attractions along with salvaged rides, games, and costumes. Upon my arrival in the Bay Area suburb of El Cerrito, however, I was surprised to find myself at the doorstep of Lander International, an altogether ordinary office building on an entirely unplayful commercial strip. Surely I had made a mistake. Richard himself soon appeared to clear up the confusion; in addition to his work with the museum, he is CEO of the world's largest internal audit recruiting firm. The museum is contained in three rooms out back. Business is done out front. Richard's days are spent moving back and forth between the two realms, interviewing job candidates one moment and toying with old carny games the next.

Richard Tuck wouldn't have it any other way. A doughy fifty-seven-year-old who favors Disney T-shirts and exclamations like "golly" and "neat," he says he feels entirely at ease shifting between work and play throughout the day. "I created my environment so it *all* feels like play to me," he says, sitting behind his desk with hands crossed contentedly over his belly. "To tell you the truth, I can't tell you when I'm working and playing."

After spending thirty years interviewing job candidates, Richard is convinced the same goes for most passionate people. To the truly engaged, work and play are one and the same. That guiding principle is more than just wishful thinking, he says; it has had a direct role in shaping Lander's screening process and its continued success (*Inc.* magazine named Lander as one of the five hundred fastest-growing companies in America in 1998, with revenues of $2.5 million). Unlike his competitors, Richard rejects formal behavioral tests and methodical interview techniques. Too technical, he says, too worklike. He doesn't even put much credence in job experience—he'll gloss over a candidate's job history in two minutes and then spend a few hours talking about an outside interest, be it an applicant's Third World travels or Richard's involvement with Circus Chimera, a hundred-member troupe that spent three months camping in his backyard. Richard says he knows he's found a good worker when "their face lights up, their voice goes up an octave, and they're a kid again," he says. "I look for the spark. If a person has it, they're ignitable—they know what it is to go into hyperdrive. And given the right circumstances, they can't help bring that to their work."

On Purposeful Play and Pointless Play

The ineffable spark Richard Tuck looks for in job applicants has been a subject of inquiry by psychologists for decades, foremost among them Mihaly Csikszentmihalyi, an authority on the superconcentrated mental state he calls "flow." People in flow—musicians, surgeons, chess players, and especially, children at play—lose all sense of space and time by focusing their attention on a succession of difficult but doable challenges. Flow is inseparable from play, he writes, the engine of creativity and the key to true happiness.

But if play is flow and flow is the constant testing and stretching of one's capabilities, what does it mean that rejuveniles prefer pastimes meant (at least originally) for children? Is it because their capabilities are child-sized? Do they gravitate to games they've previously mastered to avoid trying anything more demanding or complicated? Is enthusiasm for child's play a sign, then, of one's basic stuntedness, laziness, or both?

Perhaps, but only if you assume that the function of play is to improve oneself. Oftentimes, play isn't improving in the least. And for adults whose lives are otherwise entirely goal-oriented, pointlessness can be a source of tremendous relief. It's a release valve, a destressor. Writer Sarah Vowell reached that conclusion while in the throes of an obsession with a coin-operated game called Pop-A-Shot. A staple of carnivals and video game parlors, Pop-A-Shot is a sort of miniature caged basketball court in which the objective is to dunk as many baskets in forty seconds as possible. Here's an excerpt from Vowell's 2002 essay on Pop-A-Shot:

> I think Pop-A-Shot's a baby game. That's why I love it. Unlike the game of basketball itself, Pop-A-Shot has no standard socially redeeming value whatsoever. Pop-A-Shot is not about teamwork or getting along or working together. Pop-A-Shot is not about getting exercise or fresh air. It takes place in fluorescent-lit bowling alleys or darkened bars. It costs money. At the end of a game, one does not swig Gatorade. One sips bourbon or margaritas or munches cup-

cakes . . . In other words, Pop-A-Shot has no point at all. And that, for me, is the point. My life is full of points—the deadlines and bills and recycling and phone calls. I have come to appreciate, to depend on, this one dumb-ass little passion. Because every time a basketball slides off my fingertips and drops perfectly, flawlessly, into that hole, well, swish, happiness found.

Other adults have discovered hidden points in apparently pointless kid games. Bernie DeKoven is a perpetually jolly author, educator, and "fun coach"—for $150 a month, he'll act as your personal advisor on the "art and science of making things more fun." DeKoven first became interested in the appeal of kids' games while working as a school administrator in Pennsylvania. Putting together a curriculum of games for children, DeKoven played a game of Duck Duck Goose with a group of teachers. Far from being the simpleminded chase game he'd remembered, DeKoven discovered that Duck Duck Goose owed its fun to an array of subtle nonverbal cues that players use to project willingness, timidity, and aggression.

DeKoven went on to join the New Games Movement, a decidedly rejuvenile counterculture tradition of the mid-seventies famous for filling the play times of hippie children with parachutes, earth balls, and other rainbow-colored, noncompetitive doodads. He also turned a twenty-five-acre farm in eastern Pennsylvania into a compound called the Games Preserve, complete with puzzles, flying rings, air hockey tables, board games, and other kid-friendly diversions. Adults who signed up for a play retreat spent a few hours or a weekend playing and drawing lessons from kid games in postgame powwows. Today DeKoven offers much the same curriculum at the famed northern California personal improvement mecca, the Esalen Institute (a similar program, called Play for Adults, is offered at

New York's Omega Institute). At the end of these marathon play sessions, participants aren't doing baby talk or teasing or otherwise giving in to long-suppressed immaturity. Quite the opposite, DeKoven says. "One of the key discoveries of this sort of play is that you're not a child anymore—you're better than that," he says. "As an adult, you have so much more to be engaged in because your powers are more varied and more profound. These games have a way of highlighting those new powers."

The Irresistible Lure of the Big Red Ball, Part One

For most rejuveniles, however, child's play isn't about personal growth. It's simply a hoot. Standing on the sidelines of a Hollywood gymnasium wearing a green terry-cloth headband, striped tube socks, and a rhinestone bracelet, Tobias McKinney describes his devotion to a game that this thirty-one-year-old should probably have outgrown decades ago: dodgeball. The gladiator contest of the grade-school set, dodgeball is played by two teams who face off over the centerline of a gymnasium and attempt to hit each other with eight rubber playground balls. The rules are simple: You get hit, you're out. If a ball you throw is caught, you're out and one of your previously hit opponents is back in the game. The first team to send all the opponents to the sidelines wins. When remembered by adults at all, dodgeball is as likely to produce shudders of humiliation as waves of nostalgia. "My memories are not fond," said Tobias. "I was a weak and puny kid. I just remember being circled by bigger kids and getting pelted. It was not fun."

The scars of childhood didn't stop Tobias from going

along with a friend who, one day in the fall of 2003, announced he wanted to organize an adult dodgeball game. Michael Costanza is a Florida native who moved to Los Angeles partly to work in film production and partly because "in L.A. you can earn a living as an adult and live as a kid." He got the idea to play dodgeball one day while watching an adult softball game. The players, many of whom wore replicas of major league uniforms, were all very serious. At one point, a woman playing catcher failed to block the plate and allowed a run to score, provoking an angry tirade from her teammates. Appalled by the intensity and competitiveness of the game, Costanza remembered how "stupid and silly it had been playing dodgeball at summer camp."

Michael dreamed up the Los Angeles Dodgeball Society. He asked Tobias to be his "poster boy," photographing the six-foot-five actor in all his sweatband-and-tube-sock glory. To further set the tone, Michael brought along a boom box and played a mix tape featuring the eighties novelty hit "Pac Man Fever" and the soundtrack to the Jim Henson cult show *Fraggle Rock*. He also made it a point to divide the players randomly instead of using the traditional schoolyard system of having team captains assemble their teams one player at a time. "You never really get over being the last person picked," he says. "Kids might be like, 'I don't want the fat kid, or the nerd, or the kid who eats his scabs.' I wanted to use what I know as an adult to make this childlike thing better and less cruel."

The players loved it. Those with painful memories of grade-school dodgeball found a sort of redemption; the schoolyard champions relived glory years. Within a few months, Michael was hosting three coed dodgeball events a week. Tobias, meanwhile, discovered that the game that had brought him so much humiliation as a kid was earning him welcome attention as an adult. A photo of Tobias on the Society website caught the attention of producers of *Dodgeball,* a 2004 movie about rival gym owners who face off in a televised dodgeball tournament. Tobias was cast as a member of a German team coached by David Hasselhoff. A few months later, he and other individual players took home the championship during *Extreme Dodgeball,* a program for the Game Show Network. In the wake of all the exposure, adult dodgeball leagues began popping up all over, and plans were announced to create a professional association known as the United States Dodgeball League. The appeal is simple, a league official told *Newsweek:* "Life is hard for adults, and [dodgeball] gives an opportunity to act like children."

Listening to Tobias riff about his love of dodgeball—he insists mention be made of a move he developed known as the McKinney Kamikaze Kill—it's hard to avoid the conclusion that this is mostly, for this player anyway, a big goof, a silly lark that's helpful in carving out a niche in a town abounding in gimmickry. He's playing at playing. Others appear to similarly treat the game more as fashion accessory than opportunity to play, loaded with no more meaning than the Hello Kitty tattoo on the ankle of one player or the Boy Scout uniform that a thirty-two-year-old sometimes wears to games.

But the moment the whistle blows and the actual play begins, any consideration of fashion vaporizes. You simply can't maintain irony playing dodgeball. The squeal of tennis shoes, the musical *thwong* of the playground balls bouncing off the scuffed gym floor, the menace of a phalanx of blank-faced boys advancing toward you—suddenly, you're twelve again, gripped by the same pack mentality, the same terror at being singled out, the same weird thrill of hurling an object, however big and bouncy, at another person (and are you actually targeting that particular guy because he looked at you funny before the game and, well, *you'll show him*? And might you be picking on that one girl because you want her to notice you because, um, *she looks nice*?).

There are a few lawyers here, a schoolteacher, even a couple of accountants, but there's no talk of work or family. A guy in a T-shirt printed with a cartoon of a smoking bunny talks of the ex–javelin thrower whose dodgeball tosses have been clocked at fifty-five miles per hour. A waitress pulls up her sweats and shows off a purple bruise she got the week before, grinning like a kid recovering from a bit of rough-and-tumble play. "You get whacked and it stings, but it isn't so bad," she says. "Once you get hit in the face, you're fine."

Such bravado is put to the test a few days later when a few players meet early to play a pickup game against a team of actual kids. A group of jocks from a nearby Catholic high school heard about the game and thought it would be funny to play against a bunch of "goofy old guys." Their confidence is shattered quickly. It takes less than three minutes for the grown-ups to pick off the kids and send them, red-faced and dumbfounded, to the sideline. "I thought it would be more like Four Square maybe, or Candyland," says one of the kids, a senior named Matthew Delphey. "But I was very wrong. These guys are hardcore."

The Irresistible Lure of the Big Red Ball, Part Two

Dodgeball's kinder, wimpier cousin is the game of kickball. An elementary school fixture since the 1970s, kickball might be described as softball for dummies. Two teams take turns attempting to advance players around four bases; the crucial difference in kickball is that the small, hard baseball is replaced with a big rubber playground ball. There are no gloves, no bats, no uniforms. It's a good game for kids because it requires little training and even less actual athletic ability. Which, it turns out, also makes it a great game for rejuveniles.

I can't pretend to be even remotely impartial about kickball. I adore the game. And not only because I met a deeply funny and beautiful woman playing kickball in the mid-nineties; not only because I proposed to that woman by planting a diamond ring inside a kickball and dropping to one knee on home plate; not only because our first child spent much of his infancy in a homemade onesie printed with a big red ball; but also because it's a terrific game. It's almost entirely graceless and offers a near-perfect blend of silliness and seriousness. One moment you're arguing about the Infield Dog Rule, a rarely applied article of our unwritten rule book that stipulates what happens when a ball bounces off an animal (play on; you can check on your pet after the ball is dead). A moment later you're cheering for a skinny girl outfielder who just trapped a fly ball for a crucial third out.

The ball is central to the game's appeal, symbolically and otherwise. For one thing, it's hard to get excessively competitive about a game so completely oriented around something so big and cheerful and red—a cartoon polka dot. The ridiculous size and unwieldiness of the kickball also acts as a great equalizer. Ten inches in diameter, as soft to the touch as an inner tube, it can't be handled with anything remotely resembling finesse. You don't catch a kickball so much as enfold it. ("Let it mush into your gut" is the advice of a Baltimore coach.) Hulking men aren't much better at kickball than waifish women. Staring up at a descending kickball, we're all as small and silly as fifth-graders.

Adult videogamers or toy collectors often talk about what they do as if they were Smithsonian curators or Pentagon strategists. Kickballers are different. They revel in the fact that the game is played by kids. It turns out that the group I joined in Los Angeles was part of a mysterious adult kickball outbreak. In public parks across the country, egged on by a media that just can't resist color features on kooky adults playing a kids' game, dozens of adult kickball leagues formed in the late 1990s, some more organized than others, all pretty much dedicated to the childlike essence of the game. Kickballers in Milwaukee compete in a tournament known as "The Big Wheel 500." The top prize is known as the Golden Lunchbox. In Baltimore, a league of 1,200 players plays while waving rubber chickens and blasting show tunes. Team names in other leagues express kickball's juvenile spirit: Afterschool Special, the Big Kids, the Playground Bullies, the Milk Money Millionaires.

"Kickballers share a kid mentality," says Jimmy Walicek, the former IT consultant from Washington, D.C., whose barroom reminiscing led to the formation of the World Adult Kickball Association in 1998. Their stated mission: "to provide and promote the joy of kickball to those young at heart" (but not *literally* young—the league is specifically for players twenty-one or older). "We all played as kids and all remember a time when our only real responsibility was to have fun."

Jimmy lost his day job during the dot-com bust and devoted himself full time to the league. Within two years, more than one hundred kickball teams were playing in Washington,

D.C., alone. By 2004, the WAKA was sponsoring leagues in twenty cities as far away as Bombay, and Jimmy had four employees, a line of official merchandise, and a roster of corporate sponsors (Miller Light: the official beverage of kickball!). It's not lost on Jimmy that unleashing his inner child had somehow become a very grown-up business.

Just don't accuse him of being a grown-up. At thirty-two, Jimmy is a husband and new father, but like most rejuveniles, he bristles at the suggestion that he's a grown-up. "I don't want to grow up—not ever," he says. "I don't want to be smashing beer cans against my head at fifty. But I don't buy the idea that you have to act a certain way as you get older. You need to take responsibility and understand the consequences of your actions, but I never want to lose that childlike perspective."

Spaldeens, Street Games, and the Predictable Superiority of Boomer Rejuveniles

Just as adults of a certain age reflexively feel good about any game involving a big red playground ball, so too do other grown-ups get misty at the sight of the small, spongy pink ball known as the spaldeen. An essential accessory of urban kids in the fifties and sixties—they were sold for a quarter at most corner candy shops—the bubblegum-colored spaldeen (so named because that's how many New Yorkers pronounced the name of the manufacturer, Spalding) was used in a variety of kid games, from stickball and Stoopball to Box Ball and Hit the Penny.

For kids who grew up in certain big-city neighborhoods, the spaldeen has taken on a near-mythic quality. My father-in-law, for one, goes into a narcotic glaze at the mention of the spaldeen, incanting the names of a dozen spaldeen-specific games indigenous to the streets of the Bronx, from Slug to Curves to the decidedly un-PC I Declare War. That same spirit is at the heart of the children's book *Last Licks: A Spaldeen Story,* which is devoted to explaining the wonders of the spaldeen to kids unlucky enough to have been born after the manufacturer moved operations to Taiwan in 1978. Even literary heavyweights have been touched by spaldeen fever: In his novel *Underworld,* Don DeLillo ruminates at length on "the Hi-bounce rubber ball, the pink spaldeen," marveling at how kids would "adapt to available surfaces, using curbstones, stoops and manhole covers. They take the pockmarked world and turn a delicate inversion, making something brainy and rule-bound and smooth," he wrote. "Then [they] spend the rest of their lives trying to repeat the process."

Many adults aren't content to sit back and reminisce; they want to get out and *play.* In New York City, players can choose between three adult stickball leagues and as many annual tournaments. Just as they did as kids, they use broom handles for bats and fire hydrants and manhole covers as bases. The city has a stickball hall of fame (enshrined in the City of New York Museum), an official "commissioner of stickball" (Guardian Angels founder Curtis Sliwa, who has lobbied to make stickball an Olympic sport, telling the *Daily News* that "foreigners would take to it the way they do to dirty-water hot dogs, knishes, and french fries"), and even an official stickball street (Steve Mercado Stickball Boulevard in the Bronx, named after the head of an adult stickball league killed in the 9-11 attacks). Recognizing opportunity in the wave of spaldeen-specific nostalgia, Spalding reintroduced the ball in 1999, cranking out more than two million in the first year alone. "We were flooded with calls, letters, and e-mails from people thanking us for bringing it back," a Spalding spokesman told trade journal *Promo* magazine. "They remembered it from their childhood."

Clearly, there's something about the spaldeen that resists being tossed aside in maturity. Actor and director Rob Reiner developed an attachment to the spaldeen as a boy in New York; he now calls it "perhaps the greatest ball ever made." (Reiner's rejuvenile credentials were established in the 1986 boy weepie *Stand By Me,* the story of five friends summed up by the tagline "Nothing that happens after you're twelve matters very much.") Over the years, Reiner has often used studio back lots to re-create favorite spaldeen games, the movie-set stoops standing in for the real ones of his hometown. "I'm a fifty-three-year-old man," he wrote in a 2001 essay. "I've made my career working in Hollywood. And it has been a good life. But the truth is, nothing compares with being a kid and growing up in New York . . . Imagination and a spaldeen could keep you occupied forever."

Spaldeen-specific nostalgia inevitably leads to the remembrance of other street games, from hopscotch and marbles to Pie Tin Frisbee and Ringoleavio. Once remembered, these games have a way of lodging themselves in the adult mind, becoming for many synonymous with all that is good and lost about childhood. Thirty-some years after playing stickball off a supermarket wall in Queens, New York, childhood buddies Michael Greene and Mark Pesner created Streetplay, a website devoted to the promotion and preservation of mostly forgotten street games. The site includes detailed game descriptions, photo galleries, and message boards filled with discussion of such hotly disputed topics as the proper amount of Fox's U-Bet syrup in an egg cream soda. Mostly, though, the site broadcasts urgent calls to revive favorite games of childhood. Passive nostalgia isn't enough. Adults are encouraged to print out rule sheets, fashion new stickball bats, and reclaim the games of their childhoods.

When these messages are read, another major theme emerges. Adult lovers of street games can't help comparing the games of their youth to the vastly inferior sorts of things kids today do for fun. In the same spirit that Boomer-age adults love to compare their beloved Beatles and Rolling Stones to Britney and Eminem, street game buffs always seem to conclude their praise of Fivebox or Stoopball with two words that instantly communicate fogeydom: *kids today*. As in, *Kids today are too busy simulating heinous atrocities on their PlayStations to appreciate the simple glory of Ace-King-Queen*. Or, *Kids today are too busy doing drills in soccer practice to come up with something as ingenious as I Declare War*. The fact that so few kids today enjoy unstructured, unsupervised play is truly "one of the great losses as a society," notes Hillary Clinton, that standard-bearer of Boomer parents, in a 1999 essay about her childhood love of kickball, softball, and a team game known as Chase and Run. "I'm hopeful that we can regain the joy and experience of free play and neighborhood games that were taken for granted growing up in my generation. That would be one of the best gifts we could give our children."

All of which can easily be chalked up to yet another outbreak of Boomer superiority. Just as many adults born between 1946 and 1964 believe the politics they embraced in college were unprecedented and the social changes they forced as adults will be etched in eternity—so too do they now believe that the games they played as runny-nosed ten-year-olds are sacrosanct. The most maddening thing about this particular form of Boomer self-importance is that it's not all wrong.

The street games played in the fifties and sixties are indeed a marvel of resourcefulness and creativity. Of course, the very idea that old-time play trumps modern play is basically ridiculous, because there's no way to measure that essential X factor of fun. But if you had, say, a radar gun that could calculate the precise amount of fun that Eisenhower-era street kids had compared with millennium suburbanites, is there any question who would earn the higher score?

The big difference, of course, is that street games of the fifties and sixties belonged entirely to kids. They were played without supervision, uniforms, or even equipment. Kids invented the rules, managed the teams, and even observed seasons for one game or another. Kids were the game designers, agents, and commissioners. Add to that the inarguable splendor of the spaldeen, which is indeed a magnificent object, a twenty-five-cent icon of an age when kids' games were far freer, wilder, and more inventive than most played today.

Extremely Rejuvenile

Rejuveniles need not look back to the past century for kid-centered, kid-controlled child's play. For many of today's kids, play is even more wildly unregulated and hazardous than it was for the street kids of the fifties. For them, play is less about following adult instructions than it is about finding the most hazardous thing in their environment and then proceeding to fuck with it.

Which brings us to skateboarding, snowboarding, BMX-ing, and the other pastimes variously described as "extreme." The growth of extreme sports has been explosive: Skate-boarding, which in the mid-1970s was something California surfers did to keep in shape when the waves were lame, is now the single most popular leisure activity among Americans aged seven to seventeen. According to Rod Warnick, a professor of recreation, sports, and tourism at the University of Massachusetts at Amherst, the number of kids under the age of eighteen who skate now stands well over ten million, about two million more than the number of kids who play Little League. There have been parallel leaps in the number of young snowboarders and paintballers, and corresponding drops in the number of people pursuing less daredevil activities like tennis and aerobics.

Kids are powering this shift toward riskier, more free-form play, but they haven't managed to keep it to themselves. Increasingly, adults are picking up the extreme habits of kids. Call it the trickle-up effect of childhood play—kids find some new way to risk life and limb, and pretty soon their elders are looking to muscle in on the action. That's what's happened in snowboarding, which began as a teen phenomenon and is still identified as the rowdy kid brother of skiing. More than thirty years after a Vermont teenager strapped two skis together to see what it would be like to "surf" down a mountain, the ranks of snowboarders includes paunchy CEOs and perky grandparents. There are twenty-three competitive snowboarders over the age of sixty in the U.S. alone. These older snowboarders have a name: "grays on trays." And ski resorts around the world have transformed themselves to reflect the change, carving out special playgroundlike "freestyle" areas complete with piped-in rock music and ramps, rails, and half-pipes.

Older thrill seekers may pick up their enthusiasm from kids, but that doesn't mean they stop being old. Their tolerance for discomfort is lower, their appetite for luxury keener, and their gear-head tendencies more advanced. Teen snowboarders might be willing to crash on a friend's floor after a punishing day on the slopes, but grays on trays are more likely to head for a place like the Block Hotel in Lake Tahoe, a snowboarder resort that offers its guests complimentary protein bars at check-in and surround sound in every room. Teen skate rats might take pride in pulling big tricks on a battered hand-me-down deck, but a fortysomething skateboarder of means will have a hard time resisting the Street Carver, a cast-aluminum $500 board produced by BMW.

Kids aren't even part of the business model for a new-fangled pogo stick called the Flybar, a high-performance aluminum "exercise and stunt bar" that sells for $300 and sends riders soaring six feet in the air. "This is a pogo stick for the twenty-two-and-up crowd," says principal Dave Jargowsky. "Pogo sticking was fun for kids who basically wanted to see how many times they could jump up and down without falling. This is a whole different experience for a whole new breed of rider."

A visit to one of the hundreds of paintball fields that have popped up in the past decade confirms the generational divide. First played in the woods of New Hampshire, paintball now is played by more than eleven million people worldwide. Younger paintballers typically show up for battle in jeans and smudged goggles. Their older counterparts, meanwhile, are prone to fashion themselves as sci-fi soldiers on a post-apocalyptic wasteland, equipped with muscle-molded chestplates and $1,500 guns with names like the Maverick, the Intimidator, and the Evil Omen. (Sales of paintball gear now total more than $600 million a year.) For older players, paintball is more than an excuse to play dress-up—it's also a rare arena where they can hang out unselfconsciously with kids.

"I'm forty-eight years old, but at a paintball event I can sit around with twelve-year-olds and we talk equipment, tactics, and tell stories from past games," army veteran–turned-paintballer James Helton told the *Kansas City Star*. "It's as much a social event as a sport."

Taken together, extreme sports represent a return to the sort of risky, messy, free-form play that activists campaigned against a century ago. The similarities are especially apparent in the case of Parkour, the free-form urban daredevil sport most obviously inspired by skateboarding, Spider-Man cartoons, and kung fu movies, but which also takes its cue from older traditions of street games, hooliganism, and creative vagrancy. Accounts of life in city centers around the turn of the century include colorful anecdotes of kids jumping on and off moving cars (a trick known as "flipping"), hanging off fire escapes, riding the fenders of streetcars, and sliding across blocks of ice filched from the back of delivery trucks. "Children made good use of the available space, the streets and sidewalks as well as the doorways, gutters, stoops and inside stairways," notes historian David Nasaw in *Children of the City,* his account of urban childhood of the 1900s. "The intensity with which the children threw themselves into their games startled middle class observers. But this intensity was just the outward manifestation of their capacity for putting the adult world at a distance."

While today's extreme-sports fans are every bit as intense as the street hooligans of the 1900s, they part company with their forebears on one crucial point: Grown-ups are welcome along for the ride. Sebastien Foucan, one half of the French duo responsible for Parkour, has kept up with the sport well into his thirties, despite settling down with a wife and young daughter. The superstar of SuperMoto, a form of motorcycle racing that combines track speeds with dirt bike jumps and spills, is Jeff Ward, a forty-three-year-old who competes in events that draw competitors as young as fourteen.

Then there's Tony Hawk, the thirty-seven-year-old skateboarding mogul who continues to skate while parenting three kids and heading a company that generates an estimated $250 million a year. In part, that success is a result of his phenomenal skating record—among the eighty tricks he's invented is the 900, a two-and-a-half-revolution feat that no other skater has been able to duplicate—and partly due to a squeaky-clean image that has attracted multimillion-dollar endorsement deals for everything from sneakers to snack foods. When not trying out new tricks on a private vert ramp, he loves surfing and playing video games (he was heavily involved in the development of both Tony Hawk's Pro Skater and Tony Hawk Underground).

Hawk himself credits his success to his knack for staying in sync with the "12.5-year-old suburban male" who represents his core audience. The youthful part of him is kept alive by his eleven-year-old son and the pure act of skating. "Skating is a huge part of me," he says in an e-mail. "It transcends age."

Age might not make a difference to Hawk, but even he acknowledges that skating skews young for a reason. The fun of skating as a kid had a lot to do with the fact, he says, that "no one was telling me how to do it. I didn't have to show up for practice every day." Besides that, it was a whole lot more exciting than anything going on within the high school athletic department. "Skating is constant action, constant excitement," he says. "It's nonstop. Someone drops in. Boom. It's on. They're in the air. They're flying. That's exactly how I was when I was younger. I mean, I feel like I was in that frame of mind back then—where I needed constant stimulation. I needed to seek thrills. And I probably would have been diagnosed with ADD."

Older skaters have discovered, Hawk says, that they don't necessarily have to force that thrill-seeking impulse into permanent remission. "As skating grew, skaters realized that it is possible to keep improving their skills as they got older," he says. "It is now even possible to make a living at it if you have the skills, instead of having to find a 'real' job."

The very idea that an adult can still devote himself to nose grinds and frontside ollies is indeed a potent fantasy for many adults. Pat Hawk, Tony's sister and business manager, describes her brother's adult fan base as "rabid." Some of those adults simply love what Hawk represents. ("He skates for a living and gets to fly around in a private jet," says Pat. "How cool is that?") Other fans are former skaters reliving their skating years through their kids—they're the dads who not only know what a Boom Boom Huck Jam is but are the first to volunteer to carpool the kids. And then there are those who, like Hawk, are determined to keep skating through marriages, kids, careers, and stiff joints.

Dale Anthony was forty-five years old, thick around the middle and suffering from sciatica, when he decided the time had come to revive a teenage passion for skating. As a kid, Dale says, he was something of a "ruffian." Playtime usually meant throwing snowballs at passing cars or snooping around abandoned houses near his home in rural Massachusetts. He started skateboarding in high school after buying a board with new polyurethane wheels and a look at *SkateBoarder* magazine, which celebrated the antics of longhaired skate rebels like

Tony Alva and Jay Adams (who, the magazine reported, once got a ticket for skating on the freeway and allegedly "skate-snatched a wig off a bald woman's head").

Dale skated through college at Northeastern University, spending late nights in the parking lot of Fenway Park, where a sloped buffer offered a "beautiful asphalt wave." "I loved everything about skating," he says. "I loved the look, the talk, the feel. But when I grew up, I was the only one doing it. I was basically a freak."

He gave it up after getting married and settling into a job. Years passed. He took up the more mature pastime of jogging. One marriage ended, another began. Then one night, Dale stayed up late to watch a rented video: *Dogtown and Z-Boys,* Stacy Peralta's vivid 2001 account of the Zephyr skating team, a group of Southern California street kids who revolutionized the sport thirty years ago. Watching archival footage of his teenage heroes doing aerials off the lips of empty swimming pools and making a playground of parking lots and concrete stairways, Dale felt a familiar tug of excitement. "I was so worked up when it ended that I rewinded it and watched it again," he remembers. "I couldn't sleep all night long. I decided right there I had to get back."

On a trip to a local skate shop, Dale discovered his situation wasn't totally unique. The success of *Dogtown* helped spawn a huge revival of so-called old-school skating. The skateboard industry is still geared primarily toward kids, who prefer punk rock fashions and straight, slightly concave decks introduced in the eighties. But increasingly, the kid gear is sharing display space with sportswear and equipment designed for a more kick-back, longhaired, surf-the-asphalt seventies aesthetic. Manufacturers have revived long-stagnant brands like Kryptonics and Z-Flex, reintroduced the classic "pig" shape favored by older skaters, and brought back such vintage fashions as slip-on checkerboard Vans. To a skater like Dale, the mystique of this stuff is intense—all that's missing is the Allman Brothers blaring from a parked car, a can of warm soda, and he's smack dab, as he frequently says, "back in the day."

After a few hours listening to Dale talk about the old-school revival, his brother-in-law invited him to build a skate ramp in his backyard. Dale jumped at the offer, returning in a few weeks with a truckful of plywood and sheet metal and building a six-foot-high, twenty-foot-long "beast." It turned out to be an ideal arrangement, both for Dale and his two teen nephews. "They love having this gigantic pipe in their back-yard," he says. "But they're not half as stoked as I am. The most fun I have is when I'm alone and I can really cut loose. And I love showing up with my boards, doing my thing, and then driving away."

Far from feeling embarrassed by his hobby, Dale takes pride in the fact that he's a forty-seven-year-old skate rat. "I like the sense of otherness," he says. "I like that all my friends at work are golfing and I'm limping from a fall on my skate-board. I know a lot of people look at me like I'm trying to prove something. But I just love the rush, the freedom, the feeling like if I don't pull something off I'm going to die—that's a great feeling."

Nowadays far older skaters are concluding that they don't necessarily have to give up that surge of freedom and wild-ness. Liz Bevington is a German émigré who started skating more than twenty years ago when her seven-year-old son wanted to learn. He liked skating; his mom *loved* it. "I got young again," she says. Today, her son is grown and has little time to skate. Meanwhile his eighty-year-old mom spends most of her days atop a custom board based on the first deck she bought for her son, carving up the boardwalk near her home in Santa Monica, California, skating with the rest of the kids. She avoids ramps and slaloms and the like—"Tricks are for kids," she says—but the simple act of scooting from one place to another atop a skateboard connects her to an essential part of herself. "I'm not too comfortable with older people," she says. "They talk too much about their aches and pains. I get 'em too, but I forget about 'em . . . Fun is what keeps me going."

Child's Play as Pure Play

Octogenarian skateboarders. Fiftysomething skippers. Thirtysomething tag players. Regarded in passing, in the newspaper stories and TV news segments they so often attract, such characters mostly come off as harmless kooks whose love of child's play is of no more consequence than an enthusiasm for German shepherds or hats. For some observers, however, adults who indulge in child's play are nothing less than poster children for a culture in crisis. The fact that so many adults feel no censure whatsoever in flying so furiously in the face of long-standing age norms is offered as proof of how superficial, overindulged, and spoiled we have become.

"In most cultural contexts, play prepares children to move into adult roles," says Bryan Page, chair of the Department of Anthropology at the University of Miami. "Now the whole thing has been reversed—play is now the primary thing and adult roles and working have become repulsive. We have huge numbers of people now who are just counting the minutes until they can be released from their jobs to do what they really want, which is play."

To Page and his compatriots, the specter of adults at play is just another sad symptom of a profoundly frivolous age. Americans, for instance, shell out more than $600 billion a year on recreation, which, according to the U.S. Department of Commerce, includes movie tickets, video games, toys and sports supplies, stereo and video equipment, and trips to amusement parks. That's roughly equal to the entire U.S. budget deficit. Considering that expenditure in an era of deep social division and political strife, it's easy to start thinking of the whole of Western society as a well-meaning but hopelessly spoiled child whose homework is piling up while he clings, desperately, to wasteful, self-indulgent nonsense.

But are we really so playful? While it's true that well-off Westerners spend more on stuff we don't strictly need, it's also true we're working harder than ever. Our play, in other words, is counterbalanced by increasingly large workloads. Americans, for one, work more than citizens of any nation in the world, at least three and a half weeks a year more than the Japanese. Meanwhile diary studies indicate that people in most modern nations have between twenty-eight and forty-two hours a week of free time, a figure that's held steady since the 1930s, says Geoffrey Godbey, a professor at Penn State University who has devoted much of his career to studying how people spend their days. Surveys consistently show that we're dissatisfied with our free time, feeling increasingly hurried and crunched. That dissatisfaction is almost certainly due to changes in how we divide and perceive our time. While the ratio of hours spent working and playing has not changed much over the years, our days are chopped into increasingly smaller chunks as our capacity to multitask blurs the boundaries between business and pleasure. Just as work has become more like play, play has become more like work. We fill downtime at the office playing online poker or watching short movies on the Web, haul home stacks of paper for the weekend, hop on and off e-mail while looking after the kids, and treat social gatherings as prime opportunities to network.

But even as work has seeped into our leisure time and vice versa, there's no doubt which part of our lives means more to us. Labor has lost the power to define us the way it once did, back when tradesmen or factory workers or insurance adjusters could expect to hold the same basic job decade after decade. In a world where career paths increasingly fluctuate between contract gigs, moonlight assignments, and lateral moves, we define ourselves more by what we do *outside* work. The carpenter wears yoga togs. The lawyer loves NASCAR. The schoolteacher lives for poker. Our energy, our community spirit, and even our spiritual feeling spring from our free time like never before. We once played in order to become better workers. Now we work to get back to the crucial business of play.

It should be clear, though, that not all play is created equal. There's a big difference between the sort of spontaneous, imaginative play embraced by rejuveniles and what play theorist Gwen Gordon calls "the enemy of play": recreation. The sad fact is that many adults begin an urge to reconnect with some basic, playful part of themselves, only to end up zoning out with video games, vegging out on a luxury cruise, or going ballistic during competitive sports. Some adults have a talent for turning even the most childlike pastimes into exercises in adult efficiency, improvement, and status-accrual. Witness the owners of fifteen-pound bicycles who can't imagine riding without microcomputer systems that track pedal cadence, altitude, and heart rate. These adults play to lose weight, blow off steam, or spend "quality time" with the kids, in the process barely glancing up against the pulsating anarchic force of true play.

Spontaneous, creative play is now becoming scarce even among children. At the same time that rejuveniles have rediscovered the joys of child's play, too many kids are confined to domestic safe zones or enrolled in soccer clinics, piano lessons, and French tutorials designed to enhance future college applications. Then we all complain about how busy we are and how fast our kids are growing up.

So maybe rejuveniles' love of child's play isn't so kooky and meaningless after all. It's certainly not a harbinger of the downfall of Western civilization. In its freest forms, it can even approach the profound. True play, the kind that comes naturally to children, is mysterious, improvisational, energizing. It relies on flexibility and movement (an object with play isn't fixed; it has wiggle room). The adults who bring themselves to chase, skip, leap, or holler with the completeness and abandon of children tap in to this creative force. In so doing, they strike blows against the forces of rigidity, regularity, and routine. Child's play enacted by adults can certainly look undignified. It might even appear desperate. But at root, it's something else: a ridiculous skipping frontside ollie cat leap toward an essential mystery of life that adults have for too long been discouraged from exploring.

THREE

the lure of the toy

IF TOYS R US,
AS THOSE FAMOUS AMERICAN
PHILOSOPHER-RETAILERS PUT IT,
THEN WHO R WE?

— Pat Kane, *The Play Ethic*

Thankfully, one needn't growl like a cougar or risk bodily harm on a hydraulic pogo stick to reexperience the joy of childhood play. Such activities may be the purest expressions of the rejuvenile impulse, but they are by no means the most common. For one thing, childhood play is entirely too *active* a proposition for many grown-ups, some of whom never cared much for schoolyard play to begin with. Others have lost the youthful ability to run around for hours on end fueled by nothing but OJ and string cheese. That's where toys come in. A much easier, more manageable method for achieving playfulness in adulthood - revolves around toys. Searching for, acquiring, and getting reacquainted with childhood toys like Legos, action figures, or paper dolls is for many a gateway into the rejuvenile mind-set.

And happily for rejuveniles, there has never been a busier or more accepting time for adult toy lovers. Not long ago, grown-ups who refused to stash away favorite playthings could expect to be gently humored, isolated, or even ridiculed. John Darcy Noble, a British toy collector, curator, and dollmaker, recalled coming to America in 1960 and encountering blank stares and statements of concern when he spoke of his love of toys. "I was thought to be verging on lunacy," he recalled.

Some of that stigma persists today. "I am painfully aware that 99.9 percent of the world's population finds it odd—bizarre or mentally deranged even—that a grown man would be purchasing toys for himself," collector Chad Rushing wrote on an Internet posting board for die-hard fans of Transformers, robotic toys from the eighties that have become a favorite collector's item. "I'm sure this labels me as a 'freak' in the eyes of people at work . . . but I like to think that's their problem, not mine. I mean, how could anyone possibly find golf, the stock market, home electronics, or barhopping more interesting than robots raging to destroy the evil forces of another group of robots?"

Today, thanks to the Internet and a culture subdividing into ever more specialized niches, there's a community of toy lovers for every adult personality. Whimsical antique collectors gather at auction houses to peer over bifocals at $100,000 Jumeaus and Brus dolls. Mild-mannered computer geeks in tight-fitting windbreakers and close-cropped beards hoard resin action figures of their favorite anime superheroes. Ex-urban church ladies clog the phone lines of QVC to complete their collection of Marie Osmond Signature dolls. And then, of course, there are the grizzled grease monkeys who spend hours hunched over model train layouts.

Many adult toy lovers say they take profound comfort in recapturing childhood experiences, or in finally getting their hands on stuff they couldn't afford or were denied as kids: "It's never too late to have a happy childhood," announces a popular bumper sticker.

One such rejuvenile is Ali Rushfield, a thirty-three-year-old screenwriter who says the most significant relationship in her life began in college when she became attached to a stuffed animal she called simply E, whom she described in a

rejuvenile

2004 monologue as "my companion, my muse, my stuffed frog puppet doll." Her attachment to E did not weaken in the years since college, even as she adopted an otherwise adult lifestyle ("I no longer wake up at noon or have Cap'n Crunch for dinner or try pills meant for someone's cat just to see what will happen," she says). She admits that she sometimes worries about her relationship with E—she describes a particularly poignant moment of doubt driving to work and realizing she'd secured her frog puppet with the passenger's-side seat belt— but she's now made peace with the fact that she's a grown-up with a puppet sidekick. "I've decided not to give E up, no matter what other people think or how old I get," she says. "I have stopped trying to find clear answers to this question and have simply accepted and embraced my reality—an E-less world is not a world where I want to live."

On its surface, Ali's bond with a stuffed frog might seem like a hipster lark, or perhaps even a sign of deep dysfunction. But to my mind, it's a classic rejuvenile maneuver, a way of maintaining wonder, trust, and silliness in a world where these qualities are often in short supply.

But just as there are different sorts of rejuvenile, there are divergent categories of adult toy lover. In one camp we find hard-core collectors and eBay gold-star honorees who regard toys as artifacts, exhibits in their own personal pop culture archive. These are the mint-in-the-box fetishists who would never dream of breaking a factory seal for the chance to crawl around in the backyard with that Boba Fett figure. They catalog their collections, display favorite items in Lucite boxes, and negotiate complex trade agreements with other collectors. They like toys just fine, but for all intents and purposes they might as well be collecting stamps or coins or Olympic pins.

But of course they're *not* collecting stamps or coins or

pins; their choice tells us something about what truly matters to them. Stamps, coins, and pins serve entirely different functions from dolls, windup toys, or action figures. A bobblehead on a dashboard, a Barrel of Monkeys on a desktop, a Barbie in a boudoir—a toy that belongs to an adult is an announcement: This adult isn't done playing. There's fun here. "Toy collectors get to relive their childhood, enjoy it again, go back to a simpler time when they didn't have a mortgage and health insurance and all that stuff," says Leonard Lee, editor of *Toy Review* magazine, one of the dozens of specialty publications catering to the toy-loving adult.

For most adult toy lovers, toys are a simple announcement. I'm thinking here of the carriers of Magic Eight Ball key chains who want to be regarded as the sort of serendipitous free spirits who might consult a plastic oracle at any given moment ("Will I find a parking spot? Outlook good!"). These are the professionals who keep a color-gradated stack of board games in their mid-century living rooms for their aesthetic value and the administrators whose offices are adorned with precious Madame Alexander dolls, the better to communicate that fanciful imaginative powers are at work here. It makes no difference that these toys are rarely, if ever, played with—in fact, it's probably better that they aren't, since things always seem to get broken, knocked over, or drooled upon on those occasions when someone brings a kid to the office and the doll's caretaker is put in the awkward position of stepping in and asking the child if she would mind terribly much putting that precious dolly back on the credenza where she found it.

There's one more class of adult toy lover for whom toys are far more than decorative. These are the grown-ups whose childhoods were molded by epic encounters with Lincoln Logs, Rubik's Cubes, and Koosh Balls. As they grew up, toys didn't go away; they just got fancier, pricier, and more plentiful. Now the trunks of their VW Beetles are stocked with Chinese fighting kites or radio-controlled ATVs, and their spare bedrooms overflow with enough dolls and doodads to crowd out memories of the meager toy chests of their childhoods. Among the high-profile toy lovers are comic Tom Green, who according to an account in *People* magazine keeps a room in his Beverly Hills estate stocked with Tonka trucks, coloring books, and board games (his favorite: Hungry Hungry Hippo).

Such eccentricities aren't limited to celebrities. David Brooks is a forty-two-year-old graduate of Wharton Business School whose passion for toys was the subject of a 2003 *Washington Times* story. Browsing his local toy store searching for a hobby "other than watching television," Brooks picked up a box of K'Nex, plastic building blocks aimed at the preteen set. Within a few months his K'Nex habit had become so intense that he decided to take a year off work, rent an office to house his works in progress, and devote himself entirely to "life as a K'Nex developer."

Such habits trigger alarm bells in some quarters—the *Washington Times,* for one, used Brooks's story to launch into a discussion of how traditional adulthood is under attack by "radical feminism, the New Left, and the sexual revolution," thus giving rise to the nightmarish image of a fellowship of young women popping birth control pills, anti-globalization activists, and Wharton MBAs obsessed by pieces of connectable plastic. But if there is a cabal inciting adults to rediscover toys, the ringleaders are to be found in the toy industry, which is desperate to open up new markets for products losing favor among children.

The toy industry has in fact taken dramatic steps in recent

years to court adult consumers, creating products and campaigns specifically targeted at Hot Wheel collectors, senior American Girl enthusiasts, and mature Nerf tossers. What is known in the industry as the collector market represents a big opportunity in a notoriously slow-growth industry, says Reyne Rice, a toy trend specialist for the Toy Industry Association. Americans spend in the neigborhood of $20 billion on toys every year. That makes Americans the toy hog of the world—with 4.5 percent of the world's population, the U.S. buys 45 percent of the world's toy production.

Despite that haul, the U.S. toy industry hasn't experienced significant growth in more than twenty years. That's partly because of competition from video games, but also due to a phenomenon known in the industry as "age compression" or, more conversationally, KGOY (which stands for "kids grow older younger"). Beginning in the mid-eighties, parents reported that kids who once were content playing with blocks, action figures, or dolls until the age of fourteen were suddenly tossing those toys aside at eight, declaring them "too babyish." Toymakers have responded with so-called Tween Toys— handheld gadgets, fashion accessories, and the like—but not before taking a big hit. According to Brian Goldner, president of toys at Hasbro, Tweens cost the industry more than $1.2 billion between 1999 and 2003.

As kids became a less reliable source of revenue, the industry began selling in earnest to adults, appealing to their increasing appetite for fun and thus transforming the previously fringe world of collecting into a mass-market phenomenon. As Goldner observes, "Kids are getting older faster, but adults are getting younger later."

The first thing toymakers did to appeal to this new market was to muscle into traditionally toy-free environments. Auto supply shops, pharmacies, stationery stores, electronic outlets, pancake houses—all have witnessed invasions of plush and plastic. Walk into the downtown Denver outlet of Linens 'n Things and you'll find a Dora the Explorer Activity Belt Pouch next to the chenille throws and modular wine racks. Venture into the Discount Auto Parts in Pembroke Pines, Florida, and pick up a Lego Racer along with your spark plugs. "We plan to sell product to every nook and cranny in the world," a Hasbro senior vice president told the industry journal *Playthings*.

From Average Adult to AFOL

Just as it's becoming more common to find toys in everyday adult surroundings, so too is it becoming more common to find adults entirely devoted to toys. Jake McKee was working as a computer programmer in Dallas when he found himself obsessing about a new line of Lego blocks shaped like *Star Wars* spacecraft. Jake was twenty-four at the time. He'd long ago stashed away his childhood toys in favor of more adult interests, like photography. But something about the idea of a Lego X-Wing fighter thrilled him to the core. On the day the toys were released, he found himself canceling plans with friends so he could scour the city's toy stores until he'd acquired all ten sets. "It was a total rush," he says. "It was like smoking your first cigarette."

The experience triggered a cascade of pleasant memories. He recalled being eight or nine, sitting in the back of his parents' car, twirling the propellers of a yellow rescue helicopter. He recalled lying on the floor of his bedroom fiddling with a toy car that looked just like one from his favorite TV program, a Saturday morning cartoon called *Mobile Armor Strike Kommand*. Then there was the miraculous day that his mother, who generally disapproved of war toys and military play, gave in and allowed him to buy a G.I. Joe. "I remember walking toward the cash register of the department store, keeping my head down and trying not to get too excited because then she might change her mind," he says.

Wondering if he could track down that same toy, Jake was surprised to discover a huge and thriving G.I. Joe subculture online. The three-inch-tall plastic soldier Jake remembered from the early 1980s was now selling for more than one hundred dollars. That was a bargain compared with the foot-high figures from the original line, which boasted such features as facial hair and Kung Fu Grip. The rarest figures, such as a G.I. Nurse Action Girl that came complete with wooden crutches and a tiny glass bottle of plasma, fetched upward of $5,000.

Jake enjoyed learning about G.I. Joe collectors, but on reflection he realized he wasn't one himself. The G.I. Joe world was all about buy, sell, trade, and repair—the ultimate goal being the achievement of a vaunted condition known as "display status." That was all well and good, but it had little to do with what so excited him about toys in the first place. He didn't want to collect—he wanted to create.

So Jake dove headfirst into his Lego habit, setting aside a spare room in his apartment for his rapidly mounting haul. On the Internet, Jake found an encouraging community of enthusiasts known as AFOL (Adult Fans of Lego). While Jake was never comfortable with the G.I. Joe crowd, he felt an instant allegiance to the AFOL. Within a year, he'd opened an online marketplace for fellow fans to buy, sell, and trade pieces. Then, just two years after he'd snapped together his first brick as a grown-up, Lego hired Jake as its official ambassador to the AFOL community.

Today, Jake's life revolves around Lego (the word is a Danish combination of "play well" and the Latin for "connect"). His personal stash now numbers more than 100,000 pieces, but Jake says it never seems quite enough. One day on a visit to his mother's house, he unearthed an old bucket of Legos that was stashed at the back of a closet. "I was like 'OK, where's the rest of it?'" he recalls. "I couldn't believe this little bucket was the whole thing. In my mind I had this gigantic collection. It's almost as if now, as an adult, I'm trying to match in reality what I'm carrying around in my head. I'm fighting to build it up to the once-grand level it was."

Of Dolls, Men, and Eccentric Rejuvenile Forefathers

While grown-up Lego lovers and mature G.I. Joe buffs may seem like uniquely modern creations—products of an intensely commercial, relentlessly trivial age—adult interest in toys is hardly new. As noted by Gary Cross in *Kids' Stuff,* his 1998 history of toys: "Only in modern times have toys become primarily objects for children, props in a play world separated from adults." In medieval times, adults routinely played with stilts, whistles, hoops, and sticks. German artisans built the first dollhouses in the 1500s as showcases for refined aristocratic tastes. The first toy soldiers were made for the amusement of gentlemen who never dreamed of leaving such playthings to their young sons or daughters. As recently as the nineteenth century, it was perfectly acceptable for even the most educated and cultured to profess a love for things we would now consider highly juvenile, including jumping jacks, air rifles, and paper dolls.

That all changed, like so much else, with the onset of the Industrial Revolution. As we've seen, the dawn of the twentieth century witnessed a seismic shift in the understanding of childhood and adulthood. Respectable adults suddenly had better things to do than prance about on stilts. And children, who up to that point had been hustled off to the fields or factories the moment they could grip a scythe or man an assembly line, were first granted the special status they now enjoy. That new status brought significant benefits—the abolition of infanticide, stricter child labor laws, and so on—but surely one of the advances most widely cheered by children themselves was the sudden and dramatic supply of toys.

Those toys came courtesy of a burgeoning industry of amusement, which began with factories using scrap materials to turn out batches of cheap children's playthings. Farm equipment manufacturers started producing Flexible Flyers. Manufacturers produced miniatures of their adult products for kids. With toys sold in separate sections of new department stores and catalogs, the lines were drawn—toys were for kids, and adults were expected to outgrow them as they matured.

Adult attachment to toys was indulged by the occasional fad—grown-ups made a run on yo-yos in the 1920s, bought 32 million boxes of Silly Putty in the early fifties, and later spun Hula-Hoops at cocktail parties. Most were content with these brief infatuations. Still, the occasional outcast refused to give up his childhood attachment to toys, often in spite of enormous social pressure. John Darcy Noble was a fussy British eccentric who shared his lifetime friend Quentin Crisp's extravagant tastes—in college, he wore a long beard, pirate boots, and was known to arrive at social functions carrying a monkey on his shoulder. As a curator at the Museum of the City of New York, he helped advance a radical notion: that toys are not only instruments of fun but artifacts that contain deep truths about our societies and selves. And unlike the majority of collectors and toy snobs who have since created a rich market for antique toys, Noble loved toys as playthings first and foremost. He summed up his radical enthusiasm for toys to a reporter for the *Los Angeles Times* after retiring from his museum post:

> I believe play is a natural human activity, and what's wrong with this world is that people have stopped playing. The most they do is play cards or watch other people play on television. The most highly evolved animals are always playing—monkeys, whales play all the time. Only stupid humanity has stopped playing. The whole stupid world has gone crackers.

The son of a suburban London blacksmith, Noble began collecting toys at the age of six when he traded a puzzle for a ceramic whistle with a schoolmate. He soon began a brisk trade in rare and unusual dolls, picture books, and artifacts. As an art student and schoolteacher during the worst years of World War II, Noble became increasingly obsessed with old toys. The contrast between his interests and the world around him could not have been greater. Under skies he later described as "made hideous with anti-aircraft gunfire," Noble rummaged through junkshops and antique outlets in search of nursery room castoffs. "Every new find, every fresh old doll looked at with my innocent eyes could open up a rich field for speculation and wonder," he later wrote.

In a 1998 article for *Dolls* magazine titled "How to Collect

Dolls If You Are Very, Very Poor" (which he was for most of his life, calling his poverty a "great inconvenience"), Noble described a china doll he found on the back of a shelf during an antique auction. Underneath a crude homemade dress, Noble discovered a figure whittled from a wood peg and bits of whale ivory and was inspired to make a forensic analysis of the doll. Noting the heavy quality of the paint and the unusually large screws holding the prefabricated china head in place, Noble speculated that "the doll's head must have been bought by a Yankee seaman on shore leave and taken off to sea with him to be turned into a doll for a little sister perhaps, or a daughter. His patience with all his clumsy materials is very touching—For me, she is a very special treasure but I often think when playing with her (and she is delightful to play with) how very much more precious she must have been to the little Yankee girl who was her first owner."

Even as he identified with the first recipient of the doll, Noble's allegiance was plainly to the sailor who created it, since what toys revealed about adults was always much more interesting to Noble than what they said about children. "Toys weren't bought by children," he once told the *New York Times*. "They were bought by parents who had social standards."

This particular interest underlies Noble's fascination with toys from the eighteenth century, a time when adults still cherished toys with something like his own fervor. That love was infectious. By the time of his death in 2003 at the age of eighty, he had become the leading figure in a thriving subculture of antique toy lovers, each of whom has his or her own particular specialty. Today there are whole societies devoted to the collection and preservation of German peg woodens, papier-mâchés, and French bisques. Noble's stature is perhaps greatest among paper doll collectors, a group of about one thousand enthusiasts who represent the thin upper crust of the adult toy market.

Unlike so many other rejuveniles, who so often use toys as talismans to summon their own childhoods, paper doll collectors aren't all that interested in their own pasts. The dolls they prize most of all are rare and delicate artifacts of adult wish fulfillment. Ladies of the eighteenth and nineteenth centuries treated paper dolls as barometers of style in much the same way modern women regard fashion magazines and advertising, snipping paper figures and outfits from Sunday newspaper supplements. Today's paper doll collectors aren't inclined to wistful daydreaming about the wonders of childhood—they're much too busy swooning over the extravagance of period fashions and the artistry of Edwardian draftsmanship.

Interest in paper dolls seems no different from any other absurdly specialized interest in a rapidly fragmenting culture. It's easy to leave it at that—to lump the paper doll crowd together with the AFOL and G.I. Joe enthusiasts in a category of adults with a weakness for kids' stuff. But the paper doll enthusiasts are special, if only for the fact that the objects of their attention were created for adults. Paper doll collectors aren't trying to return to a childhood when they were free to play. They are reprising an era in which adults were free to play just as children.

Here Come the Doll Ladies

Still, trade in paper dolls is minuscule compared with the shockingly robust market for collectible dolls. Nominally, such dolls are for kids—specifically, the angel-faced preteens who appear on the covers of collectible catalogs with ribbons in their pulled-back hair. Browse the places where high-end dolls are sold, however, and you soon discover that real-life girls and their parents are equaled in number—and far surpassed in enthusiasm—by women of a certain age whose appetite for dolls has only intensified over the years. These might be called the Doll Ladies—intensely motivated, hyperfeminine sorts who arrange vacations around Barbie conventions and spend late nights studying eBay auction reports. For Doll Ladies, there is nothing so magnificent as glistening sienna curls, hand-painted rosebud smiles, or tiny porcelain tea sets.

Many Doll Ladies are childless, or else the mothers of children who have long since grown up. Retired widows, chubby old ladies, people with nothing better to do: These are the common stereotypes, notes doll writer Denise Van Patten, despite the fact that many Doll Ladies are well-educated and accomplished women for whom dolls are an enriching (though often private) hobby. Whether married or widowed, employed or not, actual children are beside the point—kids could never hope to lay their sticky paws on a Doll Lady's pristine stash of gowned princesses, antique teddy bears, or mint-in-the-box Chatty Cathys. Children may be the subject and inspiration for many dolls, but kids could never adequately appreciate the myriad Doll Lady specialties; one might collect cloth dolls, angel dolls, nun dolls, or Santa dolls. Some concentrate on Sasha dolls, spookily realistic Swiss figures popular in the mid-sixties. Others devote themselves to Franklin Mint fashion dolls of iconic female figures like Princess Di and Marilyn Monroe. Many more focus on celebrity doll designers like Richard Simmons and Jane Seymour, who have both lent their names to lines aimed squarely at the Doll Lady demographic.

Extreme, often grotesque cuteness is the defining characteristic of many of these dolls. Richard Simmons lives up to his reputation with a line known as his Collection of the Masters series. His "reminder angels" are dimpled, aw-shucks senior citizens that come complete with messages such as "Hug your cat" and "Spread holiday cheer." Many other collectibles are embodiments of a hyperfeminine ideal. Doll designer Helen Kish, who specializes in statuesque ladies of perfect proportions in elegant dress, sums up her dolls thusly: "Expressions of Facets of Eternal Femininity."

Not all Doll Ladies hoard their collections for themselves; some share their collection with their offspring. For these Doll Lady moms, a cabinet packed with American Girl dolls is not an absurd indulgence but the tangible expression of a deep intergenerational connection. American Girl is particularly adept at encouraging Doll Lady moms to shell out on behalf of their children. Eleven million American Girl dolls have sold since 1986, along with one hundred million books about the dolls, mostly through catalog sales. Mothers and daughters carefully pick over American Girl catalogs and devour American Girl books that detail the backstory of each character—from the travails of Depression-era sweetheart Kit Kittredge to the triumphs of California surfer girl Kailey—absorbing it all with the abandon of schoolgirls on a sleepover.

It's hard to imagine this sort of mother-daughter-doll bond existing ten or twenty years ago. Most obviously, it reflects the lengths today's upper-middle-class parents are willing to go to please their children. In an age when retail superstores are stocked to the rafters with ballerinas and princesses that can be had for the price of a Happy Meal, it simply takes more to impress a kid.

But the fact that many parents go to heretofore unimagined extremes to satisfy their children is less important than the fact that many of them are prepared to go to extremes to satisfy themselves. One need look no further for proof than Fifth Avenue in New York, which has in recent years become a haven for Doll Ladies. Occupying one square block, surrounded by crisp red awnings and uniformed doormen, you'll find American Girl Place, the Neiman Marcus of the doll world. Walnut displays are packed with row upon row of American Girl dolls, along with books, gadgets, and clothes. In one area, moms compare their children against a selection of hair colors and body types to create a personalized American Girl, which comes dressed in a special outfit that is naturally also available in sizes for girls (with adult sizes in the works, if history is any guide). Upstairs, there's a "hospital" for broken dolls, a Doll Hair Salon, and a white-tablecloth café that features pop-out seats to accommodate dolls. Little girls surely appreciate the cushy surroundings, but one look at the starry-eyed expressions of the adult chaperones and it's clear: This is all about the moms.

A few blocks away, mothers and daughters indulge in an even girlier, more elaborate fantasyworld at Cinderella's Princess Court, an enclosed "guest experience" contained within Disney's flagship New York store. For eighty dollars a head, little princesses and their larger companions sip tea, assemble toy tiaras, and confer with Disney's strike team of star princesses on the four "princess principles" (intelligence, grace, thoughtfulness, and honesty). For girls, the experience is nothing if not intense. My own daughter, a three-year-old human tornado, turned positively zombielike holding a beloved

111

Snow White doll on a visit to the Princess Tea, a road-show version of the Princess Court. Even more bizarre was the effect on my mother, a sixtysomething feminist who spent the afternoon in a long fit of giggles and gushing.

Much has been made about how the success of the repackaged princesses—merchandise related to the eight Disney heroines generated more than $2.5 billion for Disney in 2004—signals a welcome return to wholesome imagery in a market overrun by sexualized, rebellious figures. It's true that princesses represent a pointed response to such miniskirted, midriff-bearing hoochie mamas as the Bratz and My Scene dolls. But while Bratz owe their success to what those in the industry call "the nag factor"—kids' ability to get parents to buy what they want—there's no need for nagging when it comes to the princesses. The crown-and-scepter fantasy is as potent for women as girls. The arch formality, the promise of ugly-duckling transformations, the cheerful supremacy of pink—for many women, the princess universe offers an intoxicating inversion of modern hard-charging gender-neutrality. A few steps behind every girl in a Snow White dress, there's a Doll Lady listening in, shelling out, and sharing in the fantasy. "I already have a crown at home and a dress," thirty-one-year-old Dona Kronrad told the *New York Times* as she accompanied her six-year-old stepdaughter to the opening of the princess superstore. "I'm going to be Cinderella."

As far as dolls adored by adults go, the reigning queen is Barbie, the foot-high icon of prefeminist American conformity and still the most successful branded toy in history. Introduced in 1959 at a time when girl toys meant baby dolls or kitchen sets, Barbie was a little lady, a miniature mannequin on which girls could hang their adult fantasies, provided they all revolved around clothes, kids, and Ken. Playing with Barbie—

posing her, undressing her, even defacing her—offered girls a chance to assume grown-up roles, however phony. Barbie gave girls a sense of mastery over that most terrifying inevitability: their own maturity. According to Mattel's official Barbie biography, creator Ruth Handler was inspired to make a Barbie one day while watching her daughter play: "It hit her—why not make a teenage doll that little girls could play and dream about the future with? Ruth recognized the value of helping children realize their dreams and goals through play."

In fact, Barbie appears to have been more a product of appropriation than inspiration; according to other accounts, Handler got the idea while vacationing in Germany and spotting a Bild Lilli doll, a female figure based on a risqué Marlene Dietrich–esque comic strip character. Sold in tobacco shops, Bild Lilli was busty, blond, and marketed as a novelty item for men. Handler and her husband, however, saw a broader appeal. They snatched up the rights to Bild Lilli, made a close copy, gave her their daughter's name, and released her into the U.S. market. She was an immediate hit among Baby Boom girls, who saw in Barbie the promise of a fun-loving, va-va-voom future. Today Barbie is sold in 140 countries, with sales totaling more than $1.5 billion a year.

If Barbie was used in her heyday to transport girls to an imaginary future, today she's also used to transport women back to an imaginary past. Beginning in the eighties, adult collectors began paying top dollar for vintage Barbies at specialty shops and flea markets. Mattel soon began courting this adult market, operating Barbie collectible boutiques in department stores and releasing limited-edition Barbies in conjunction with designers including Bob Mackie, Donna Karan, and Paul Frank. A 1992 ad campaign featured photos of adoring women posing with their collectible figures, over the tagline

"Because you're never too old for Barbie." Barbie's time machine, it was discovered, operates in both directions.

Thus the circle closed; a toy originally created overseas for adults became a plaything for children and was finally taken up by adults again.

The Toy Generations

Barbie's evolution from kid toy to adult collectible is closely aligned with another progression: the aging of the Baby Boomers. In keeping with their abiding fixation on youth (see also Rolling Stones, Harley-Davidson, Viagra), the 76 million adults born between 1946 and 1964 were the first generation to carry childhood toys into adulthood, creating a market for toys not as playthings but as tools for summoning that most fetishized Boomer sensation, nostalgia. That acceptance has been inherited by younger adults, many of whom look on toys not just as evocative keepsakes but as props in their everyday lives.

No doubt Baby Boomers' embrace of toys has something to do with the fact that they "grew up with more manufactured toys than any generation before them," as noted by Robert Thompson, media professor at Syracuse University. That formative exposure clearly made a deep impression; just as Boomers never quite got over Woodstock or the VW Bug, they've clung tightly to their childhood toys, with their favorites emerging as the "classics" of all subsequent generations. G.I. Joe and Barbie have been repackaged and "updated" dozens of times (see Ferrari Barbie, and the G.I. Joe Search and Rescue Firefighter), beating back the challenges of knockoff Tammys, Mistys, Fighting Yanks, and Action Soldiers.

Twister and Slinky have entangled kids for a half century. Mr. Potato Head and Rock 'Em Sock 'Em Robots have stuck around, even appearing as supporting players in the *Toy Story* movies. The list of surviving Boomer toys goes on and on, from Colorforms and Tonka trucks to Silly Putty and Magic Rocks.

Boomers do far more than buy these toys for their children and grandkids; they also buy them for themselves. Just as adult demand for Barbie and G.I. Joe took off in the eighties, collectible markets simultaneously emerged for every sort of Boomer plaything. Hot Wheels and Matchbox cars, the die-cast metal miniature vehicles, are now treated as precious gems by collectors, with pieces assigned ratings as nuanced and specific as those applied to diamonds dug from South African mines. A C10+ rating, for instance, describes a Matchbox still in its original packaging with none of the paint chips or scratches known as "playwear." Such a rating can translate into big money when describing rare or unusual models—the ultimate example being a mini pink Volkswagen bus known as the Beach Bomb that sold to a Washington real estate agent for $70,000. For serious die-cast collectors, life becomes an obsessive search for the perfect C10+, a quest that has as much to do with an appreciation for the craft of toymaking as a rejuvenile compulsion to satisfy childhood desires never quite fulfilled.

Taking their cue from these collectors, toy manufacturers rushed to release new versions of classic toys for those with a more casual interest. In 2002, Philadelphia publisher Running Press released its quintessentially rejuvenile Executive Set— childhood playthings repackaged to fit in traditional adult surroundings, complete with pseudoscholarly booklets and faux-sophisticated touches. The Executive Set Sea-Monkey included a "high design squeegee" and a tank accented with gold and black trim and topped with a Baroque ornamental handle. Pieces in the Tinker Toy Executive Set were cast in "elegant cherry and ebony finishes," suitable for display in the most austere professional environment. Even the colorful simians in the classic Barrel of Monkeys got a makeover, recast in steely gray and housed in an attaché-black barrel. "Play at your desk!" went the pitch. "No guilt attached!"

Then there's the Easy-Bake Oven, the toy kitchen appliance introduced in 1963 with its woefully inadequate light-bulb heat source. Thirty years later, wistful Boomers looking for a taste of their own childhoods had driven up the price of vintage avocado and harvest-gold Easy-Bakes on eBay to fifty dollars. Partly to commemorate the fortieth anniversary of the toy, Hasbro authorized the *Easy-Bake Oven Gourmet Cookbook,* in which notable chefs contributed recipes to be prepared exclusively with the children's toy. Celebrity chef Bobby Flay whipped up a Queso Fundido with Roasted Poblano Vinaigrette, while Tom Douglas offered a recipe for Palace Olive Poppers—dishes that would likely go over better at a dinner party than a playdate.

But if toys are mainly totems of nostalgia for Boomers, they're much more for adults of subsequent generations. For members of Gen X—that tiresome, fuzzily defined classification most often used to describe people whose teen years touched the eighties—toys are increasingly ordinary parts of adult life. These are the parents who log long hours of play-time with their kids' action figures; the professionals who work out weekend aggressions with Super Soaker squirt guns (ideally the Triple Aggressor, whose shooting range is comparable to some ICBMs); the twenty-nine-year-old men who make up the booming video game industry's median. For these Xers, playing with toys isn't about reclaiming youth. It's just another entertainment option. And if that entertainment option happens to upend traditional notions of adulthood, so be it.

"I'm not interested in recapturing childhood at all," insists forty-one-year-old Spartaco Albertarelli, head designer for KidultGame, a Milan-based company that creates games for adults under the motto "Never stop playing." Says Albertarelli: "This is very important to understand. We don't want to stop time or to fight against our age. We're adults who simply want to keep playing because we like it."

That same matter-of-factness is characteristic of the many Gen Xers who collect action heroes, play card games like Magic: The Gathering, or otherwise amass knickknacks from the worlds of superheroes, sci-fi, and fantasy. To the adults who inhabit this province of Geek Nation, there's nothing inherently juvenile about action figures or trading cards—indeed, many can only barely be described as toys. Take, for instance, the output of Todd McFarlane, a comic book artist turned action figure mogul who is heralded by competitors as the Picasso of his field. McFarlane generates an estimated $25 million a year producing sculptural, realistic-down-to-the-last-freckle action figures based on rock stars Ozzy Osbourne and Jerry Garcia; characters from horror movies *Halloween* and *Nightmare on Elm Street*; and athletes Jorge Posada and Shaquille O'Neal (the one athlete who might actually play with his own action figure, possessing as he does an off-court affinity for go-carts, food fights, and roller coasters). McFarlane's creations typically end up on cubicle dividers and beside stereo units, making what McFarlane told *Vanity Fair* is a clear announcement about the owner: "I don't know the words 'responsibility' and 'adulthood' quite as well as I should.

I'm out from Mom and Dad's grasp, much as I love them, but I'm not going to *be* them."

While specialty toymakers like McFarlane create tchotchkes for postadolescents, big toymakers have bridged the generation gap, selling toys to both kids and adults. The secret to what toymakers reverently call "the bi-modal brand" was revealed in 2001 to American Greetings, which owns the rights to Care Bears, Strawberry Shortcake, and Holly Hobbie, cartoon characters that at the time were considered the Lynda Carters and Don Johnsons of the kiddie set—that is, icons of the eighties that had long since passed out of the public eye. In a poll of more than one thousand American women, however, American Greetings learned that not only were these supposedly washed-up characters fondly remembered, "purchase interest" was identical among women who wanted to buy a doll for their child and those women who wanted to rekindle a love affair of their own.

New lines of Care Bears and Strawberry Shortcake toys were big sellers, their jaunty expressions printed on everything from hoodie sweatshirts to bottles of "bedtime body mist." The advertising campaign cannily exploited the dolls' appeal to parents. "Who knew you and your daughter would have the same best friend?" was the tagline in a Strawberry Shortcake ad. In 2006 American Greetings unveils a new line of Holly Hobbie & Friends, in a "contemporary fresh style" that replaces the distinctly seventies brand of calico-print, big-eyed girls. The characters hit a trifecta in toy terms, appealing to three separate groups: young girls for whom the characters are a novelty, teens who embrace them as kitschy and ironic, and adults who fondly remember them from childhood.

In the wake of such success, toy stores have been flooded with other so-called retro toys. Teenage Mutant Ninja Turtles were revived, along with Cabbage Patch Dolls, My Little Pony, Rainbow Bright, He-Man, Masters of the Universe. In the U.K., cartoon characters Bagpuss and Zippy were unearthed from the cartoon scrap heap—nowadays it is hard to find a kiddie character from seventies and eighties kids' TV that hasn't been yanked out of retirement and given a quick makeover. In his new incarnation, He-Man lost his unfashionable pageboy haircut and got a chiseled, Pilates-enhanced physique. The new Strawberry Shortcake lost her pantaloons and bonnet and picked up a striped T-shirt and blue jeans. To toymakers like Hasbro's Goldner, the success of such retro toys rests largely on how parents react when kids mention the familiar name. "It's not like your kid is asking you, 'I want that newfangled thing I saw on TV,'" says Goldner. "When an eight-year-old little girl asks her thirtysomething mom for My Little Pony, there's no translation necessary. She gets it right off the bat. She feels good."

Toys as Weapons of Rebellion

Bill Manspeaker was looking for a camper shell to go with his 1979 Ford Bronco when he came across a model that did a nifty trick. Turn a few handles, fold it down, and presto: What was a camper shell became a ramp, perfect for lugging motorcycles (Bill has five) or classic cabinet video games (ten). Moving such bulky stuff would be a cinch thanks to an automotive accessory that resembled nothing so much as the die-cast Transformer robots he began collecting as a kid. The designers of the camper shell may have been aware of the connection, judging from the product's brand name: The Toybox.

That clinched it for Bill, a forty-two-year-old club owner

and sometime musician who lives by a simple, three-part credo: "Always be the loudest. Always make people laugh. And always have the most toys." Living up to this motto involves a few sacrifices. Bill doesn't have many things most adults his age treat as essential—a home phone, for instance, or an appointment book. What he does have are thousands upon thousands of toys. His home and office overflow with action figures, slot cars, puzzles, board games, and video game consoles.

Unlike most adults with a toy habit, Bill is not at all curatorial. He doesn't seek out particularly valuable or unusual toys. He doesn't display his toys like objets d'art or catalog them like rare fossils. He buys toys at chain toy stores, avoiding online marketplaces that require a delay of gratification. To him, having a toy the moment you want it is the whole point. "When you're a kid, you get excited when Christmas is coming because of all the toys you're gonna get," he says. "But the great thing about being an adult is [that] I can go to the store anytime I want with my own money and I can get it myself."

Often that thing is something he's seen advertised on TV. Bill is fully aware that his obsession is nurtured and exploited by marketers. "I'm no different really than most adults; it's just they're interested in Range Rovers and flat-screen TVs," he says. "I'd just rather buy little plastic things instead of big metal things."

While he treasures a few toys from childhood—his most prized possession is a rocking horse named Blaze that he was given when he was five—he doesn't understand toy enthusiasts whose goal is the reconstitution of their entire childhood toy collection. To Bill, toys aren't kitschy artifacts or totems in a personal museum of childhood memory; they're just fantastic junk. This immediately becomes clear on a visit to a Hollywood storefront loft that he shares with his giant pet iguana Jug Jug, a tankful of fire belly frogs, and, until recently, a shark named Mystic. (It died when the filter on his tank broke; not knowing what to do with a dead reef shark, he wrapped it in cellophane and stored it in the freezer.)

Upstairs, row upon row of action figures are displayed over a bed used during visits from his nine-year-old son, Damien Hellion. Thanks to his dad's handiwork, Damien has three options for going from his room to the main floor. He can take the stairs. He can hop on a yellow slide that spirals around the loft and empties into the kitchen. Or he can roll out of bed, swing on a latticework of ropes, and drop down onto a sixteen-foot circular trampoline.

Bill still occasionally performs with a band that was known as Green Jell-O until a lawsuit from Kraft Foods forced a name change; they're now known by the more generic Green Jelly. The band, which enjoyed a run of success in the early 1990s, was known mostly for animated videos and bizarre stage shows, in which members assumed superhero alter egos. Green Jelly drew heavily on Bill's love of toys, junk food, and Saturday morning cartoons, and in the process created a small but colorful genre of alternative rock that might be described as kiddie punk (other bands in this category include the monster-mash metal band G'War, art-noise thrashers Imperial Butt Wizards, and Toydeath, an Australian trio that creates dense electronic music using samples from sound chips found in toys). Green Jelly's hit song was a thrash metal anthem called "Three Little Pigs." The band once released a video called "Cereal Killer" in which popular Kellogg's breakfast cereal icons were comically dismembered.

Bill realized just how deep his attachment to kiddie culture

121

went when he bought a pair of DVDs of two favorite childhood shows: *The Flintstones* and *The Munsters*. He'd never stopped loving *The Flintstones,* going so far as to build a replica of the Flintstones house out of foam and PVC pipe for a Green Jelly number called "Anarchy in Bedrock." But watching the actual programs for the first time in over thirty years, he was shocked by just how formative they had been for him. Fred Flintstone and Herman Munster were more than just funny characters on TV, he says—they were role models, authority figures, perhaps even stand-ins for Bill's father, who died when he was an infant. "I got all my weird mannerisms from those guys," he says.

With a toga-wearing caveman and a dim-witted gravedigger as father figures, it makes a certain sense that Bill grew up wholly uninterested in the usual trappings of adulthood. Most nights, after closing his nightclub in Hollywood, Bill stays up until dawn to watch the first traffic reports on the local news. "Just before going to bed, I love to see everyone stuck in traffic," he says. "It's like, 'Good night, suckers.'"

Asked if he's an adult, Bill makes a face like he needs to spit. "No way," he says. "I'm not responsible and I'm not going to be on time and I'm going to come home with chocolate cake on my shirt," he says. "I'm gonna miss my gas payment to buy a dirt bike."

The Toyification of Everyday Stuff

Even those adults who haven't seen an action figure since blowing up their last G.I. Joe are making room in their lives for toys—often without knowing it. Cell phones, automobiles, even housewares—all have been transformed in recent years from purely utilitarian to positively toylike.

Call it toyification. Squint while browsing through Target and you'd be forgiven for thinking you'd somehow wandered into a Toys "R" Us. Vacuums come in candy-apple red and baby blue. A laundry contraption called Buzz! comes complete with a magic wand attachment made to "blast stains." A thermoelectric cooler looks just like an olde-tyme fridge at $^1/_{10}$th scale, with a tiny latch and handle suitable for a Raggedy Ann. A brush for washing vegetables (could there possibly be a task less appealing to the inner child?) has been molded into the shape of a purple duck, with bristles sticking out of its head in a cheerful tuft.

Conventional, unadorned versions of these things are still available, of course. But why buy a plain old aluminum-sided toaster when you can get the Michael Graves version, the one with the white plastic form that looks like a fluffy cartoon cloud? Much has been made of how such objects demonstrate the popularization of high design. And it's certainly true that mass-market aesthetics have become more sophisticated. But most Target shoppers couldn't give a hoot if this cherry-stained hardwood Monopoly set was designed by Michael Graves or if that striped shower curtain was created by Cynthia Rowley—what draws them in is the simple, childlike responses they stir.

Toyification is perhaps no more plainly visible than on the road. For decades, automobiles were the ultimate adult consumer good. Ever since the Model T (which, Henry Ford famously declared, "you could get in any color, as long as it was black"), cars were cast as manifestations of adult ideals. Reliability, performance, safety—these were the bedrock qualities motorists looked for in the first decades of the automobile. A more youthful energy surfaced in the fifties, as car manufacturers followed the lead of teenaged customizers, who saw their cars as expressions of freedom, rebellion, and sex appeal. If hot rods of the *American Graffiti* era captured an essentially adolescent impulse, many of today's cars seem to embody the inner lives of tiny tots. Alongside mammoth SUVs and aggressive proto–station wagons dart swarms of compacts as speedy and nimble as go-carts. Automotive magazines that once rhapsodized over horsepower, dependability, and high performance now herald the latest superminis as sassy, cool, and gadget-packed. A review in *BusinessWeek* described a new Micra Mini as "huggable."

This trend toward car cuteness can be traced to the 1998 release of the redesigned Volkswagen Beetle, a bright and shiny bauble amid clusters of hard-edged rectangles. With its red and purple interior lights, mesh storage pockets, and dashboard bud vase, the new Beetle was even more polka-dot-like than the model beloved by Flower Children. More recently, the Volkswagen marketing department ran a campaign that made the aesthetic explicit, selling Jettas with the slogan "All grown up. Sort of." As part of the campaign, guerrilla marketers were dispatched to pass out coloring books, mix-and-match tile puzzles, and DVD copies of a short film about a young man confronted by an agent from the "Federal Commission on Adulthood." (The best way to outfox the agent, the ad suggests: Buy a Jetta.)

Volkswagen's success in courting the rejuvenile market has spawned a slew of imitators. The PT Cruiser gained a rabid following thanks to a design that looks like nothing so much as a die-cast metal London cab, perfect for rolling around the kitchen floor. The Mini Cooper captured attention

partly for its diminutive profile, but also for its Mod cool ca-
chet (the tagline: "Don't let big happen to you"). And the Toyota Scion came complete with bright interior stripes, gigantic
built-in speakers, and a sleek, *Millennium Falcon*–esque dashboard, all in an effort to reach what Toyota called "an emerging new buyer group in the marketplace."

Car manufacturers often take a circuitous route in pitch-
ing these youthful cars to adults. The Honda Element is
a Lego-shaped mini truck introduced in 2002 as a "combination dorm room/base camp for active young buyers," and
subsequently marketed at extreme sports and surfing events,
according to American Honda Motor Company spokesman
Andy Boyd. It was all part of Honda's plan to reach buyers
who hadn't seen the inside of a dorm room since the Reagan
administration. The average age of Element drivers, Mr. Boyd
says, was forty. "That's exactly what we anticipated," he said.
"It's a new definition of the family buyer—someone who
doesn't want to give up their individual character even though
they're getting older."

The rejuvenile impulse is also at work in the design and
marketing of cars at the opposite end of the size spectrum.
The Hummer might not fit into anyone's toy cabinet, but it
still owes a good share of its appeal to the childish (okay, boy-
ish) feelings it stirs in consumers. For one thing, it dwarfs even
the largest adult, re-creating a child's vantage point as deftly as
the enormous rocking chair Lily Tomlin used in her Edith
Ann sketches. Even in its more modest G2 model (Only
6,700 pounds! Only seven feet wide!), the Hummer still owes
its appeal to its toyishness. Gushed an auto critic from the
Toronto Sun, "The little boy that still lives within most men is
fascinated by the sheer enormity of it." He went on: "From the
deliberately aggressive military design, right down to its desert

sand paint, this vehicle makes you want to shout, 'Look at me! I've got the biggest toy in the sandbox!'"

There's been a simultaneous two-wheel drift from adult and utilitarian to childlike and playful. Take pocket rockets, two- to three-foot-high mini-motorcycles designed as squealing miniatures of high-performance racing bikes. Hundreds of thousands of these cheap, imported Mini Choppers and Super Ninjas have allowed adults to scale down full-scale motorcycle fantasies, even if riders look less like hardened pros than circus clowns yukking it up atop mini-unicycles. Ordinary bicycles, too, have veered away from the high-performance and utilitarian. It's no longer enough to rediscover a childhood love of riding a bike; the objective now is to chase down the particular make and model of bike you rode as a kid. Schwinn reintroduced its classic Stingray in 2004, complete with balloon tires, bulky fenders, and chain guards; the smaller manufacturer Nirve offered an adult-sized, pink Hello Kitty cruiser with the mouthless kitty face embossed on the rubber tires.

The Tech-Toy Connection

In previous eras, new technology was often camouflaged to blend with everyday adult surroundings. The first phonographs, radios, and televisions gained mass acceptance after manufacturers packed the mechanics into wood cabinets suitable for the living room. Likewise, the first typewriters, calculators, and copy machines were sheathed in die-cast metal cases that looked right at home next to filing cabinets and waste containers in corporate offices.

Today's computers, cell phones, and other electronic gadgets tell a different story. They are neither made nor used like furniture or hardware; instead, they bear an unmistakable resemblance to toys. Few companies have worked the tech-toy association as successfully as Apple, which rebounded from its mid-1990s slump by creating a product that directly challenged the popular image of a dark-shelled PC that sorts through deep reservoirs of code in a clumsy slog to produce spreadsheets or sales reports. The iMac was gumdrop-shaped and cheerful and could be ordered in blueberry, strawberry, tangerine, and grape (thus recasting the emotional experience of choosing a computer into the same sort of choice you once made standing on tippy-toes at the corner ice cream parlor). The same translucent, jewel-colored motif was subsequently copied by manufacturers of staplers, microwaves, and TV sets.

Riding high on this triumph of toyification, Apple has gone on to infuse its entire product line with the whimsy, cheer, and suggestiveness of playthings. Taking a page from kindergarten alphabet books, new operating systems are named after jungle cats. New components have been given the look and feel of yo-yos, or toy spacecraft. (The sci-fi influence runs deep in Apple product design. The white-shelled, streamlined iBooks, for instance, would fit right in amid the pre-grunge futuristic worlds summoned in *2001: A Space Odyssey* and *THX 1138*, seminal childhood movies for many of Apple's die-hard adult fans.) And following the success of its iPod digital music player, Apple released an even smaller, cuter, and more successful line known as the iPod Mini, which came in nursery-room shades of pink, mint green, and powder blue. In all, Apple presents its products as simple on the surface, easy on the eye, friendly in function, and yet containing limitless possibilities. Its products are no mere devices, as any fervent Mac user will attest; they are portals to worlds of wonder.

This isn't simply a matter of aesthetics. Apple's first and most lasting innovation was its graphical user interface. Before Apple, personal computers required users to learn and input specific lines of DOS code. In the early 1980s, Apple created the first viable commercial version of a system that incorporated a mouse, a desktop, and simple, cartoonlike icons that could be clicked on, dragged about, and otherwise toyed with. The actual nuts and bolts of computing were hidden behind this decorative partition, the unseen hands of code fattening up whimsical happy-face icons. Twenty years later, we take this interface for granted, but it's worth recognizing for what it is: computing as puppet show.

The toyification of computers is most plainly an act of beautification. "Adults use computers primarily to do work, stuff they don't necessarily like, so it makes sense that they try to overcompensate by making them more toylike," says Syracuse University's Thompson. "If you're in the workplace, being a keyboard jockey all day long, at least you can make this faceless, technological thing you're strapped to appear to be something a little more whimsical and a little more fun."

Cell phones, too, have in recent years been transformed into playthings by manufacturers and consumers eager to find the fun in everyday routines. When cell phones were introduced in the 1980s, they were built and marketed as essential safety gear. Ads pictured pitiful motorists, stuck in the breakdown lane, tires flat, gaskets blown, gigantic big-rigs whipping past. Having a cell phone wasn't about fun—quite the opposite. Having a cell phone was about fear, and that most adult virtue: responsibility.

How needlessly dire all that seems more than a decade later. Today cell phones come with built-in video games, cameras, text messaging features, pop-song ringtones, and a grab-bag of other useless but diverting features. Commuters kill time on subways negotiating paths for pellet-gobbling serpents or contemplating hands of virtual poker. For those who still find their cell phones too serious, accessory shops sell flashing keypads, cartoon faceplates, and so-called Fone Petz, cuddly covers in the shapes of creatures named Munchie the Manatee, Oinky the Pig, and Beary Cute. And if the idea of speaking into the belly of a stuffed animal is a mite too obvious, there are mouthpieces modeled after the big bulky landline handsets dimly remembered from their own childhoods.

Even through their central function—the ability to reach anyone anywhere at any time—cell phones have helped shape new standards of adulthood. It's worth remembering that in the late 1800s, the introduction of new gadgets like the timepiece and the telephone had a role in forging the then-novel conception of adulthood, making accountability and reliability fundamental virtues. Today, technology is helping shape our values once again. How crucial is accountability when we can so easily arrive thirty minutes late for a dinner, because, hey, we called from the car? And how important is reliability when we answer an invitation with a promise to touch base later, because why set something in stone when we're all reachable and it's far easier to keep our options open? Nowadays, flexibility and connectivity are more important than ever, a change in values that flows directly from how we make up our days on the fly, changing course based on quick catch-ups with friends and furtive glances at our PDAs. Yes, this has made us flakier, harder to pin down, maddening in our constant maneuvering.

But I for one wouldn't dream of going back to the time when human contact was so tyrannically dictated by time and space. We're freer now, less encumbered by plans, more overwhelmed by the range of available choices, each of us enacting that wonderful line from Bob Dylan: "I was so much older then, I'm younger than that now."

FOUR

uncle walt and the adult playground

IF ALL THE WORLD THOUGHT
AND ACTED AS CHILDREN,
WE'D NEVER HAVE ANY TROUBLE.
THE ONLY PITY IS EVEN KIDS
HAVE TO GROW UP.

— Walt Disney

The most popular vacation spot in America is not New York, Las Vegas, or Hawaii. These locations have their admirers, to be sure, but when it comes to the sort of appeal that draws twenty thousand new visitors each and every day, one destination is favored over all others. That place is Orlando, Florida, home to the Gatorland reptile park, the Daytona Speedway car track . . . and a little roadside attraction known as the Walt Disney World Resort.

More than 47 million tourists visit Orlando every year—that's more than the combined populations of Pennsylvania and California. They don't come for the gators. They come for the fireworks, thrill rides, miniature monuments, and well-scrubbed, ever obsequious "cast members" (Disneyspeak for employees) found inside this virtual nation-state of fantasy worlds. The WDW Resort, as it's officially called, now includes the original Magic Kingdom, the internationalist EPCOT Center, the MGM-Disney studio tour, and the faux-African savannah known as Animal Kingdom. It's a wildly disjointed place, but few who enter have any trouble under-standing what holds the dizzying assortment of attractions together. They're "family attractions," the sorts of things you want to do as a kid, or with a kid.

At least, that used to be true. Walter Elias Disney created his theme park with a simple strategy: Grab the children, and everyone else will follow. "It's sort of a kiddieland," Disney wrote in an early memo. Unlike other amusement parks, which he found distasteful—with their games of chance, menacing rides, and what he called "tough-looking people"— Disneyland would be a place where families could share wholesome, wondrous experiences. In what came to be known as the Griffith Park Credo (so named because Disney dreamed it up while sitting in Los Angeles's Griffith Park, excluded and bored, while his children rode a carousel), Disney proclaimed that in his land, everything would be for everyone. Adults could enjoy the kiddie rides, and children would be welcome on the park's few thrill rides (even the Matterhorn roller coaster imposed no minimum age and height requirements until the seventies). And so it was, at Disneyland and at the affiliate parks that sprouted up first in Orlando and then in Tokyo, Paris, and, most recently, Hong Kong. From its inception, Disneyland meant sharing an experience with children.

Fifty years later, children are only part of the story. Stand outside the turnstiles today and you'll still see plenty of kids, perched bolt upright in strollers or bunched around their parents like battalions preparing for an amphibious landing. But you'll also encounter a startlingly large share of grown-up Mouseketeers with nary a child in sight. Groups of twentysomethings rush through the gates in jogging sneakers and clip-on walkie-talkies, the better to coordinate plans to hit two dozen attractions in six hours flat. Grandparents line up for tickets in oversize foam hats (classic Mickey ears having given

133

way long ago to puffy Tigger, Goofy, and Dumbo headgear). Then there are the die-hard Disney enthusiasts, identified by their Tokyo Disney sweatshirts, bulky fanny packs, and official-issue lanyards studded with collectible pins. Of the 200,000 people who visit Walt Disney World every day, it's estimated that fully *half* are adults traveling without young children.

The same influx of adults has invaded other amusement parks, from the thirty-one roller coaster mills operated by Six Flags to smaller regional parks like Adventuredome, Hershey-Park, and Dollywood. In all, an estimated 53 million adults attended theme parks in 2004, according to *American Demographics* magazine. While it's hard to say what percentage of adults visited primarily for their own enjoyment—neither Disney nor Six Flags will release information on attendance or age makeup at its parks—there's plenty of evidence that adults are whooping it up at amusement parks like never before, along the way changing the way parks are designed, marketed, and operated.

Adult mania for roller coasters, water slides, and cartoon-themed stage shows is not lost on travel publishers. Fodor's and Birnbaum's now offer guides to Disney World especially for adults visiting for their own enjoyment (Birnbaum's is titled *Walt Disney World Without Kids: Expert Advice for Fun-Loving Adults*). These guides offer advice on senior citizen discounts, places to eat for those with mature palates, and listings of attractions adults should seek out and avoid (including Tom Sawyer's Island, which Fodor's warns "can make a pleasant interlude for adults, but which is overrun with freewheeling children all day." Beware—actual kids!). All over the country, parks now enforce strict age requirements during Halloween attractions, banning children altogether from gory commemorations of an increasingly grown-up holiday.

The shift is especially pronounced in the way parks are marketed. In 2004, Six Flags ditched previous attempts to appeal to teenagers and launched a campaign centered on a "brand character" said to embody the "spirit of the park": a spry fellow in a tux who looks not a day younger than seventy. "Our campaign research showed that today's families spend more time at work than ever before—they are overscheduled, overworked, and stressed out," a Six Flags marketing vice president said at the launch of its new mascot, Mr. Six. "What they need most, what they desire most, is playtime."

Meanwhile self-described amusement park addicts have banded together for support and encouragement. The Disney parks have spawned dozens of enthusiast clubs that organize group outings, monitor park maintenance, and compare collections of everything from pins to paper flyers. American Coaster Enthusiasts (ACE), a group of coaster fans that organizes visits to new attractions and marathon rides, now claims some eight thousand members, only a few of whom are the thrill-seeking teens to whom coasters are primarily marketed. "The middle-aged professional adult is our most common member," says ACE president Bill Linkenheimer. "Our active members include doctors, lawyers, federal agents, clergy, schoolteachers, coroners, nurses, engineers, and entrepreneurs." Other local organizations have formed to preserve, restore, or share photos and paraphernalia from demolished theme parks of yesteryear, from Euclid Beach Park in Wickliffe, Ohio, to Wonderland Park in Wichita, Kansas.

It's enough to cause hemorrhages among the Harrumphing Codgers of the world. "We have huge numbers of people who are just counting the minutes until they are released from their jobs to do what they really want to be doing—which in the extreme cases is going off to Disney World to ride the rides and doing stuff that's essentially play," says Bryan Page, anthropologist at the University of Miami. "It doesn't accomplish anything, it doesn't enhance their social standing as adults—it's just stuff they see as fun."

Few adult amusement park addicts would argue. Although all but the most hard-core are people with busy lives and strong family bonds, many admit that their ordinary lives seem comparatively inadequate—they'd much rather be riding a coaster or picking at a mound of cotton candy than pushing papers or filling orders or adding lines to their résumés.

But what environment better reflects our true inner selves: a cubicle farm or a theme park? And who's to say the fun adults experience in amusement parks is worthless? I determined to get to the root of what adults get out of places created primarily for children.

Gary and Anita, Power Couple of the Disney Enthusiasts

My search for answers begins one chilly Saturday afternoon, riding a giant caterpillar with a municipal magistrate from Ohio. The magistrate is smiling broadly, his eyes half-closed in contentment. The caterpillar rounds a corner, passes a fiberglass tree stump, and travels through an archway shaped like a watermelon rind. The air is suddenly thick with a sweet synthetic fragrance, as if someone just uncapped a thousand tubes of pink lip balm. "Watermelon!" my companion says, beaming.

The ride is Heimlich's Chew Chew Train, one of four new rides at Disney's California Adventure theme park inspired by the movie *A Bug's Life* (Heimlich was the name of the Bavarian caterpillar in the film with an insatiable appetite). Along with slow-moving bumper cars, a 3-D movie, and modified playground equipment, this new section of the park is geared for what's known in the amusement park business as "the stroller set"—small children and their parents. But as the ride shudders to a stop, forty-seven-year-old Gary Schaengold is a satisfied customer indeed. The Chew Chew Train may be two and a half minutes long and about as exciting as an escalator, but to Gary it's simply "terrific."

This sounds especially odd coming from Gary, who is by most measures a full-fledged, capital-A adult. He wears conservative clothes and wire-rimmed glasses, drives a sensible Honda Prelude, and owns a nice ranch house in Dayton, Ohio. By day, he adjudicates cases in a municipal courthouse, teaches law at the University of Dayton, and runs a private law practice. His wife, Anita, owns a jewelry store. They attend services at a local Baptist church. They're active in the state's Republican Party.

All of which tells you next to nothing about what truly matters to Gary and Anita. They are, in fact, a reigning power couple among Disney enthusiasts, those fans who have devoted much of their lives—their free time, their social circle, their disposable income, their private musings—to the Disney mythology. To hear Gary tell it, they're simply believers in "the gospel according to Disney."

Their shared obsession began one Christmas when Gary

gave Anita a set of Disney videos. Anita soon found herself preoccupied with the 1989 feature *The Little Mermaid,* in particular its red-haired heroine, Ariel. She began collecting Little Mermaid merchandise, which eventually spread to every corner of their 4,200-square-foot house. She joined, and eventually became president of, a support group called Arielholics Anonymous that includes 130 active members. Meanwhile she and Gary took a trip to one Disney park, then another, then another, until it made sense to purchase annual passes for Walt Disney World, Disneyland, Tokyo Disney, and Disneyland Paris. Nowadays Gary and Anita spend at least one weekend a month at one Disney park or another, even though it usually means taking a red-eye flight so that he can be in court at 8:00 A.M. on Monday mornings. "Starbucks helps," Gary says.

In the absence of children—"My insides aren't perfect," says Anita, "and I'm not about to spend a billion dollars trying to fix 'em"—Gary and Anita have the time and income to fully embrace their Disney obsession. Between the trips to Disney parks, the Ariel merchandise, and the projection room in the basement, it adds up. "It does require more than a modest level of income, yes," says Gary. "Luckily my wife and I do okay."

Anita, an ebullient forty-one-year-old, grew up loving roller coasters, mini golf, and video games. As she settled down and built a business, she never saw the point in giving up what she'd loved as a kid. Today, she's happiest walking down Main Street U.S.A. munching a Rice Krispies treat molded into the shape of Mickey's head. Her affection for Disney, she says, is boundless.

Not that Anita is always so carefree. At work, she's efficient and orderly and not at all childish. "I don't have time to daydream at work," she says. "It's not like I think one day I'm going to live with Uncle Walt when he gets unfrozen and turn into a mermaid. But my fantasy life keeps me sane in my real life."

Gary is equally clear about the division between his love of Disney and the demands of his adult routine. While his law partners and colleagues know about his "Disney thing," he says he keeps it mostly to himself. His weekends at the park, Gary says, recharge his batteries for the working week. "I have to deal with serious stuff twelve hours a day—this is a great escape," he says.

As he hurries through the crowds at Disneyland one afternoon, however, it becomes clear that Gary's idea of relaxation is quite different from his wife's. The two Schaengolds are two sides of the enthusiast coin; each gets something entirely different from Disney. She loves the characters, the message, "the magic." Gary, on the other hand, is captivated by the facts of the park, its history and details. On a ride through It's a Small World, Gary holds forth on the attraction's development, from its roots at the 1964–65 World's Fair in New York to the modern-day Imagineer who designed the "holiday overlay" on display today, which has upped the ride's twinkly quotient considerably. Over lunch he marvels at a display of fried cheesecake and chocolate éclairs shaped as dog bones, taking a moment to name the manager responsible for such "themed foods." He also talks about an article he's just written about the history and design of Tokyo Disney popcorn buckets.

And as much as he enjoys the rides, Gary seems happiest simply walking through the park, which he does quickly and with great purpose, slowing only to chat with cast members, pin traders, or fellow enthusiasts. Mostly, the topic is merchandise. He spends a good part of the day searching for a stuffed animal of Mickey Mouse dressed in a reindeer costume that his wife wants for Christmas. Gary clearly delights in asking shop assistants (taking pride in consulting their name tags and addressing them by name) if they would check "backstage" for the item in question. In the next hour or so, the phrase "plush Mickey reindeer" becomes a mantra, as we go from one shop to the next, where we ogle Mickey Mouse coffee tins, an $800 Donald Duck statuette, and a Snow White oil painting. We find no plush Mickey reindeer, but in the end it hardly seems to matter. It's the hunt that counts, the chance to banter with cast members like a true insider.

The highlight of the day comes when Gary meets up with an enthusiast who makes his living buying, selling, and trading Disney pins. A deal has been worked out in advance, and in a quick exchange that would look highly suspicious in any other setting, Gary hands over one hundred dollars cash for a Ziploc bag containing his own personal "holy grail," a tiny copper-colored Ariel pin that was distributed as part of a European video release. "I never thought I'd see one of these," he says. "I am now complete."

What Drives the Disnoids

In that moment, I got the feeling I'd stumbled into a basic truth about the adult appeal of Disneyland. Gary didn't say his collection was complete—he said *he* was complete. This seemed significant, but when I pressed him to explain, Gary shrank back and gave me a puzzled look. The pin was rare, he said; he was glad to have found it. He was complete. Simple.

Indeed, calm satisfaction, not wild ecstasy, best describes

the optimum emotional state of Disney enthusiasts like Gary. He and his pin-trader friends will, when pressed, talk about the childlike feelings of magic Disneyland gives them, but in truth they don't seem all that happy about the Happiest Place on Earth. But of course they are—it's just that their happiness is less about play, freedom, and excitement than contentment, completion, and safety. Their good feeling is rooted in an article of faith: Disneyland, like all Disney parks and unlike any other amusement park, presents itself as a world, one that mimics more pleasant parts of the real one, but without its infinite complications and vast possibilities. It's manageable. You can, without too much effort, master one part of that world—Collect the pins! Own the merchandise! Learn the history!—and in so doing, join a group of like-minded settlers on a patch of make-believe that has been crafted, packaged, and contained for your pleasure. (Disney storytellers excise the darker bits of European folk tales, just as the cogs and pulleys of the park are hidden behind decorative scrims and security personnel are disguised in themed costumes.) Disneyland is at once vast, containing entire "lands," mythologies, and characters, and at the same time limited and inviting and knowable. It's a small world, after all.

It is just this quality that holds certain Disney enthusiasts in such a viselike grip. Gary and Anita are dedicated, but they are not among the hardest core of the Disney enthusiast crowd. Disnoids, as they are known among park employees, are those fans of mysterious means who buy annual passes and who visit the park five, six, even seven days a week. While others drift around the park in a haze, Disnoids tend to concentrate on one favorite area or attraction. Some spend their day riding the Haunted Mansion, again and again. Some are devoted to the Matterhorn. Others are specialists in Disney napkins, flyers, and other "paper ephemera." One woman visits the park every day to ride the Indiana Jones Adventure ride (employees gave her a crystal bowl on her thousandth ride). When not at the park, they collect Disney figurines and animation cels and watch Disney-owned TV channels.

Not that all Disnoids are alike; just as Gary and Anita love the parks for different reasons, some revere the parks for their history and mythology, while others love them for their "magic." This magic may be manufactured, but enthusiasts don't seem to mind, as long as it does the trick of transporting them back to a wide-eyed, wondrous state they associate with childhood. Thirty-seven-year-old Daniel Bowen falls into the second category. President of a Disney fan club, longtime annual passholder, and collector of all things Tinkerbell (apparel, crystal figurines, animation cels), Daniel estimates that he spends 90 percent of his free time doing something Disney-related. But like Gary, he is careful to keep his private passion under wraps in his job managing a suburban superstore, where he projects the image of a dedicated, trustworthy adult. "I know most people think my love for Disney is mucho loco," he laughs.

Keeping up these appearances isn't easy for Daniel, a natural ham who says that most of the time he feels shut down and ill at ease. At Disneyland, he feels free. He feels free to wear his Tinkerbell T-shirt, free to chow down on corn dogs, free to ride the Fantasyland rides again and again ("Those are the *funnest,*" he says).

While Disnoids like Daniel have never lost their taste for fun, others are more like Gary in pursuing a Talmudic expertise about all things Disney. Just as Daniel amasses collectibles as proof of his devotion to Disney, forty-seven-year-old Al

Lutz collects intelligence—about park operations and management, maintenance, and office politics, all the insider details that most lovers of Disney willfully ignore. Al is a former music industry product manager whose devotion to the park isn't rooted in a need for escape or childlike wonder. "It's not a nostalgic or happy place for me," he says. "But it is fascinating. I see nuts and bolts. My interest is what's happening behind the scenes."

Al knows when a sidewalk is blocked, when a flower bed is replanted, when a showtime is changed. Reporting on such revelations has earned him a huge following of cranky, critical enthusiasts. His website, Miceage.com, now attracts some half-million hits a month. When paint peels on Cinderella's Castle, Al posts close-up pictures with fuming commentary. When the Entertainment Department extends the run of a parade he believes demeans the heritage of certain costumed characters, he posts a photo of a pair of *Jungle Book* bears wearing funny hats and tutus with the caption: "Oh, where did their dignity go?" To this unpaid agitator, the original Disneyland was the manifestation of a near-perfect vision of childlike wonder—and it's his job to protect it. Less apparently childlike than many of his fellow Disnoids, Al is characteristic of rejuveniles whose interest in the culture of childhood is almost entirely protective. He's a rejuvenile in the mold of Holden Caulfield, that diffident hero of American lit who railed against the phoniness of adulthood and dreamed of himself "standing on the edge of some crazy cliff," watching over a crowd of children playing on the edge of an abyss.

rejuvenile

W.W.W.D. (What Would Walt Do)?

Disney critics like Al often make reference to the original vision of Walt Disney. In him, they see a model of a driven, highly productive adult who never lost sight of the unadulterated wonder of childhood. While Disney might not deserve such blind adulation—you rarely hear much from enthusiasts about Disney's anti-Semitism or McCarthyist sympathies—this much is undoubtedly true: For Disney, theme parks were more than just an enterprise. They were a haven. And by all accounts, they did him immeasurable good.

Disney was born in 1903 with amusement parks in his blood—his father Elias was a carpenter at the 1896 World's Fair in Chicago, thus witnessing the launch of such kiddie commercial favorites as Cracker Jack, the Hershey bar, and the Ferris wheel. Despite a difficult early life—his father was abusive, his mother distant—Disney looked back on his childhood as a period of near-Edenic enchantment. At sixteen, he dropped out of high school to serve as a Red Cross ambulance driver in World War I (alongside future McDonald's mogul Ray Croc, who also built a career catering to the tastes of children). His eventual success as an animator in Hollywood was distinguished primarily by his knack for entertaining both kids and adults. Adults flocked to see *Snow White and the Seven Dwarfs* and *Pinocchio* nominally for their artistry, but mostly because Uncle Walt could be counted on to so powerfully catapult an adult psyche back to a romanticized version of childhood.

As his studio grew, Disney struggled with anxiety and isolation. While the public knew him as Uncle Walt, a jovial and good-humored Midwesterner, the truth about Disney was "less benign and a lot more interesting," writes biographer Richard Schickel. "Uncle Walt didn't have an avuncular bone in his body. Though he could manage a sort of gruff amiability with strangers, his was a withdrawn, suspicious and, above all, controlling nature." In 1931, even as Mickey Mouse had become an international star, Disney suffered a nervous breakdown and was forced to leave the studio for an extended hiatus.

Disney found relief in the most mundane way imaginable: He got himself a hobby. Ordered by a psychiatrist to take some time away from work and develop outside interests, Disney became a train buff. In 1938, animator Ward Kimball invited Disney to his house in the foothills outside Los Angeles to have a look at an old steam locomotive he'd restored to its Victorian grandeur. Pushing the throttle of the old steam train, his "expression was like a kid in a candy store," Kimball recalled. Disney soon began spending long hours in the inner office of his studio playing with model trains. He eventually built a half-mile track around his Holmby Hills estate. Weekends were spent riding the rails around his house, dressed in bib overalls and a red bandanna, setting up trains to crash and then delighting in setting them up to go around again. Disney's wife, Lillian, was none too pleased with her husband's hobby, annoyed at the time spent tinkering and the upset to her garden (he built a tunnel below it and had his lawyers draw up a formal contract legitimizing the easement). Throughout it all, however, Disney was unrepentant. "It saved my sanity," he said later.

At work, Disney often fought bitterly with his brother Roy over finances—they had a particularly nasty row over his tepidly received adaptation of *Peter Pan*. Trains offered him a refuge. A *New York Times* reporter sent to interview Disney found him "totally disinterested in movies and wholly, almost weirdly concerned with the building of a miniature railroad engine." Soon this passion led him to think beyond his own private railroad. He began making notes and sketches for what he called "Mickey Mouse Park." It would include a candy store, a hobby shop, carnival rides, a western village, a theater for "little kids' plays of all kinds"—and, most important, it would be circled by a train. In searching for property, he made it clear that it must have enough flat area for a full-scale steam railroad. Indeed, the earthen berm on which the tracks were laid became a defining feature of Disneyland, the boundary between the outside world and the Happiest Place on Earth. Today, enthusiasts speak reverently of life "within the berm."

The railway is not the only feature of the park that owes its existence to Disney's knack for channeling the impulses and memories of boyhood. Disneyland is of course a ridiculously nostalgic place, most obviously on Main Street U.S.A., that idealized small town painted in the soft whites, pinks, and yellows of movie dream sequences. Most obviously, the street is a reproduction of just the sort of town where Disney himself spent his formative years. In the same way children of the fifties now go gaga over the midcentury modern stylings they dimly remember from their own childhoods, adults in 1955 got weak in the knees at the sight of Main Street's gingerbread detailing. Margaret King, a cultural consultant who has worked for Disney and who now runs The Center for Cultural Studies & Analysis, a Philadelphia think tank, points out that Disney heightened the nostalgia through an ingenious architectural trick: "While Disneyland's forced perspective on the upper stories makes them appear taller than they are, the three-quarter scale at ground level replicates the feeling of returning to childhood haunts as an adult when 'everything looks so much smaller.' "

Disney himself spent much of his time at the park in the thrall of Main Street. After the park opened, he moved into a private apartment above the fire station. Never one to be unfaithful to theme, he had the apartment decorated in pink flocked wallpaper, thick red rugs, faux gas lamps, and even a windup phonograph. The overall impression was more whorehouse than wholesome, according to Marc Eliot's 1993 biography *Walt Disney: Hollywood's Dark Prince*. Many of Disney's employees, Eliot claims, believed their boss used the apartment for secret trysts, but the truth was much less salacious. The apartment was an exact duplication of Disney's childhood living room in Marceline, Missouri. Writes Eliot: "From within this most private retreat, sitting alone on his overstuffed sofa, a fifty-four-year-old Disney joyfully ruled the kingdom of his past: the eternal land of his imagination east of Once-Upon-a-Time and down a ways from Never-Never Land."

That's a scary picture. The same is true of much of Disney's work—his ingenuity at unearthing the past, cleaning it up, and displaying it for maximum effect had a way of backfiring, kicking up clouds of uneasiness that linger long after the enchantment is gone. (I suspect I'm not the only kid who had nightmares starring Disney's animatronic Mr. Lincoln.) So it is with many of Disneyland's most ardent adult fans, whose devotion to Disney's childlike ideal might begin in cheerfulness and childlike wonder but often transforms into something sad, strange, or desperate.

Which brings us, inevitably, to Michael Jackson, King of the Disnoids and poster boy for the rejuvenile gone wrong. Jackson's zeal for Disney is well known. Even at the height of his fame, Jackson kept up an intense study of Disney's life and work, once going so far as to track down and personally interview a studio masseuse in hopes of gaining insight into Uncle Walt's private musings. Then there's Neverland Ranch, Jackson's 2,700-acre compound built in the image of the Magic Kingdom, complete with steam engine, roller coaster, and European carousel. Neverland is undoubtedly Disney-esque, but with its menagerie of exotic animals and man-made lake dotted with paddleboats and Jet Skis, the overall impact is more jumbled, with one guest describing it as "Salvador Dalí–meets–Richie Rich comic book." To wit: In the master bed-room, Jackson displays a bizarre reproduction of da Vinci's *The Last Supper* with himself in Jesus' spot and Disney appear-ing as a disciple (others at the table include Charlie Chaplin, Elvis Presley, and Little Richard).

In an argument that figured prominently in his defense against molestation charges, Jackson says he embraces juvenile amusements because he never got a chance to as a child; while other kids went to school, played with toys, and watched Dis-ney cartoons, Jackson was trapped in a grueling regimen of rehearsal and performance, prodded and sometimes beaten by a controlling and berating father. At other times, Jackson has cast himself as a defender of the childlike ideal, a rejuvenile mogul in the mold of Disney, whom Jackson idolizes for his tenacity in the face of skeptics. "They laughed at Walt Dis-ney," Jackson said in a 2004 interview with filmmaker Brett Ratner. "[He] shaped and changed our culture, our customs, the way we live, the way we do things . . . I think God plants seeds through people on the earth. And . . . I'm one to bring some bliss and escapism, some joy, some magic."

Still, it's hard to reconcile Disney's rejuvenile tendencies with Jackson's. For all his attention to fantasy and imagination, Disney ultimately emerged from his childhood apartment, ran his park, made his movies, and created an empire along the way. Disney might have been a boy, but he was also a man. He simply never let a developmental stage slip by without making it a part of his character. Infant, boy, teenager, man—he stubbornly refused to let one cancel out the rest. In the Disney myth, not even death matters so much, as stories of his cryogenic preservation keep alive the hope that Uncle Walt will somehow cheat the ultimate milestone of maturity.

Jackson, meanwhile, appears permanently fixated on fantasy. One look at his face confirms that. Much has been made about how Jackson's misadventures in plastic surgery have blurred the boundaries of race, gender, and age. What is this creature: Black or white? Man or woman? Boy or man? Look closely at those huge oval eyes and simplified, stylized features and you soon recognize another major influence. Jackson is turning himself into a Disney character.

The Corporate Embrace of the Childlike

Perhaps the most unsettling thing about Jackson's Disney obsession is how close to home it hits. The objects of Jackson's adulation are not, after all, figments of a perverse imagination but wholesome icons of childhood that many adults still cherish. Evidence of the strength of those bonds among everyday adults is plentiful at the parks themselves, which have only grown in popularity in the fifty years since Disneyland opened, thanks in large part to the fact that each successive generation seems to absorb a little more of Disney's willful ignorance of traditional age norms. Kids who grew up making pilgrimages to Disneyland make it a point to return as adults, with or without kids in tow.

This shift has not gone unnoticed by the Walt Disney Company, which in the mid-nineties began taking dramatic steps to appeal more directly to adult tastes. In Orlando, nightclubs and higher-end restaurants were added, along with a deluxe spa and even an adult education center. Today guests to the Magic Kingdom can take a class in cardiovascular fitness at the Disney Institute, enjoy a gourmet meal, and dance the night away at the House of Blues. Elsewhere at the resort there's a recreation center for off-duty military personnel and six separate convention centers, which host trade shows and annual meetings for the likes of the Plastics Processing Industry and the Insulation Contractors Association of America (because what better way to complement a long day of seminars than with a frolic around the Happiest Place on Earth?).

And when the day is done, the most dedicated rejuveniles return to another recent addition to WDW—the Pop Century Resort. Opened in 2003, the hotel was billed as a "nostalgic journey through decades of the past century." One step onto the grounds, however, and it's clear that this monument to the twentieth century isn't likely to include shrines to the Bay of Pigs, say, or the Great Depression. Instead, there's a four-story-high yo-yo, a set of Rubik's Cubes embedded into the stairwells, and a colossal can of Play-Doh. Underneath the gigantic Big Wheel and dwarfed by the preposterously large foosball table, it's impossible not to feel awestruck and utterly small. Somewhere Fred "The Kid" Thompson is laughing—a hundred years after his plans for Toyland Grown Up were abandoned as the fevered dream of a madman, Disney has done it.

But Disney's most audacious attempt to cater to adults is surely Fairy Tale Weddings, an event-planning service that hosts some one thousand ceremonies on the grounds of Disney resorts every year. Putting its distinctive childlike spin on what has become one of the last remaining rites of passage into adulthood, Disney freely mixes the trappings of traditional matrimony with characters and images drawn from Disney mythology. While some couples elect to exchange vows inside a Disney hotel, at a mature remove from the actual park, more adventurous brides don cartoon-blue gowns and arrive at the foot of Cinderella's Castle aboard a glass coach drawn by miniature white ponies. J. C. Boyle, an analyst with the Center for Cultural Studies & Analysis, recalls stopping to watch a bridal party inside Disney World, milling around as they waited to have their pictures taken. "The groomsmen all had on these white tuxedos and they were standing around in a semicircle, doing that awkward thing guys do when they're talking and they don't know what to do with their hands," he says. "And right there with them was Mickey Mouse, dressed in an identical white tuxedo, nodding along with his hands dangling just like everyone else. And no one thinks this is weird—he was just one of the family."

The success of Fairy Tale Weddings emboldened Disney CEO Michael Eisner to appeal even more directly to adults. The monument to this approach is California Adventure, a $700 million adjunct to Disneyland which when opened in 2001 was notable mainly for how little there was for kids to do. Visitors could stroll along a faux boardwalk, stop for a cocktail at one of several bars, catch a meal at a restaurant run by celebrity chef Wolfgang Puck, or take a tour of a working bakery (cannily exploiting the innate satisfaction in watching someone *knead*). The logic was straightforward:

If more adults are coming, Disney should give them things adults like.

The logic was utterly wrong. California Adventure was an immediate flop, with adults as well as kids complaining about an oversupply of stores and restaurants and a shortage of rides and attractions. In its first year of operation, attendance fell some two million short of projections. Attendance continued to decline the year after, and picked up only after a new thrill ride was installed, Wolfgang Puck pulled out, and Imagineers scrambled to add kiddie attractions. The ultimate lesson: The best way to appeal to adult visitors is to ignore them completely. Adult visitors don't come for placid promenading, fine dining, or vicarious thrills. They come for fun of their own. They come for stomach-churning thrill rides, parades, corn dogs . . . and maybe even a spin on a ride like Heimlich's Chew Chew Train.

The Rise of the Kid–Adult Hybrid

Changes at California Adventure put the park back in line with the philosophy that made Disney successful in the first place, described in 1968 by biographer Richard Schickel as "so pervasive and persuasive that it forces first the child, then the parent to pay it heed—and money." This encompassing approach has had a dramatic impact far outside the parks, most notably in movies and on TV. Disney wasn't the first to create entertainment that appealed to both kids and adults, but he set the standard for high-end kids' entertainment that grown-ups unashamedly want to see.

This blurring of demographics has worked in both personal and commercial ways. For one, it's made kids more

sophisticated and adults more childlike. Before Disney, pop
culture for kids was most often cut-rate, condescending, and
devoid of adult themes. After Disney, the ante was upped.
Cheaply made, cynically produced movies still got churned
out (a lot by Disney himself), but kids and adults now knew
that just around the corner was an epic release packed with
production values and themes that would resonate across the
age spectrum.

The success of this formula is most plainly seen in motion
pictures. The biggest filmmakers of the past thirty years have
all shamelessly borrowed from Disney's playbook. The list of
the highest-grossing worldwide films is now essentially a catalog of kid-adult hybrids. You've got your Star Wars movies,
your Harry Potters, your Nemos and Shreks and Spider-
Mans. The only movie in the top ten all-time top-grossers that
even remotely resembles a movie for grown-ups is *Titanic,*
which at least included a few mustaches and pinafores. On
television, programs including *The Simpsons, Buffy the Vampire
Slayer,* and *SpongeBob SquarePants* have carefully straddled the
line between children and adults. Often, that line is an explicit theme and source of endless go-to gags. "SpongeBob is
an adult character who acts like a child," Stephen Hillenburg,
creator of SpongeBob, remarked in an interview included on
the DVD of *The SpongeBob Movie.* "The show is all about not
losing your childlike sense in life. It can be helpful in solving
problems. It also can cause trouble."

And just as the sweet, clueless SpongeBob taps in to a previous era's ideal of innocent youth and the savvy Bart Simpson
satirizes that ideal, these characters exert influence over adults,
who prize their remove from the stark realities of adulthood.
Asked in 2000 to identify the preeminent icon of the twentieth
century, British adults aged 18 to 35 picked Bart Simpson

over Nelson Mandela, Mother Teresa, and Princess Diana (also in the top ten: video game starlet Lara Croft).

Cartoon characters and video game figures as twentieth-century icons? Much of the credit (and blame) goes to Uncle Walt.

FIVE

boomerangers, twixters, and panic over grown-up kids

WE DO NOT GROW ABSOLUTELY,
CHRONOLOGICALLY. WE GROW
SOMETIMES IN ONE DIMENSION,
AND NOT IN ANOTHER; UNEVENLY.
WE GROW PARTIALLY. WE ARE
RELATIVE. WE ARE MATURE IN ONE
REALM, CHILDISH IN ANOTHER.

— Anaïs Nin

Rejuveniles are easiest to spot at play, whether cavorting through the Magic Kingdom, hurling a playground ball, or wolfing down a gourmet cupcake. But the fact that a certain subset of adults has developed a taste for childlike leisure is not the whole story. Being a rejuvenile is not simply a matter of a preference for certain hobbies, movies, or snacks. It is also a matter of bigger choices: when to leave home, when to get married, when and if to have children, and even what kind of parent to be.

On all these scores, adults are making drastically different choices than they have in decades past. They are putting off marriage, delaying parenthood, and forgoing children altogether. They are choosing to live with parents longer and forming surrogate families of friends and roommates. They are redefining gender roles and carving out increasingly large chunks of family life for play and fun. The choices they're making aren't all rejuvenile—that is, they're not all calculated to protect some treasured aspect of childhood. But that's often their effect. Living alone, living with parents, living with roommates, waiting to have children—choices based on practical economic and social realities have had an unexpected consequence: They've created ideal conditions for the rejuvenile. Indeed many of the deepest conflicts and richest obsessions of rejuveniles aren't rooted in their innate love of fun and games but arise from their shifting place in the domestic universe.

Clearly, rejuveniles have been shaped by momentous social change. Lengthening life spans, for one. Americans can now expect to live a full thirty years longer than they could in 1900, and in an era when reaching the one-hundred-year mark is not unreasonable, why settle down at eighteen or twenty-one? Increased mobility also plays a part; the average American now relocates eleven times in his or her life, giving traditions governing "proper" adult behavior less chance to take root. The late-seventies spike in divorce rates is also at work. Adults with vivid memories of their own parents' bitter splits tend to approach family life with extreme caution and then throw themselves into parenthood with zeal, treating it as a chance to relive and improve on their own childhoods.

But rejuveniles are also active participants in social change— and sometimes, as we'll soon see, they're both *acted upon* and *actors*. A growing mass of adults are surveying the prospects of maturity, pivoting on their heels, and announcing, simply, Not me. No way, no how. I know better. I will not marry first thing out of school. I will change jobs, switch careers, and relocate until I find what I'm looking for. I will handpick responsibilities one at a time instead of accepting wholesale sets of obligations at predetermined points in life. And when I do settle down to raise a family, I will hang on tight to those things that have always made me happy.

These sorts of choices are being made most obviously by people in their twenties and thirties. These are the over-educated itinerants who "boomerang" back to their parents' house, the determined singles who rail against what author

Sasha Cagen calls "the tyranny of coupledom," and the co-habiting unmarrieds who describe their arrangement as "playing house." Mostly, these are people whose own parents were married with kids, mortgages, and picket fences when they were their age. Now that their time has come, however, they face the frontier of family life with the trepidation of Arctic explorers. Before they head out into the chilly unknown, they fortify themselves with the comforts of home and the cama-raderie of friends, accumulating multiple degrees, high-interest debt, and checkered romantic histories. They travel in packs of other not-quite-grown-ups, dipping their toes into one en-thusiasm, romance, and job after another. These are the job hoppers, the speed daters, the subscribers to Friendster, and the loyal viewers of *Friends,* the people who took to heart the adage "Follow your bliss"—which sounded deep and wise coming from Joseph Campbell on PBS but which has sent them unexpectedly far afield of most things resembling tradi-tional adulthood.

Together, they're pushing back the statistical goalposts of maturity. They're taking longer to finish school, longer to find a mate, longer to have kids. Thirty years ago, the average age of American women at their first marriage was twenty-one. Most had a baby a year later. Nowadays the median age for marriage is twenty-five for women and twenty-seven for men. The average is far higher for the well off and for those in big metropolitan areas; in New York, for example, some 41 percent of people age thirty to thirty-four have never mar-ried, and according to some reports, the middle and upper classes now defer childbirth ten to twenty years later than their parents.

Such changes have become a hot topic for sociologists and a flash point for tradition-minded critics. All agree that a distinct new stage of life has taken shape between adolescence and adulthood, even if no one quite knows what to call it. Author Gail Sheehy dubs it "provisional adulthood." Developmental psychologist Jeffrey Arnett favors the phrase "emerging adulthood." Trend spotter Faith Popcorn calls the phase in which young adults return to their parents' homes "B2B," or "back-to-bedroom."

In most accounts, the people inspiring all these neologisms don't come off particularly well. They're painted either as shallow drifters who honestly believe "it's all about me," or mooching hangers-on who lack the gung-ho of generations past. One of the earliest such accounts came in 1986 from Susan Littwin, whose book *The Postponed Generation* railed against young adults more interested in "finding themselves" than in "facing reality." Young people, she wrote, duck out of committed relationships and avoid long-term commitments for the most shallow, self-serving reasons. "They don't want to reach beyond the piping hot, fast fantasy of pop music, television and sports," she wrote. "To do so would mean identifying with adults and assuming responsibility. Quadraphonic sound is so much better."

Littwin was quick to name the culprit: overindulgence. This theme has since become a conservative rallying cry—the young adults of today, this theory goes, came of age in the sixties and seventies and were thus raised in a bubble of warm self-esteem. They were showered in praise, given shiny trophies for "participation," and shielded from the harsh vicissitudes of life by hippie-dippie parents more interested in "validating" their feelings than in teaching responsibility. It's no wonder, then, that such privileged princes and princesses now are taking so long to begin the hard business of adulthood. They just can't get over the indignity, Littwin writes, that "no one cares if they can paint or run a mock constitutional convention or work on relationships or jog six miles."

That same reproachful tone resurfaced in a 2005 *Time* magazine cover feature on Twixters, its name for those who inhabit "a strange, transitional never-never land between adolescence and adulthood in which people stall for a few extra years, putting off the iron cage of adult responsibility that constantly threatens to crash down on them." Under a cover photo of a starry-eyed twentysomething sitting in a sandbox (plastic pail and shovel at the ready) was the headline "They Just Won't Grow Up." Among the young people profiled was a twenty-seven-year-old insurance claims adjuster with a characteristic take on the prospects of adulthood: "I don't ever want a lawn," he said. "I don't ever want to drive two hours to get to work. I do not want to be a parent. I mean, hell, why would I? There's so much fun to be had while you're young."

The story triggered a hearty round of tsk-tsking from commentators, who laid blame for the phenomenon at the feet of overly permissive parents. "The problem is, growing up is easier and cushier than ever," syndicated columnist and former Reagan staffer Betsy Hart wrote. "No one is making them leave the family nest, it's incredibly cushy there, and why in the world would you go through the hard work of building your own nest when you have access to a much fancier one ready-made?" Conservative talk show host and freelance columnist Kay Daly went one step further, arguing that the Twixters' predicament was a product of their own feckless pursuit of pleasure. "Apparently years of instant gratification, whether through the endless barrage of video games or parents wracked by guilt over divorce or time consuming careers, has now taken its toll," she wrote.

Such overheated commentary can be taken as just another

outburst of conservative outrage over the erosion of the nuclear family, proof that certain critics will, when faced with any significant social change, find a way to blame the hippies. Never mind that the adulthood described by these commentators is so relentlessly grim—is it any wonder that young adults are avoiding "the iron cage of adult responsibility" described by *Time,* or "the real world" as described by the authors of the 1987 book *Boomerang Kids,* a place characterized by "setbacks, disappointments, consequences, and losses"?

For all their apparent indecisiveness, young adults are reasonably certain that what lies ahead for them doesn't have to be quite so dire. Which is a big part of why they're so cautious; they want to get it right. Reading the jeremiads against Our Aimless Youth, you'd never know that the vast majority of adults today *do* eventually marry and have children, or that the divorce rate is actually declining—since peaking in the U.S. at 53 percent in 1981, the rate fell to 37 percent by 2004, a shift many sociologists attribute to the extra years adults are taking to settle down. According to the National Marriage Project, getting married after the age of twenty-five dramatically reduces the chance of divorce.

So why the fuss? Perhaps what disapproving commentators are reacting to—consciously or unconsciously—is not so much the spectacle of twentysomethings who decline to marry on cue and, still worse, make no apologies for their behavior, but to a larger and more radical phenomenon. The truth is that people in their twenties and thirties are reinterpreting the very idea of adulthood—rejecting the notion of a life that proceeds neatly from one stage to the next. *Time* got it wrong. It's not that Twixters refuse to grow up—they're just growing up on their own terms, reshuffling, prolonging, and interleaving a once-predictable sequence of events that, until recently, could be counted on to usher one into a settled, stable way of life.

A generation ago, adults could expect to finish school, get married, and start a career all within a few years. Now people are living together before getting married, working while in school, continuing school while working, and taking full advantage of their immunity from the expectations inherent in being a parent, husband, or wife. They are, to borrow a sociological term, on "role hiatus," free to try things out, screw up, move back home, and try again. Along the way, they're forging a new sense of adulthood—one that has less to do with what they've achieved than how they *feel*.

Of course, most eventually get tired of dating, sick of going to bars, and bored with a life lacking long-term attachments. They build a career, find a spouse, start a family. Others, however, remain adrift, either because they waited too long—the once-overflowing dating pool is now more shallow—or because they come to sincerely value their unsettledness, not as marks of childishness but as a prize of maturity. For these rejuveniles, the old measurements of adulthood are simply out of date, as musty and laughable as Victorian etiquette guides. They might not be married, they might not have kids, they might build their life around values older people find self-serving, but they're still adults—they're just a different sort, less mature in some ways, but, it must be said, far more in others. Yes, they're less self-sufficient, but they're also more self-aware. Yes, they're less dependable, but they're also more adaptable. And yes, their crisscrossing career paths can look like proof of indecisiveness or all-around flakiness. But these same qualities can also be seen as evidence of an open and adventurous spirit, one that would rather explore and experiment than settle down, stick to it, and hope for the best. And when their time comes to settle, either with a family or on their own, they're better prepared to do it for good.

Growing Up with the Goodtime Gang

Every once in a while, Gwendolyn Sanford thinks about what her parents were doing when they were her age. At thirty, her dad was a computer salesman at a store in downtown L.A. Her mother was a dental hygienist. They'd been married twelve years and had three kids, the oldest of whom was eleven. They were, in pretty much every sense of the word, settled.

Thirty-year-old Gwendolyn, meanwhile, is almost entirely unsettled. Up until three years ago, she lived with her dad in the same neighborhood where she grew up. She isn't married, doesn't have kids, and is nowhere near ready for anything resembling an adult routine. "I do a few grown-up things," she says. "But mostly, I have fun." An ideal day might include a tap-dancing class, a trip to the park, a stop for Popsicles, and a few hours combing through the racks at thrift shops for costumes to wear with her band, a group called the Goodtime Gang that does raucous rock covers of nursery room standards like "Bingo" and "Itsy Bitsy Spider," along with original compositions that tackle such topics as human anatomy, the importance of sharing, and bugs.

The group enjoys a rabid following of Southern California preschoolers, who turn out in droves to see them play at malls, street fairs, and the occasional birthday party. But the Goodtime Gang also has a loyal adult fan base—I first saw them perform at an East L.A. nightclub that caters to a crowd of people whose idea of a stiff drink extends beyond undiluted

163

OJ. I knew it was partly just a hipster lark, a novelty night—the lineup also included a puppet show and a "conceptual art rock band" that included a nine-year-old girl on drums. But there was also something deeply heartfelt, even momentous, in the air as Gwendolyn took the stage in a Raggedy Ann dress, cartoonish pigtails, and knee-high socks and performed for an audience of adults seated cross-legged on the floor, cocktails perched on bobbing knees. Many sang along.

Talking with Gwendolyn afterward, it was clear that the act was more than just shtick. She'd written her first song for kids a year earlier at a time when she was struggling to establish herself as a solo singer-songwriter in the vein of PJ Harvey or Tom Waits. That focus changed after being approached by a filmmaker friend who needed a lighthearted kids' song for an independent feature called *Chuck and Buck*. Gwendolyn sat down and wrote "Oodly Oodly (Freedom of the Heart)," an ethereal slice of bubblegum pop that became a minor hit on alternative radio. Encouraged, she assembled a group of musician friends to record a whole record of kids' songs. It all happened naturally, she says. "This free-spirited kid inside me stepped up and took over," she says. "I can't tell you how refreshing it was to meet her at that point in my life. Here I was trying to be an adult and make a living doing serious music—and all of a sudden this little four-year-old girl pops up and says, 'Look at me!'"

Tending that inner four-year-old has become the closest thing to an adult career Gwendolyn has ever known. While she still records and performs as a solo act, the Goodtime Gang is now a cottage industry, generating CDs and DVDs and even girl-sized versions of Gwendolyn's signature dress. But while she now supports herself entirely through music, she's still a long way from settling down. She and her fiancé, a drummer named Brandon who's "just as un-grown-up as I am," are in no position to buy a house or start a family. Not that either one of them is in any hurry—Gwendolyn says they're both too happy with how things are to make any big changes. That, more than anything, has been the greatest dividend from embracing her inner four-year-old. "I've never been happier," she says. "It might sound flighty, but as soon as you make friends with the kid inside you and learn how to let them play, you just feel better. You're nicer to people. You realize they're just a kid too. The pressure is off. The pressures my parents and grandparents felt at my age—I can't imagine how that must have felt. I'm free."

Gwendolyn says she looks forward to starting a family—just not yet, not when she still has "so much left to learn." The choice to hold off on making permanent changes is, she says, in part a response to the example set by her parents, who married young, shelved their own artistic ambitions, and split up when she was a teenager. By contrast, her siblings have taken their time finding their way; her brother lived at home until he was twenty-seven, while her sister is starting out on a career as a teacher at the age of twenty-six. "We're all doing the opposite of what our parents did," she says. "We're all getting life out of our system."

For his part, Gwendolyn's father, Thom, is delighted his kids have taken a more gradual route toward adulthood, even if that meant they hung around the house a good deal longer than other kids. "We took care of each other," he says. "We'd all been through so much, and our relationship changed to the point where we were three adults living under the same roof." Thom is quick to point out that his kids paid rent and helped with household chores. They were allowed to stay, he says, because they couldn't have fully pursued their creative ambitions otherwise. "They were both serious and talented and working hard—how could I not support that?"

This is not an uncommon attitude among parents of adults who drift home. While critics take for granted that parents of Boomerang Kids can't wait for their kids to get their act together and flee the family home, studies have shown that parents are usually happy to play a closer part in their adult kids' lives. A 1996 survey of 420 families in Vancouver, for instance, found that a full 73 percent felt "very satisfied" with the arrangement. "They like the idea of having the family together," reported sociologist Barbara Mitchell. "It alleviated anxiety over what's happening to their children."

A Tale of Two Twixters: Stacy and Rachel

Struggling artists alone don't account for the sharp spike in the number of adults who depend on parents for support. Many B2Bers are still in school or working subsistence-level service jobs, while others labor in entry-level drudgery while laying the groundwork for profitable but far-off futures. All told, close to sixteen million families in the U.S. had one child or more over the age of eighteen living at home in 2003, a 14 percent jump since 1985, according to a U.S. Census American Housing Survey. And while full-blown rejuveniles like Gwendolyn account for some of that change, the vast majority of B2Bers present a more complicated picture, mixing the outward attitudes and responsibilities of adulthood with the freedoms and dependencies of youth.

Twenty-five-year-old Stacy Marble is by all appearances an independent, self-starting adult. Perpetually busy and given to superlatives—her e-mails are filled with exclamation points, and she's likely to describe wherever she ate lunch as "the best restaurant ever!"—Stacy has spent the past four years working as a special assistant to a Los Angeles city councilman, typically putting in fifty hours a week and spending much of her time planning meetings and coordinating agendas. She has an IRA and a closet full of heels and J. Crew professional suits. She can talk for hours about conditional-use permits and the workings of civic politics.

Outside work, however, she shelves her adult persona. For one thing, Stacy still lives with her parents, at the end of a leafy San Fernando Valley cul-de-sac not far from the home that appeared as the family house on *The Brady Bunch*. Free time is mostly spent with the same tight circle of friends she's known since junior high. On weekends they often get together for pajama parties complete with cupcakes and romantic movies on DVD. Most of these friends are like her, unmarried and footloose, free to pop out for a drink on a weeknight or take a few days off for a trip to Costa Rica or Vegas or New York.

A year ago things took a turn toward the permanent when she moved in with her boyfriend, heir to a family lightbulb fortune (he called himself, only half jokingly, "the lightbulb prince"). After six mostly blissful months together, he proposed. It looked like a traditional adult life was coming together. Still a few years shy of twenty-five, she saw herself quitting her job, getting pregnant, and slipping into the routines of a Brentwood housewife.

"That's when all hell broke loose," she says. Arguments over wedding plans escalated. She began to realize her fiancé was still perhaps a bit *too* attached to his parents. The wedding was called off. Stacy headed home again.

Despite how it might have looked, Stacy says the decision

167

to stay unmarried and move back to her folks' house was not an outburst of immaturity. Stacy didn't act out of a need to preserve the freedoms and comforts of youth. Quite the opposite: Becoming the lightbulb princess would have meant becoming the baby daughter of a new family. "I wasn't gaining a husband as much as I was becoming a daughter all over again," she says. "In that situation I never would have grown up."

Stacy admits she sometimes feels embarrassed about her situation, especially when she thinks about how much her parents had established for themselves when they were her age (married two years, mom working at medical office, dad for the Internal Revenue Service in the job he still has today). But in general, the arrangement works. Her parents are happy to have her at home, she says, grateful to have been given a few "bonus years." This is especially true, Stacy says, for her mom, whom she describes as "my best friend, my sister, and my therapist." It's the emotional support she gets at home, far more than the financial help, that Stacy says keeps her there. "Could I go rent a decent apartment?" she asks. "Sure. But where is it written that I can't still love my parents as an adult? Or that I can't still play with my friends?"

Many in Stacy's circle of friends see things much the same way. Rachel Zaiden is also twenty-five, also works as a political aide, and until recently still lived at home, though she felt more conflicted about it. "A little part of me cringed when someone asked where I lived," Rachel says. "I knew it wasn't uncommon, but I still worried about what other people thought."

And there's no doubt material concerns factored into Rachel's decision. Rachel's parents live in a three-story hillside modern they built themselves, complete with curved walls and pristine hardwood floors and wide canyon views. It's an

Architectural Digest sort of house, a universe or two away from the dingy starter apartments she could have afforded if she was on her own. "It sounds horrible, but my parents live in a really big, nice house and it was hard to think about spending a lot of money to live somewhere not half as nice," Rachel says.

Like Stacy, Rachel moved home after finishing college and starting work in a low-paying but highly rewarding job, as a caseworker to a California congressman. She's always been ambitious—as a teenager Rachel announced she would be the first female president of the United States, telling friends and teachers she was counting on their support come 2036. As she grew up, she worked on local political campaigns and volunteered planting trees in the Santa Monica Mountains. Her sense of social responsibility is still strong—she's just begun graduate school at the University of Southern California in the hopes of becoming a senior policy advisor. Beyond the occasional trip to the Magic Kingdom, her interests have never run toward kid stuff. She and her boyfriend have been in a "committed long-term relationship" for five years and recently moved in together; they like to take wine trips, visit museums, and spend weekends at B&Bs. All of which made the stereotype of the immature Boomerang Kid seem particularly unfair. "There's very little in my life that's actually childlike," she says.

Why, then, did she rely so much on her parents during the lean postcollegiate years? Rachel says it wasn't simply the creature comforts. It was mainly an emotional bond that kept her home, the chance to live with her parents as an adult and forge a different and better relationship. For one thing, grown-up Rachel is mellower, better able to listen and learn. She never stopped being the youngest daughter—her mom never managed to break the habit of calling her by her baby name, Nini—and she knew she relied on them in a way other twenty-five-year-olds would find deeply unacceptable. But none of that stopped her from growing up. In fact she thinks the safety net provided by her parents helped her move along a little more quickly than if she'd been out scraping by on her own, eating Top Ramen, and sweating the cable bill. She lived at home, but it didn't hold her back.

This point was driven home one day at her synagogue, where Rachel's rabbi had assembled a meeting of young adults in the congregation. Most were about twenty-two, just out of school, living at home, ambivalent about their place in the world and the dizzying array of choices available to them. Rachel recognized that feeling—it was the same one she had when she first moved back in with her parents. Now, just a few years later, she felt more confident, less anxious, "at the end of the shock of learning about the real world." And she made that adjustment under her parents' roof, proof to her that "you can develop as a mature person and still maintain a close dependent relationship with your parents."

Toppling the Grown-up Goalposts

What should we call the self-directed, socially conscious, altogether worldly twenty-five-year-old who spends her off hours giggling with junior high girlfriends? How do we reconcile her heavy load of responsibility with the fact that she sleeps in a bedroom where she once did algebra homework and snipped pictures out of *Teen Beat*? Even choices that seem on the surface sure signs of immaturity—Gwendolyn's foray into kiddie rock, for one, or Stacy's decision not to get married—are turned inside out, evidence not of disdain for adulthood but respect for it. Are they girls or women, children or grown-ups?

The confusion stems from the degree to which the markers of adulthood have shifted in recent years. One such signpost loomed especially large in the past, says Jeffrey Arnett, a developmental psychologist at the University of Maryland. "Until fairly recently, what made you an adult is whether you were married," says Arnett. "Marriage was hugely significant for most people. It was the first time they lived outside their parents' household, the first time they had sex, the first time they lived independently."

That all changed, of course, with the Pill and the sexual revolution and the spike in the divorce rate and all the other mixed blessings of the sixties and seventies. Marriage is still a significant milestone, of course, but in an era when it's considered reckless to start a family before getting a career on track, when getting established professionally often requires additional years of school and associate-level apprenticeship, when cohabiting is a routine stop on the romantic trajectory, when the bride's virginal white costume is a quaint anachronism . . . well, marriage just isn't the benchmark it once was. As noted by historian John Modell, "It has become an embarrassment to present marriage itself as a happy ending, not so much because it is not a happy event but because so often it is no longer an ending." Once a rite of passage, it now seems more like a pageant.

But if marriage isn't an entry to adulthood, what is? The next big benchmark would seem to be parenthood. Surely bearing a child and taking responsibility for a new life still counts as an etched-in-stone demarcation between youth and adulthood? Again, not so much. As the Playalong Parents we'll meet in the next chapter have discovered, having kids is

no longer seen as a mandate to become a role model of authority and seriousness; many parents now greet parenthood
as a chance to reexperience childhood all over again.

So what defines an adult now? Arnett has done more than
ten years of research on the topic, talking to thousands of
young people about what makes an adult. His conclusion:
While adulthood was once associated with marriage and parenthood, it's now synonymous with intangible qualities of
individual character. In one typical survey, Arnett and his colleagues asked people aged twenty-one through twenty-eight
to rank criteria they believed were required to achieve adulthood. Ninety-four percent of respondents listed one attribute
as essential: "accepting responsibility for one's self." Other top
qualities included "making independent decisions" and "establishing a relationship with parents as an equal adult." Near the
bottom of the list were being married (just 17 percent listed it
as essential for adulthood) and having kids (14 percent)—
right alongside "avoiding vulgar language" (17 percent) and
having "grown to full height" (13 percent).

The common theme is clear enough. Being an adult was
once about objective measurements of one's relationship to
others: You were an adult when you became a husband, wife,
father, or mother. Now adulthood is a solo journey, an un-
guided personal quest, the ultimate prize of which is to "come
into one's own"—a standard whose meaning varies significantly from person to person. By these new standards, adulthood is amorphous and intangible, a gradual psychological
transformation that can take a decade or longer to complete.

The goalposts have not just moved; they've dematerialized.

Maturity can now be achieved in situations that in previous eras would have marked you as hopelessly immature. Just
as being married with kids doesn't make you an adult any-

more, being single and unsettled doesn't make you a kid. Even the B2Bers clinging tight to mom's apron strings can achieve adulthood on the new terms—as long as they feel they're accepting responsibility for their tight grip. "I used my parents as support," said one of the adults cited in Arnett's study, who lived with his parents through college and two years afterward. "But I was able to say, 'This is what I want to do' or 'This is the direction I want to go.'" Another respondent put it plainly: "You can be an adult and still live at home and have your parents take care of you financially, if you sit down with them and have adult conversations and they respect your decisions."

Arnett and other sociologists often cite the Western emphasis on individualism for putting this new weight on the role of personal choice, and that's undoubtedly a factor. It's more than a little ironic, however, that the choices these young Western individualists make so often leave them less independent and less traditionally Western. By looking to parents for safe haven and putting more stock in psychological attributes than in familial status as determinants of adulthood, they are shifting our values, bringing the West closer to those cultures where people live with parents long into their adult lives and value character over marital status in determining maturity. In Morocco, for instance, young people are thought to enter adulthood when they gain *aql,* an Arabic term that roughly translated means "rationality and impulse control." Obtaining *aql* can take decades, even longer for young men. Meanwhile, dependence on family into adulthood is the unquestioned norm in places like China, Japan, Spain, and Italy.

Indeed, changes that critics deplore can also be viewed as a healthy embrace of interdependence. To be sure, extended stays with family often happen out of necessity. They can even be made for less than noble reasons (fear, insecurity, a reluctance to give up familiar creature comforts). But even in those circumstances, nestled in "cushy" family nests, maturity often takes root. Long-term objectives are adjusted and refined. Setbacks are weathered and overcome. Most important, family bonds often strengthen and evolve. This may be the most profound impact of the B2B phenomenon—the way it forces parents to recognize their children in adulthood, and conversely, the way it forces grown-up kids to appreciate their parents as adults. In the best circumstances, these grown-up kids leave home not only better prepared to make their own way but with a deeper understanding of how inexorably their path is intertwined with others.

This appreciation of interdependence is decidedly at odds with the sort of every-man-for-himself worldview celebrated by traditionalists. Which may be why Twixters stir such disapproval—they fly in the face of long-held Western notions that a parent's basic job is done the moment a child can pay his or her own way. Maturity, in this view, is a matter of pulling up one's bootstraps, of fighting for one's share in an unforgiving world. Rejuveniles, meanwhile, refuse to get with the program. They maintain strong ties with family while finding their own way. They try one thing, fail, then try something else. Worst of all, they seem unimpressed with the virtues of hardship—to them, suffering is vastly overrated.

Immature or Unlucky?

Twixters may take pride in their freedom, but that doesn't mean they aren't conflicted. Leading a life so awash in options comes at a price: anxiety. Many even admit to feeling ashamed that they have run so far afield of the traditional route to adulthood. This is particularly true for B2Bers—all seem keenly aware of the popular image of lackadaisical moochers so in love with Mom's lasagna that they refuse to go out and get lives of their own. So many people I interviewed for this chapter requested anonymity that I began to feel like I was writing about a shameful sexual habit or a top-secret military operation.

"I'm thirty-eight years old, single, and I live with my parents," explains a fellow we'll call Drew, who lives in his childhood bedroom in Long Island. "What that adds up to in people's minds is that I'm a loser. That's not great for self-esteem, believe me."

Drew isn't convinced, however, that his domestic recidivism is a result of immaturity, even if the particulars of his life so far haven't exactly added up to a rock-steady adulthood. After graduating college, Drew took a computer job in Washington, D.C., where he shared a house with three roommates. It was a kind of Twixter paradise: a run-down mansion in a tony neighborhood with rats in the basement, hair in the sinks, and parties on weekends filled with other free spirits who worked hard and played harder. That went on for five years, until Drew headed for California, where he joined a booming tech start-up and tried his hand at surfing. By 2001, he was working crazy hours at a job in San Francisco developing streaming-video software, paying $2,500 rent for an apartment in Pacific Heights, and feeling like a newly minted Master of the Universe.

Drew blames the post-9-11 economic downturn for his parallel personal downturn. The start-up went bust, and after a difficult year scrounging for work in California and back in D.C., he accepted his parents' invitation to move home. They welcomed him back, even installed a new flat-screen TV in the family room, which was especially nice since it covered some of the tiny dents in the walls Drew recognized as evidence of epic penny fights that he and his little brother waged as kids.

Drew has been looking for work for a year now, lately concentrating on firms that design and maintain back-end databases for financial traders. He's been discouraged, however, by how much of this work has been outsourced to cheaper international subcontractors or else taken up by "naive young college graduates or guys they bring over to work three thousand miles away from home." With plenty of time between scouring the want ads and the occasional interview, he often finds himself mulling over what went wrong, how his own faults landed him in this fix. Lately he's found himself agreeing with his dad, who makes no secret of his opinion that Drew suffers from unrealistic expectations, that he has spent too much time playing and not enough working, that he needs to—and here the dagger twists in—grow up.

To Drew, his situation isn't a result of immaturity so much as hard economic realities. Sure, he might have saved more when he had the chance, spent less eating out, taken fewer cabs, but it's doubtful anything he did would have prevented him from being cast aside by a convulsing industry. He's human flotsam in the turbulence of the global economy. And adding insult to injury, he's called childish by those insulated from the storm.

Of course, this will sound like more self-involved sniveling to those complaining about the aimlessness of youth [see Richard Melheim's *101 Ways to Get Your Adult Children to Move Out (and Make Them Think It Was Their Idea)*]. It's not that these critics don't recognize some economic part of the equation—

but the only factor they care to discuss is the voracious consumerism of the people who land back home. It is certainly true that Drew likes his parents' flat-screen TV very much and Rachel enjoys the view from her childhood bedroom. Easy to mock, yes. Yet setting aside for a moment the hypocrisy of Boomer-aged, Lexus-driving adults complaining about the consumerism of the kids they raised, it seems to me we're better off asking a bigger question: Aren't there other, vastly more significant economic forces at work here? The fact is, Drew and many more of his unsettled peers would be only too happy to buy a home, pay off their debt, and find the right someone—but they simply can't afford it. The rapid run-up in the housing market, for one, has made even a starter home a pipe dream for all but the most firmly established, just as actual earnings have dipped, tuition has increased, and the job market has turned more volatile. Meanwhile young adults have taken a cue from the federal government, running up record personal debt with credit cards handed out on college campuses like candy canes at Christmas. Adulthood is just plain expensive. As put by Frank Furstenberg, head of a MacArthur Foundation study of the "adultolescent" phenomenon: "The conveyor belt that transported adolescents into adulthood has broken down."

Reached at his office at the University of Pennsylvania, Furstenberg is quick to express contempt for the suggestion that aimless adults are too busy indulging their inner children to get serious about adulthood. (He bristled when told the name of this book, taking offense at the pejorative whiff of "juvenile": "I hate your title on principle," he announced. "It's demeaning.") Today's young adults, Furstenberg says, literally can't grow up according to the standards set by generations past. And it's not for lack of trying. "Young adults are working

177

harder and longer than ever," he says. "But they're now in an economy where it's difficult to get at twenty-two or twenty-five what you got thirty or forty years ago."

That's a theme that comes up again and again talking to the young and unsettled—sure, they're ambivalent about adulthood, in part because it seems so permanent and deathly serious, but also because it's so difficult to obtain. So they make the best of what's available, be it the temporary-contract gig or the twin bed in the refinished basement. Thus do economic forces shape the rejuvenile identity. Drew, for one, says he felt far more adult when he was "working hard and solving problems." Now that he's out of work and home, the dynamic is reversed. Surrounded by a house filled with childhood memories, comforted by the support of a loving family that isn't shy about reminding him how grateful he should be, he feels more like a kid than ever. It's enough to drive a man to stickball.

Why the Lady Painting a Butterfly on Your Daughter's Face Thinks You Are a Dolt

If some rejuveniles are made, others are born. Amanda Cohen was an unsettled, childlike adult ten years before *Time* dubbed her a Twixter. She's still one now at the age of thirty-five, long after she was supposed to have grown out of it. Amanda is a talkative New Englander with a thick shock of dark hair and the big, expressive eyes of a slapstick comic. She's entirely comfortable with the fact that she's spent most of her adult life skipping from one thing to another. "I live by randomness," she says with pride. She's worked in radio, waited tables, sold magazine subscriptions, studied graphic design, and done stand-up comedy. She's lived in four apartments in three cities having shared a place with an old friend, a place with a boyfriend, and a place with an ex-boyfriend who had taken up with the old friend. Eventually she concluded that the only roommates she wanted were Mr. Potato Head and a few Godzilla dolls.

While friends from childhood have settled down and become more enmeshed in family life, Amanda has kept her life mostly unencumbered and her interests almost entirely kid-centric. She loves cult kiddie programs like *Land of the Lost* and *H.R. Pufnstuf* and counts herself among the most devoted members of a small but rabid adult fan base of novelty songwriter "Weird Al" Yankovic. She reads the Harry Potter books and science fiction. She enjoys carnivals and circuses. She supports this thoroughly rejuvenile lifestyle with an appropriately rejuvenile job: painting faces at children's birthday parties and at a fifties-themed restaurant in downtown Chicago, where on a typical weekend she paints in the neighborhood of three hundred kids. (Her philosophy: "If it holds still, I will paint it.") She loves the work, partly because she's such a natural with children—"I never lower myself to 'kid level,' " she says. "It helps that I'm already there." But more than that, she appreciates the job because it provides a steady living. Since starting her face-painting business four years ago, she's built up a nice 401(k) and IRA, and has socked away savings for the down payment on a house. "Like a garbageman, I've got incredible job security," she says. "There will always be junk and there will always be kids."

Somewhere along the line she came to terms with the fact that she was never going to go the traditional adult route. All the supposedly naturally occurring impulses of maturity— the ones that drive women toward what pollsters call "the magic M's: marriage, munchkins, mortgages"—simply never kicked in for Amanda. And while her life is filled with children and childlike stuff, she emphatically does not see herself as childish. She pays her way, works hard, and knows herself well enough to say that she simply wouldn't be happy as a mother or a wife—a realization she counts as one of her most mature decisions. "I've broken up with guys who told me I needed to settle down," she says. "That just isn't going to happen. I'm as settled as I'm ever going to get."

Part of the reason she's remained so resolutely single, she says, is the scarcity of like-minded men. It's not that she hasn't met and even dated lots of men her age who fit the rejuvenile profile. But over the course of several very awkward encounters, she's stumbled into a sad rejuvenile truism: When a man gets in touch with his inner child, he's likely to take up paintball, or mountain climbing, or German death metal. He starts wearing baggy pants and bill-backward baseball caps. He might even say "rad." In short, he reverts back to the age when girls were gross and fun was had primarily in the company of other boys. Women, meanwhile, are more likely to be drawn to things boys avoided like the plague. Like pajama parties. Or puppets. Or tap dancing.

Male or female, people with childlike tastes are no more immature than any other group of adults, Amanda says. Her circle of friends includes puppeteers, toy collectors, party clowns, and obsessive fans of sci-fi, animation, and Weird Al. As might be expected, there are some flaky, irresponsible personalities in that mix, people who "complain they don't have money for bus fare but then turn around and spend a hundred dollars on a new Transformer for their collection." But there are also sensible and responsible sorts who, like her, never "want to become jaded or lose a sense of wonder or innocence."

Those are qualities she rarely sees in the more conventional adults she encounters in her job. From beneath her pink beret, other adults seem harried, frantic, and unhappy, driven mostly by convention and compulsion. She's particularly mystified by the affluent suburbanites who dress their children in identical designer outfits and who all seem to pick from the same list of a dozen baby names (top of the list: Connor, Ashley, and Mavis). "They all seem pretty miserable," she says. "I know they must be satisfied, but that's definitely not for me."

In Which the Author Revisits His Twixter Years

I have a friend who refers to his postcollege experience as his "formative floundering years." That's what they are for most of us: formative and floundering.

Mine were marked by the usual mix of uncertainty, heartache, and self-involvement. It was, in retrospect, the typical Twixter bumpy ride—after college, I tried living with a girlfriend, living alone, and living with roommates. I moved from Montreal to Toronto to Cape Cod, where I managed to find a nice place to live and a good job I worked hard to get. So I did the obvious thing: quit, broke my lease, sold all my belongings, and took off for Europe, planning never to return. I drifted back to my hometown, Los Angeles, a year later, moving into a duplex with three high school friends and two chickens (don't ask). We called our place the Halfway House, a nod to the fact that this was, for all of us, a temporary stopover between now and . . . whatever came next. I drove a

$300 car nicknamed Doug, wrote for a throwaway weekly newspaper, and kept my distance from anything that suggested long-term responsibility. At one point I actually wore a T-shirt printed with the now-cringe-inducing catchphrase *whatever.*

I never thought about it in these terms at the time, but it's clear to me now, safe behind the psychic barricades that stand between my twenty-six- and thirty-six-year-old selves, that the fun of those years wasn't all that different from the fun of being a teenager. Which is to say, there were episodes of hilarity and fun set against a backdrop of high anxiety. On the plus side, it was a Pippi Longstocking existence, just us kids in a big place of our own with almost no authority to speak of. We had our day jobs to worry about, and our various creative endeavors—one roommate played bass in a power pop band, another worked as an animator on *The Simpsons,* another had plans to open a café that sold nothing but empanadas—but all in all, we did what we pleased. Our free time was filled with crushes and breakups, movies and video games, road trips and theme parties (the most memorable of which was a prom for grown-ups—I wore a blue ruffled tuxedo shirt and posed with my date in front of a pink heart crudely painted on a roll of butcher paper). We shared a dense vocabulary of in-jokes and felt privately superior to those who didn't understand our references. We stayed up late drinking wine and smoking pot and talking about this or that social slight or messy breakup.

On weekends, I'd sometimes take walks around the neighborhood with my roommate Paul, a lean, bald, and effortlessly hip man-child we called Wrinkle P. At the time Wrinkle was working behind the bar at a place called Big Daddy's and spending his days lounging at a local coffee shop. As we wandered through the surrounding streets of grand old houses filled with families and flower arrangements and people whose lives seemed entirely alien to us, we each played a game. Wrinkle's was physical—he leaped over the manicured hedges and tumbled on the lawns, jumping on telephone poles and sliding across sewer grates. It was a noisy routine, acrobatic and obnoxious and hostile to property lines and basic rules of propriety. We loved it. My game, meanwhile, was mental. It was called Come the Revolution. The L.A. riots were still fresh in everyone's minds, and I liked to imagine what would happen if another one broke out. I pictured all the homeowners fleeing at the first sign of trouble, leaving me and my vastly more street-smart, revolution-friendly roommates (ha!) the pick of whatever home struck our fancy. "Come the revolution," I'd say, squinting across an impossibly vast lawn to a Spanish bungalow shrouded in rhododendron, "that shit is *mine!*"

I mention this because it shows how ridiculous we all were (or at least *I* was; Paul's neighborhood gymnastics were indisputably cool—Parkour before there was a name for it!). It also neatly encapsulates how permanent our situation felt at the time—it was all a joke, of course, but it was, as they say in comedy, "kidding on the square"—the "square" being the fact that in some deep part of myself I actually thought that the only way I would ever find a way out of the Halfway House and into something more permanent was through the violent displacement of my neighbors.

Of course, it wasn't a riot that propelled me out but the usual thing—I fell in love and coupled up. Before I knew it, all those adult trappings that had seemed so utterly unobtainable and unnecessary began to rapidly accumulate. I got a serious job, got married, had a kid, then another. We moved to a Spanish house on a bluff covered in (of course) rhododendron.

rejuvenile

So, pampered postadolescents from affluent L.A. screw around before buckling down and growing up: end of story, right? Not exactly—not for me, or anyone else at the Halfway House. A few years after moving into the house on the bluff, I looked around at the great pileup of my kids' toys, the huge collection of my wife's beloved children's books, and the display of sad-clown paintings and wondered: Where had "adulthood" gone? Marriage, parenthood, home ownership—none of those things had made me an adult. I grew up, of course. I cultivated a social conscience, volunteering at a public school and for political campaigns. I got more serious, was less given to melancholy, and was far busier (so much busier! Is that what adulthood boils down to, a lack of time?). I learned to stop worrying and love my minivan. But mostly, even today in the house on the bluff, I still feel more like the kid on the sidewalk outside, staring in.

Meanwhile my friends from the Halfway House have made similarly ambiguous trade-offs with adulthood. Paul is still Wrinkle P, still single, still working at a bar—and astonishingly, still living at the Halfway House. But he's also grown up: He got sober, bought the bar, and got serious with a long-time girlfriend. My best friend the musician traded his bass for a banjo and joined an Irish punk band that now makes an astonishing living touring the world. The *Simpsons* animator got married, then divorced, and is now back on her own and has recently found success selling hand-knit baby clothes in the colors of Neapolitan ice cream.

In short, none of us grew up in the way we expected to. We grew just as Anaïs Nin said we would—mature in some realms, childish in others, our own Neapolitan swirl of identity.

SIX

playalong parents and the proudly childfree

SALLY SAID, "COME MOTHER.
COME AND SEE FATHER.
SEE FATHER JUMP AND PLAY.
OH, OH. FATHER IS FUNNY."

— Dick and Jane, *We Come and Go*, 1940

The moment of reckoning comes for every new parent, usually soon after arriving home with a freshly hatched newborn. I can still vividly recall the morning my wife and I brought our first son, Charlie, home from the hospital. We stood around our dining room table where he sat dozing in his infant car seat. Staring down at his grapefruit-sized head flopping disconcertingly off to the side, there was a long moment of silence. We looked at each other with a mix of wonder and panic. We were alone now. Our parents, our pediatrician, the experts expounding theories in the stack of parenting books by our bedside—no one could help us now. From this moment on, this tiny helpless creature, the one with the pulsing oval on his forehead so vulnerable it could be dented by a change in wind direction, was dependent on us for his very survival (cue sinking sensation in stomach).

Such an experience seems biologically designed to weld shut the neural pathways responsible for any remaining childlike tendencies. The gurgle and shrieks of an infant may sound incoherent to a nonparent, but they are loud and clear commands to a new dad or mom. Indeed, the job requirements of parenthood are mostly synonymous with qualities commonly associated with adulthood: dependability, responsibility, diligence, patience, authority. In becoming a parent, the conventional story line goes, you become, inevitably, an adult and, in the process, you cancel out your kidhood. End of story.

This has been a basic assumption for generations, most plainly articulated in advice aimed at young people considering the challenges of a new family. "Yesterday you were a boy, and today you're a man," stated a 1987 advice manual titled *Coping with School Age Fatherhood*. "As much as you may wish otherwise, and be assured there will be many times, you will be a man from now on until the last day of your life. This is a fact that cannot be changed."

A 1959 guidebook for teenagers titled *Your Happiest Years,* written by that figurehead of endless adolescence, Dick Clark, also hammered home the idea that adulthood begins at the onset of parenthood. Warning young readers what lay ahead when they became parents, Clark wrote that the typical father spent his days hard at work "competing with hundreds of thousands of other fathers all trying to earn enough money to meet the bills now due." He might get the occasional night out "with the boys," but his life was otherwise consumed with chores and worry. While his children lay in their beds at night, sleeping off another day of carefree fun, the dad tosses and turns, "trying to figure a way to increase your allowance the two dollars that you argued for."

To such a beleaguered provider, there was simply no room for the friends or trivial amusements that consume the typical teen. "Things that seem so important to you now hardly seem to make an impression on him," Clark told his young readers. "He can pass up an important sports contest, and if he didn't get to the local movie on a night when all the crowd was going he wouldn't bat an eyelash. Don't make the mistake of thinking that these things were never important to him. They were, but there came a time when the things he is doing now seemed even more attractive than his personal social life."

This portrait of the typical fifties dad is surely exaggerated, coming as it does in a book that shamelessly cloaks authoritarian fearmongering in the guise of casual, just-us-kids pep talks. But the picture Clark paints still illustrates a long-held assumption about growing up: Parenthood is a life sentence of maturity, with no possibility of parole.

If that was true a half century ago, it is much less true today. There are still plenty of duty-bound dads and moms who live in an entirely separate realm from their kids. Many others, however, make it a point to hop the generational divide. They may maintain adult responsibilities, but that doesn't stop them from immersing themselves in their children's world. They work hard, worry plenty, and spend their share of sleepless nights mulling over household finances — but unlike the parents described by Clark, they don't confuse these acts with parenting. After all, they were doing their share of working and worrying long before they had kids. (Unlike the parents of the fifties, who on average had their first kid between the ages of twenty and twenty-four, today's parents have spent a decade or more fending for themselves before having kids.) Responsibility and obligation might be essential ingredients of parenthood, but to many of today's parents they are not the essence of it.

So what *is* the essence? Talk to parents today and you hear more about connection than obligation, more about availability than leadership, more about participation than provision. These are the Playalong Parents, moms and dads whose idea of parenting does not exclude — indeed it is centered on —

Wiffle ball tournaments, princess tea parties, and cartoon marathons. Unlike parents of previous eras who regarded their children's activities from a lofty distance, these parents jump in and join the fun. Most partner in their kids' playtime in the hopes of forging closer bonds with their kids. Others look to childhood play to ease the pressures of their workaday routines. And many have simply discovered that having kids is a perfect excuse for experiencing childhood all over again.

Still, Playalong Parents walk a fine line. On the one hand, we understand, from the moment we lay eyes on our newborns, that we have been drafted into a mandatory service of protection. Our first and most important job is to help our kids grow up strong and healthy—to prepare them for what lies ahead. But we also want to avoid being distant, duty-bound, or dictatorial. The most idealistic among us share a deep-seated commitment to appreciating our children for who they are—not just as incomplete adults in constant need of instruction and improvement but as people in their own right who might even teach us a thing or two. We hope their spirit will rub off on us. We want, in short, to be both parent and playmate.

Tension created by these contradictory goals sends us hurtling back and forth between roles and headlong into questions that rarely occurred to parents of yore. We ask ourselves: Is my ability to enforce household rules undermined by my ability to blow big bubbles? Is my kid's ability to play on her own undermined by the presence of a parent? And perhaps most distressing of all: What if my kid has no interest at all in the things I'm so eager to do again?

Gymbo Is a Friend of Mine

One measure of how playful many parents have become can be found in the pages of childrearing manuals. While still dominated by guidelines for feeding and sleep, parenting books have lately become sources of affectionate anecdotes attesting to the transformative power of parent-child play. These stories are particularly popular in books describing the spiritual dimensions of parenting. In the 2004 book *Sacred Parenting: How Raising Children Shapes Our Souls,* Cary Thomas describes ducking out of work early to join his young son in a game of football and stumbling into something close to transcendence. "Only rarely do you find something so right and so fulfilling that you don't think you should be doing anything else," he wrote. "I stretched out, a small step from heaven, in a place called contentment—not because of a call from a publisher, a job promotion, or a raise, but because a four-year-old had called with a simple question: 'Dad, would you come home early and play football with me today?' "

To a parent like this, the point of play is deeper than mere enjoyment. It's about bridging the gap that separates parents from offspring. In the 1997 book *Everyday Blessings: The Inner Work of Mindful Parenting,* authors Myla Kabat-Zinn and Jon Kabat-Zinn lovingly describe an evening playing catch with their teenage daughter: "As we throw the ball back and forth and listen to the thud in the gloves, and the sharp crack when it goes over my head and hits the wooden fence behind me, it feels as if we've been doing this forever. Time falls away."

No doubt parents have always derived pleasure from playing with their children. What is perhaps different now is how much meaning they're investing in the experience. For these parents, play with kids has moved from diversion to priority.

In his book *The Play Ethic,* Pat Kane describes coming home from a grueling day at his job editing a Scottish newspaper supplement to find his three-year-old daughter stacking Duplo blocks into a castle. Joining her on the carpet, he found the process of stacking bricks was a sort of Zen meditation on impermanence.

"She doesn't worry about excess, or asymmetry, or redundancy," he wrote. "She has no fixed plan, other than which might emerge from the methodical snapping of plastic to plastic, blue to yellow to red, the long infrastructural one hanging by just one nubble from the transparent decorative brick—but that's all right, even as the whole thing inevitably falls, helped on its way by some gleeful bashing from her. And from those pieces, irreducible and always usable, you make something new. Create, destroy, create."

This is no mere anecdote to Kane; it's a crystallization of what he calls a "vital matrix of love, care, and communication." To him, parents who take time to play with their kids are engaged in something far more radical than the loosening up of traditional family roles. They're making a "new culture of mutual enjoyment between parent and child."

If Kane is the high-minded philosopher of this new culture of mutual enjoyment, the indoor play center is its teeming marketplace. The indoor play center is the industry name for those brightly lit, heavily padded minigymnasiums that have popped up by the thousands in minimalls and storefronts over the past ten years. And for Playalong Parents, the weekly appointment at Bright Child or Little Planet or Mumbo Jumbo Children's Indoor Play Center is the highlight of their parenting routine. They're the parents buried up to their bald spots in a pit of colored plastic balls or feverishly making their way through the two-story tube crawl, arthritic knees and pungent

rejuvenile

kid-odors be damned. They're the ones who flock by the thousands to Gymboree, which with more than five hundred "directed parent-child developmental play programs" in twenty-six countries around the world, is the McDonald's of the indoor play center biz. Visitors stash their shoes in cubbies, smear their hands in antibacterial gel, and take turns rolling on tangerine and purple tumble mats, singing along to "Itsy Bitsy Spider," and applauding the appearance of a clown puppet named Gymbo.

"The most important way for young children to learn is through play," declares *Baby Play,* Gymboree's official compendium of activities and songs. "Of course parents benefit from play, too." Not all elders, of course, find it so easy to get with the program; some hang back with pained expressions while counting down to dismissal. Still, a good number look positively giddy as they grab hold of a corner of parachute or jump up and down on a minitrampoline. For these parents, improving dexterity and coordination are not the real reasons they block out an hour for Gymboree every week. They're here for a second go at nursery school.

Full disclosure: I am acquainted with Gymbo. You might even say Gymbo is a friend of mine. Time with my kids is often spent splayed on the carpet, stacking blocks or arranging rubber dinosaurs or poking at the keys of a minisynthesizer, activities whose enjoyment is diminished only slightly by the discovery that my playmates have drifted off (to file credit card receipts or catch *American Masters* on PBS, undoubtedly). At the park, I'm the dad in the middle of a thicket of kids, playing pirates or Duck Duck Goose or Four Square. I'm occasionally joined on the slide or monkey bars by another adult, but mostly the parents and nannies sit off to the side, occasionally shooting me an overly cheerful, slightly suspicious look: "Freak or fun guy?" Once satisfied that I'm harmless, they go back to chatting, reading, and offering up sippy cups and graham crackers. To which I respond: What fun is that?

I mostly play with oblivious pride, assuming that of course it's good that I'm spending such concentrated time with my kids. When asked why I choose to run around like a camp counselor when I could be catching up on neighborhood gossip like any normal adult, I explain that it's all about *being* with my kids. It's about sharing an experience. When pressed, I might even argue that playing with my kids presents opportunities to reinforce the occasional life lesson ("If you throw sand at Dylan, he won't share his toy truck") or social skill ("If you want to play with Gilda's Barbie cell phone, you should look her in the eye and say 'please' "). But the truth is, I don't play to teach. I play for the same reason my kids do— because it's fun. I enjoy jungle gyms. I like to swing. And I can't get enough of the way new playgrounds' mammary-soft padding feels underfoot.

The same need to play along isn't confined to the playground. I'm also an eager partner in my kids' consumption of music, TV, movies, books, comics, and the like. Again, my motives are easily justifiable: I pay close attention to the media my kids are exposed to in the interests of weeding out stuff I find objectionable. It just so happens that this requires *constant and careful* attention. But although I do care about shielding my kids from sexualized teen pop, hyperviolent cartoons, and commercials for fast foods they shouldn't eat or toys they shouldn't play with, the truth is that my attention to kiddie media is mostly motivated by a need to entertain myself.

Thus my kids are intimately familiar with movies my wife

and I enjoy watching over and over again as much as they do (the shortlist: *Willy Wonka and the Chocolate Factory, The Point,* and *Babe*). And thus have my children never heard a note sung by the kid troubadour Raffi. And thus was born my family's strict No Barney policy. I'm sure there's nothing particularly wrong with Raffi or Barney—I just can't stand them. (What is it about Barney that stirs such passionate aversion in even the most indulgent parent? The writer Adam Gopnik devoted an entire chapter to just this topic in his 2000 book *From Paris to the Moon,* saying he and his wife moved to Paris with a single purpose: to escape that "man in a cheap dinosaur suit singing doggerel in an adenoidal voice.")

The same impulse behind the No Barney policy has figured in many choices my wife and I have made as parents, including a hotly debated decision to share our bed with our kids well into their toddler years. To those who told us we risked giving our children sleeping disorders, we cited La Leche League studies and talked about how children and parents have been "co-sleepers" for centuries; only modern Westerners, we said with modern Western indignation, have barbarously shuttled their babies off to cribs. But the truth is, high-minded platitudes of child development were the last things on our minds when we settled in beside our kids at night. We wanted nothing more than to connect with our children, even in sleep. We simply enjoyed cuddling. And up until our daughter developed the habit of jamming her little pajama'd feet into our stomachs at three in the morning, it seemed like the easiest and most natural thing in the world. They were happy; so were we. It's true that we mourned the loss of some of what might be called marital intimacy—but we figured that's why God created afternoon naps.

In Which Experts Inveigh Against
Parent-Child Play

As harmless as it might seem to sleep, play, and watch TV with one's own children, Playalong Parents find themselves in the thick of a debate that has been raging among psychologists, fundamentalists, and cognitive scientists since the early part of the twentieth century. As described by Ann Hulbert in *Raising America,* the debate pits the "child-centered" or "soft" school, which stresses parent-child bonding and open communication, against the "parent-centered" or "hard" school, which holds that discipline and clear division of mother-father roles are essential in the rearing of productive and moral adults. While both schools are relatively quiet on the subject of parent-child play—the topic tends to get lost amid thunderous debates over potty-training, spanking, and sex education—a few experts from both sides have turned their attention to Playalong Parents and their impact on child development.

Not surprisingly, Playalong Parents get a firmer rap from the "hard" experts, who believe parents have become entirely too chummy with their children. Some "parent-centered" experts argue that parents who allow themselves to join their children's fun simply make the basic job of running a family more difficult. In the aptly titled *Cheap Psychological Tricks for Parents,* psychologist Perry W. Buffington describes techniques to help parents "marshal your troops"—none of which are even remotely playful. "For parents to be effective, they must be leaders, exerting responsible power over children," Buffington proclaims.

Playalong Parents get an even sterner rebuke from traditionalists who believe parents—especially dads—betray their children, not to mention their masculine birthrights, by whooping it up with their kids. In *A Father's Book of Wisdom,* published in 2000, H. Jackson Brown put it bluntly: "Fathers are pals nowadays because they don't have the guts to be fathers."

Apparently, falling into "pal behavior" is one of the seven worst things parents do, according to a 1999 book by "Christian therapists" John and Linda Friel. The mom who spends time playing with her children communicates a clear message: "I'm too scared to make adult friends. I'm too scared to even address the problem. I don't have anything to do with my life when I'm not at work."

John Rosemond, publisher of the magazine *Traditional Families* and author of eleven books on childrearing (including *Parent Power!, To Spank or Not to Spank,* and *Because I Said So!*), agrees that parents now spend much more time and energy playing with their kids than they did in the fifties, which he calls "the last decade when parents raised their kids with any common sense at all." He has a vivid boyhood memory of his own mother setting him up with the materials for making papier-mâché and promptly vanishing, getting back to her housework and leaving him to it. "Today a mother would spend the next two hours making little animals with her kid," he says. "That constitutes good parenting according to the nouveau standard."

And to Rosemond, that new standard—which he sums up as "psychological propaganda about the need to bond with your child"—has only created confusion for children and stress for adults. It's not that parents should never play with kids, Rosemond says. "If a dad wants to take his son outside and play catch, fine," he says. (Presumably it's okay too for

Mom to take a break from mopping to join her daughter in a brief tea party.) The problem, he says, is the constancy of that play and the way it blurs the boundaries between parent and child. Parents who play with their kids, he says, "cannot adequately serve as authority figures. It doesn't work in the military or in business—why should it in the family?"

It's certainly true that the breakdown in traditional roles has left today's parents more unsure than ever. Rosemond is also right that well-meaning parents often go overboard in attempts to relate to their kids—witness the mother who dresses herself in the same designer getups as her teenage daughter, or the father who chatters nonstop with his sons about sports or video games.

It seems to me, however, that "hard" experts like Rosemond are entirely too quick to tout family roles of the fifties as all-purpose solutions to the problems inherent in parent-child play. Yes, traditional roles were simpler and more stable. Kids played, moms nurtured, dads provided. But didn't these families include a fair number of unfulfilled, pill-popping housewives and remote, rotting-from-the-inside company men (to say nothing of their embittered, soon-to-be Flower Children)? It's just plain unrealistic to think that open-minded, dual-income families of today will find harmony by reverting to an *Ozzie and Harriet* ideal. The genie is out of the bottle. And while its playful presence may upset traditionalists, families are simply having too much fun to stuff it back in.

Playful Parents get a warmer reception from the "child-centered" experts, who are far more concerned with pressures of conformity and early achievement than threats to parental authority. It's no wonder they aren't particularly worried about parents who spend hours playing Monopoly Junior with their kids. "Attachment parenting" guru William Sears advises parents to put down their work and play Ping-Pong with their kids, so as to "enjoy the precious moments while they last." A few proponents of the "soft" school have even designed protocols around parent-child play, such as the "floor time model" devised by psychiatrist Stanley Greenspan, which calls on parents to spend at least thirty minutes a day in one-on-one interplay with children.

William Crain, a developmental psychologist at the City College of New York and author of the 2003 book *Reclaiming Childhood,* argues that as long as parents let their kids direct the play and know when to step aside, parent-child play can actually enhance parental authority. "A child gets a kick out of a powerful person who's playing along," he says. "It promotes a deeper respect for a parent. It may not be the sort of respect that comes from fear or the threat of force. But kids will respect the parent who plays along. They like them."

The danger comes when Playalong Parents slip into the role of coach or instructor. Parents who drill their kids on athletic fields or "help" their kids with drawing or model making aren't really playing themselves, he says, and they're certainly not making their child's play any more enjoyable. In play, he says, parents should heed the advice of Ralph Waldo Emerson, who said, "Be not too much his parent. Trespass not on his solitude."

"You've got to know when to back off," says Crain. "Most kids will let you know right away when you're too involved. If you just give them opportunities to play on their own and naturally develop, they'll grow in incredible ways."

America Loves the Skateboarding Mom

For Barbara Odanaka, becoming a mother triggered a rejuvenile reckoning. Odanaka is fit and easygoing with curly blond hair that she bleaches a few times a year—"because we should all have the same hair color we had when we were ten," she says. Friends call her Barb. In 1993, she gave up a job as a newspaper sports reporter and spent a year backpacking around the world with her husband. When they returned home, they bought a place in an Orange County housing development called Top of the World and settled down to have a baby. The pregnancy was difficult. Barb spent six weeks in the hospital on bed rest before delivering a three-pound baby boy. She felt immense relief when she came home with her new son Jack, but soon that feeling was blotted out by near-constant anxiety. Her therapist called it postpartum depression. For Barb, however, it was less about a shift in hormones than a shift in circumstances. Barb had grown up feeling perpetually young, free, and cared for—one result of being the pampered youngest of five children. "My family never stopped treating me as the baby," she says. "And I think I always relished that." Now, in what felt like the blink of an eye, she was an Orange County stay-at-home mom, a career and travel and independence behind her. As she confronted what she called "the minivan existence," she felt unfit, unprepared, and utterly unhappy.

She tried to find relief through long walks with her son Jack. But he hated the jostle of the jogging stroller and cried hysterically from the moment she strapped him in to the moment she returned home. Her therapist gave her a simple assignment: Find something that once gave you joy and do it for ten minutes a day. "My husband hoped it would be sex, but I had another idea," she says. "Skateboarding."

Barbara originally took up skating at the age of ten, when her parents gave her an oak and walnut laminated Super Surfer skateboard for Christmas. She was soon sneaking out at night with neighborhood boys to race down the steep hills around her house. Some of her most vivid childhood memories revolve around an empty reservoir hidden in a grove of eucalyptus trees. She eventually earned a spot on a competitive team sponsored by a local skate shop. But at thirteen, in a half-hearted stab at maturity, she allowed herself to be convinced by the coach of her high school track team to quit skating altogether. She shouldn't endanger her prospects as a runner, he said, with something as risky and ridiculous as skateboarding.

And that was that. Over the next twenty years she occasionally daydreamed about skating, imagining herself skating this storm drain or that asphalt embankment, but it never occurred to her to take it up again. Now that she was a mom, however, it felt absolutely right. In the early evenings when her husband got home from work, she buckled Jack in the back of her Volvo wagon, picked up her new Sector Nine longboard, and headed for the hills, where she would slalom her way down the same streets she ripped up as a preteen. Soon she was scuffing up the hardwood floors of her house and putting in so much time on the streets that neighborhood kids often rang the bell to ask if "Mrs. Odanaka could come out to skate."

For Barb, skating was exciting in a way that nothing in her new adult life was. She finished her nightly sessions of "zoom and follow" feeling refreshed and more present for her family. Some moms knit, some shop, some scrapbook—but Barb realized she needed something more removed from her daily existence. "As an adult I appreciate the thrill more because it is so shockingly different from my regular life," she says. "It's such a rush. When you're skating, if you're not focused you can totally eat it. You have to be entirely in the moment. You can't be thinking about changing the poopy diaper." Beyond that, there's something about risking great bodily harm, Barb says, that makes you feel twenty years younger, which she sees as a reward in itself. "Let's face it: Who wants to get old?" she asks. "I choose to avoid the face-lift and boob job route. It may not keep me young chronologically, but it does emotionally."

Ironically, the boy in the Odanaka household has shown no interest in skating. Jack is nine now and has grown up studious and serious and much more interested in indoor solitary pursuits than outdoor exertions. While Mom is out with the neighborhood skate rats, Jack can often be found inside studying periodic tables or diagramming molecules. Barb says the role reversal actually works, in its way. When Jack seems overly preoccupied or stressed out, she relieves the tension with a pillow fight. When she ventures out to skate without her helmet, he hides her board in the backyard bushes. And when the time comes to work through family disagreements, she works hard to avoid being "reactive fifties mom," allowing her son a role in making decisions. "It's a whole different philosophy," she says. "You've got to see things through his eyes."

So Barb has given up her "grand visions" of mother and son skating or surfing together (which seems much too hazardous to Jack, she says: "He worries about the bacteria count in the water"). Still, she's found other ways to play with her son, joining him in word games and storytelling and even inviting him to a weekly writers' group to share his poetry.

At the same time, she carves out time for herself to skate, which has become much more than a ten-minute-a-day stress reliever for Barb. It's now a calling. A few years after Jack was born, Barb decided to start writing again, this time for kids. Her first project was, naturally, *Skateboard Mom,* a picture book about a mother who swipes her son's skateboard. She also formed a group called the International Society of Skateboarding Moms, which grew to three hundred members and hosted occasional events like the Mighty Mama Skate-o-Rama, a skate park get-together held across the country on, naturally, Mother's Day.

To Barb, skateboarding is not so much a way to connect with her kid as a way to connect with herself, which in turn relieves the stress of her stay-at-home mothering routine ("It's Prozac on wheels," she says). She knows Jack still has mixed feelings about her skating—mainly because it takes her away from him—but she says he's come to accept it. On those mornings when she's on the way out with her board, she reminds him that skateboarding makes her happy. "That makes me a happier mom," she says. To which Jack nods sagely and hands her the wristguards.

At the same time, Barb hasn't entirely given up hope that her son will grow to appreciate the glories of skating. He recently accompanied her on a weekend trip to a skate camp, where Barb practiced ollies and ramp dropping and Jack performed the duties of a skate caddy. On the last morning, Jack ran up to his mom, looked her in the eye, and said something she never thought she'd hear: "Will you teach me to skate the ramp?"

A generation ago, skateboarding moms like the women in Barb's group would likely have been greeted by other parents with puzzlement, if not ridicule. Today, playful parents of all sorts are celebrated as quasi-celebrities. Barb has strutted her stuff on *Good Morning America,* told her story on National Public Radio, and been profiled in newspapers across the country. Like Kim the skipper, Tobias the dodgeballer, and Kate the tag-player, Barb has forged a media persona thanks to a rejuvenile passion. These playful adults actively seek and enjoy the attention of other adults in much the way of kids at the playground, who like swinging on the monkey bars fine, but who *love* swinging on the monkey bars when an adult is nearby, oohing and aahing.

This bid for attention is relatively harmless—a natural response to a culture that puts such a heavy premium on the attention of the media. More problematic is the impact playful parents have on their children, especially those who, like Barb's son, aren't keen to play along. The dynamic between Barb and her son Jack turns out to be common in rejuvenile families: wacky parents, serious kids. Or a variation: parents heavily into make-believe play who spawn kids who come out of the womb kicking balls and running races. For the Playalong Parent, this is surely the cruelest irony—having your childlike enthusiasm rejected by your own child.

The Cruelest Irony

I have a friend named Josh Fouts who runs a center on public diplomacy at the University of Southern California. He's serious, sober-minded, and also, as it happens, a total *Star Wars* freak. As a kid, he "amassed every single *Star Wars* toy known to fandom," dressed up in a homemade Darth Vader costume on Halloween, and even, for a time, slept on *Star Wars* bedsheets. As Josh grew up, his fandom extended to other TV shows and toys of his youth. In his twenties, he amassed a not insignificant collection of Oscar the Grouch merchandise.

"*Sesame Street* is my Rolling Stones," he explained. Entering the workforce and getting married only deepened his appreciation for kid-targeted pop culture. A few years ago, Josh and his wife had their first child. "One of my first thoughts was, 'Great! A boy! We can play action figures together!'" he said.

Josh went on an epic action-figure-collecting binge. And while his infant son showed only passing interest in the new complete sets of G.I. Joe, *Planet of the Apes,* and *Star Trek* dolls, Josh told me at the time he would occasionally sneak outside with a toy or two after a hard day at work. "I deal with a level of stress at work that makes being able to play with my G.I. Joe soldiers in the sand hill in my backyard seem really desirable," he said.

Over the last few years, however, Josh's tune has changed noticeably. His son August is nearly four now and entering what should be prime action-figure years, but to Josh's dismay, playtime for August doesn't mean the same things as it does for Daddy. August mostly likes to run around the house until he drops to the floor in exhaustion. Josh's precious action figures sit idly by while August turns cartwheels and tears around the house—Josh has come to accept that while he is "a toy doll geek who lives in a fantasyworld of green army men and Han Solo," his son has the makings of a jock.

More distressingly, Josh has come to see fatherhood less as a never-ending playdate than a tough job requiring an even temper and an iron will. For now, it's clear that his playful tendencies aren't much use. "Without thinking about it, I've become exactly what I never thought I'd be—the heavy," he says. "I've had to draw certain lines. And it turns out I have a hard time crossing them once they've been set down. When my kid is having a tantrum and I send him to his room and he's banging on his door, calling me 'stupid daddy,' I have a hard time going back to being playful happy Dad."

But just because parenting has turned out to be less playful than he expected doesn't mean that Josh has stopped playing. Not long ago a colleague at work turned him on to an online video game in which players interact as characters from the *Star Wars* universe. It's a ridiculously involved game that mixes the occasional light-saber duel with highly mundane activities like washing dishes. Josh was hooked instantly and was soon spending an hour or two a night playing. Last summer he even attended a fan festival with two thousand other players. "I expected a ton of guys in Coke bottle glasses and women who belonged at the Renaissance Faire," he says. Instead, the hard-core fans included a broad spectrum of personalities, including a huge share of harried dads and moms living out childhood fantasies after tucking their children in bed at night.

Hopping Boomer Boundaries

Why are so many parents suddenly putting such a high priority on playtime—their kids' and their own? Clearly, large generational shifts are at work. More than half of parents of kids under eighteen today were born between 1965 and 1979, making them members of the endlessly analyzed Generation X. In parenting, as in most things, Gen X defies broad categorization, but it's worth noting one big Gen X character trait that helps explain playalong parenting: Boomer backlash.

One of the first things you hear when talking to Playalong Parents is that their approach to parenting is a direct response to—or, more accurately, rebellion against—the way they themselves were raised. These are the latchkey kids and the children of divorce, the kids whose Boomer parents embraced above all the virtues of independence, individuality, and self-esteem. "I'm a Special Person," read the slogan on a T-shirt given to a certain twelve-year-old boy (me) that had un-intended real-world consequences (unanimous rejection by peers). Many of today's parents look back in astonishment at the leeway they were afforded by parents whose childrearing duties too often took a backseat to their own epic quests for self-actualization.

Modern-day traditionalists like James Dobson, self-styled General Patton of the modern "hard" school of parenting, have made much of this more permissive Boomer style of par-enting, arguing that the spirit so vividly captured in the 1972 production *Free to Be You and Me* amounted to little more than a justification for selfishness. It's true that Boomers have al-ways had a particular talent for putting their needs first. But it's unfair to suggest that the working moms and dads of the six-ties and seventies cared about their kids any less than tradi-tion-minded parents. For one thing, their choices were born out of genuine idealism and an honest attempt to improve upon the *Father Knows Best* ideals of their own childhoods. As the writer Thomas de Zengotita puts it, Boomer parents "couldn't just move, unreflexively, into adult roles they had thrown so radically into question when they were young. They couldn't pretend that they took such roles for granted, accepted traditional definitions of them—because they didn't and were proud of it." Just as the heavily involved, playful par-ents of today seek to right the perceived wrongs of their own upbringings, Boomer parents formed their childrearing ideals in contrast to those of a previous era, which they perceived as overly strict and authoritarian. Today we're witnessing the latest attempt to compensate for a previous generation's blind spots, a process that's bound to result in an entirely new set of parenting mistakes (which will in turn inspire resentment among the next generation, and so on).

One prime example of this shift is seen in the premium parents today put on time with kids. While Boomer parents invented the idea of "quality time," which confined the parent-child relationship to periodic appointments, today's parents seem intent on building their lives around time with their children. A 2004 survey by the Boston marketing research firm Reach Advisors reported that twice as many Gen X moms as Boomer mothers spent twelve hours a day or more with their children. The split is comparable for dads—half of Gen X fathers spend three to six hours a day with their children, compared with 39 percent of Boomer dads. Even more significantly, while Boomer parents reported being perfectly happy with the amount of time they spent with their kids, Gen Xers wanted more.

Many of these parents are "child-centered" idealists who stress connecting and sharing with kids in a way their more distant Boomer parents never managed. But backlash against Boomers isn't limited to the progressive-minded. Matt Stone and Trey Parker, the neoconservative thirtysomethings responsible for the cartoon series *South Park,* credit the success of their program to a "philosophical underpinning" that directly challenges Boomer notions of childhood and responsibility. "We grew up around all these hippies, just going, you know, 'Society's so messed up, man—our only hope is the innocence and purity of the child,'" Parker said on *60 Minutes.* "And it's like, 'No, dude, you got it backwards. Our only hope is society, really.'"

rejuvenile

Whether they idealize their kids like "child-centered" parents or hold them accountable like "parent-centered" ones, nearly all take pride in how intimately involved they are in their kids' lives. Belinda Miller is a thirty-nine-year-old new mom from Portland, Oregon, who says her approach to parenting couldn't be more different from that of her parents. Whereas she was pretty much left to her own devices as a kid, Belinda makes it a point to engage in her daughter's play in a way her own parents never did. Like many other parents her age, she has taught herself and her daughter sign language in an attempt to open lines of communication as soon as humanly possible. Belinda looks back on the "space" she was given as a kid and shakes her head in wonder—she was baby-sitting at ten and was free to wander around her neighborhood long before hitting puberty. "Now my mom comes over and sees me down on the floor playing with my daughter Georgia and can't understand what I'm doing," she says. "She tells me, 'I put you in a playpen for hours and you loved it.' I can't even imagine putting Georgia in a playpen for more than five minutes. I want to experience every moment I can with her." (Surely the playpen—that plastic mesh enclosure separating parents from whatever it is their kids are doing—is the antithesis of everything the Playalong Parent stands for.)

Her husband, Hova Najarian, had a similar moment recently while leafing through a reissue of the old *Storybook Treasury of Dick and Jane and Friends*. At one point in the book, the children lure their pipe-smoking, fedora-wearing pop into a game of jump rope. "It's played as this big funny thing—like such a thing was completely outrageous," he says. "Looking at it now, it's not funny at all. It's normal. I play with my kid all the time."

Still, it's one thing to maintain closeness with a toddler;

Belinda fears it will get harder as her daughter grows into a semiautonomous adolescent. There simply aren't many good models of parents who managed to be both fun and firm, goofy and great. "I know we can be fun," she says. "But frankly I have no idea if we can be the disciplinarians we need to be."

I understand that worry completely. It's a credibility problem. How can you expect to enforce the No Roughhousing in the Living Room Rule after you mistakenly bump over an heirloom lamp during a game involving a rolled-up sock and a frying pan? After your daughter hears you bray like a horsey for the five hundredth time, will she grasp the intended seriousness of your occasional hard-won word of wisdom?

These worries may be natural, but it's not clear they have much validity in the trenches of parenthood. Playalong Parents report that switching roles is a natural part of their dynamic, that play in no way undermines their standing as heads of the household. Tea parties with imaginary friends are interrupted for pointed reminders about not pouring sugar on the carpet. Board games are put on hold when tantrums erupt. And by most accounts, kids accept these stops and starts without any confusion. That's because kids, unlike most adults, do not assume that play undercuts authority. Many parents who routinely play with their kids report that they have a relatively *easy* time enforcing rules and imparting lessons.

"We spend a lot of time playing and reading and talking, but when she does something wrong, I won't hesitate to stop and correct her," says stay-at-home dad Jake Austen. "I can switch gears to mean dad real quickly."

Other Playalong Parents try to avoid constantly switching gears, opting instead to integrate their parental duties into their playful selves. These are the cool parents, the children of

209

rigid disciplinarians who made a solemn vow that when they grew up, things would be different. Dean Dryer is a thirty-nine-year-old gymnastics coach from Tampa, Florida, who often plays card games like Magic: The Gathering and Yu-Gi-Oh with his ten-year-old son Garrett. "When push comes to shove, he knows I'm the dad," he says. "I enjoy palling around with him, but we both understand it's not my job to be his buddy—it's my job to be his father."

Time spent playing is a natural part of parenting, Dean says, even if it wasn't something he experienced growing up. Dean's own father is a telephone technician who was always, it seems, busy mowing the lawn, trimming the hedges, or painting the house. Father-son relations were mostly based on the imparting of knowledge. "He loved playing professor," says Dean. "His relationship with me was about 'Be a man, learn how to change a tire.' That's not necessarily a bad relationship, but it's different than the one I have with my son. When I try to talk to my son the way my father used to talk to me, I can just see his eyes glaze over. I'll say, 'I'm just boring you to tears, aren't I, son?' And he's all, 'Yeah, dad.'"

At which point Dad might suggest a game of Parcheesi. In contrast to his workaholic dad, Dean is determinedly playful. Dean is a self-described "fantasy geek" who volunteers at science fiction conventions, keeps up with cartoons, reads young-adult fiction, and enjoys the occasional game of laser tag. But his biggest obsession by far is Dungeons & Dragons, the fantasy role-playing game that has recently enjoyed a resurgence among the over-thirty set (celebrity devotees include action hero Vin Diesel and comedian Jack Black). Dean has been playing D&D for close to thirty years, joining a weekly group that now includes the fifteen-year-old son of a friend Dean has been playing with since junior high. This familiarity with kid culture definitely comes in handy with his son and gymnastics students, Dean says. "It allows them to relate to me more," he says. "To look at me not as the enemy, you know?"

Not that Dean's interests are simply a ploy to connect with kids. He doesn't even think of his interests as particularly juvenile. D&D, for instance, is only as mature or immature as the people playing it, he says. Teen players may bicker endlessly about who killed who with what weapon, but Dean says he plays less for pretend battles than for the opportunity to stretch imaginative muscles that don't get much use in his adult life.

Connoisseurs of Kiddie Culture

It's fair to say that adults today are the most media-saturated people in history. Feeding on a smorgasbord of cable TV, the Internet, satellite radio, video games, movies-on-demand, handheld digital devices, and on and on, we're now exposed to more images and information in a day than adults twenty years ago experienced in a month. (De Zengotita compares the difference between the media of twenty years ago and the media of today to the difference between "a breeze and a hurricane.")

It's no wonder then that media plays such a prominent role in parenting. Having a kid often reawakens childlike tastes in movies, books, and TV shows, and offers parents a chance to tag along as kids take their first tentative steps into the mediascape.

It's not that previous generations didn't have their own romance with media. Boomers, for example, were raised in television's Golden Age and perfected the use of TV as babysitter. But the media of our parents' generation was far less prevalent and certainly more primitive. Many Boomers can remember marveling at TV test patterns before graduating to standard kid fare like Shari Lewis, *The Lone Ranger,* and *Howdy Doody.* By contrast, today's parents grew up with programs designed to operate on multiple levels, from *The Muppets* to *Pee Wee's Playhouse.* As a result, many Gen Xers never rejected the same shows that now keep their kids absorbed for hours on end. On the contrary, many of us spent our childfree years developing deep and discerning tastes for kiddie culture.

This certainly holds true for Belinda and Hova, kiddie connoisseurs of the first order. Long before becoming parents, the couple began volunteering at the New Jersey public radio station WFMU. Trawling the station vaults, they found themselves drawn to Disney lullabies, cartoon theme songs, and novelty 45s (two favorites: a recording of twelve thousand Girl Scouts singing "Roundup Is Here Again" and a cover of "Born to Be Wild" featuring a chorus of chickens). Children's music, they decided, was too good to be left to children. So they started *Greasy Kid Stuff,* a Saturday morning show featuring favorite kid songs along with brief interviews, snippets of storytelling, and "birthday hollers" to loyal listeners. Their motto: Hi-Fi for Small Fry. Perhaps unsurprisingly, small fry weren't the only ones who tuned in. Birthday hollers often went out to listeners celebrating their thirty-third birthday, or their forty-fifth.

Belinda and Hova never thought of the program as much more than silly. Then a few years ago, as they approached their fortieth birthdays, they decided to move out of the city and return to Belinda's hometown in Oregon, the better to raise their new baby girl. That's when they discovered an unexpected benefit of their years listening to kids' music. Without knowing it, they'd prepared themselves for one of the most daunting challenges of modern parenting: navigating the on-slaught of kiddie media.

Unlike their own parents, Belinda and Hova had no inten-tion of standing by as their firstborn dipped her toe into the fast-moving current of kiddie TV shows, playthings, music, and picture books. They took an active and discerning role—for her benefit, but also for their own. "Georgia's enjoyment comes first, but there are lots of things we simply won't allow in the house if we can't stand them," says Belinda. A talking Elmo doll, for instance, was rewrapped in the Christmas paper it arrived in and stashed in a high cabinet. "A lot of things she naturally likes make me want to retch," explains Hova. "Kids just don't have any critical apparatus yet and they're constantly exposed to really horrible stuff. It's part of our job to shield them from that."

This is roughly the same strategy employed by Jake Austen, the Chicago stay-at-home dad who, like Belinda and Hova, developed a discerning taste for kids' culture long be-fore having a kid of his own. Growing up, Jake loved Marvel comic books and theatrical rock bands like Kiss. Those inter-ests only intensified in adulthood, leading to a succession of highly rejuvenile endeavors. He now edits an underground magazine of music and comics, dons a mask and cape to per-form in a thrash-vaudeville rock band called the Goblins, and works as puppeteer and producer on a long-running public-access TV show that might be described as a cross between *American Bandstand* and *Sesame Street*.

Given these kidcentric interests, it's no surprise that Jake takes a particularly keen interest in the media his two-year-old daughter, Maya, is exposed to. He pays close attention to *Sesame Street,* buys Golden Books by the dozen, and counts his time with Maya watching *Mister Rogers' Neighborhood* as sacrosanct. He understands that his appreciation is not the same as his daughter's. While she's laughing along with the silly red monster, he might ponder the strangeness of Elmo being voiced by a husky African American. While she's diverted by the shiny wheels in a short segment of *Mister Rogers* about a bicycle factory, he's admiring the oversaturated color of the film clip. And so they pass an hour or two, each responding to separate but equal triggers of enjoyment.

That enjoyment, however, is a delicate thing. It can be cut short in a second by a note of insincerity or crassness—the most common afflictions of kid media, Jake says. He seethes at the mention of *Baby Einstein,* videos for infants that supposedly enhance a child's IQ through repetitive visuals and what Jake describes as "classical music played on an ice cream truck." But Jake reserves his most intense irritation for movies like *Aladdin* and cartoons like *The Animaniacs,* both of which mix exaggerated, colorful visuals with huge helpings of blatantly adult humor.

"There's nothing I hate more in children's entertainment than the clever adult aside," he says. "I can't stand pop culture references made for the benefit of adults that fly over the heads of kids. Half the time the remark isn't even funny—it just sounds funny. I'd rather my daughter hear a dirty joke. At least a dirty joke is actually a joke instead of a fake joke."

In this, Jake is in the minority. Most parents I know are eternally grateful that the producers of kiddie entertainment will occasionally throw a bone to the adults who happen to be watching. Not all kid content is inclusive, of course—the cable channel Nickelodeon, for one, is determinedly (with the notable exception of *SpongeBob SquarePants*) "all about the kids," says Sarah Tomassi Lindman, vice president of production and programming for the cable channel Noggin, which is targeted to preschoolers. Most producers of kiddie entertainment, however, favor the approach most often associated with the Warner Bros. animators responsible for Bugs Bunny and Elmer Fudd, exaggerated characters kids could enjoy and adults could relate to. "The people who make kids' entertainment know that parents are going to be sitting there next to them," says Lindman. "And most of them will do whatever it takes to keep them from running out of the theater screaming."

Childless, Childfree, Childlike

When she was a teenager, Rebecca Flaugh always assumed she'd get married and raise a family. She started having second thoughts while teaching Sunday school at her community church. Rebecca had always enjoyed being around kids; she's exuberant and fast-talking, the sort of person invariably described as being great with kids. Which made it all the more odd that when she tried to imagine having kids of her own, she mostly felt queasy.

Her thinking didn't change as she grew up. She's twenty-eight now and living in suburban Virginia with a job as a travel agent and all the usual trappings of adulthood. But while many of her childhood friends are up to their necks in diapers, sippy cups, and car pool schedules, Rebecca has built her life around simpler pleasures: board games, swing sets, amusement parks. She and her fiancé, a military engineer, prize their freedom to sleep until noon and then toss a playground ball around their apartment. In winter, Rebecca likes nothing better than bundling up, going outside, and launching into a snowball fight with the neighborhood kids—though she's begun to feel a little nervous about that, since "when you're a kid and you throw a snowball at a kid, it's fun. But when you're an adult and you throw a snowball at a kid, it's assault and battery."

The occasional legal worry notwithstanding, Rebecca says her life is blissfully fun and almost entirely devoid of stress. The secret, she says, is simple: The best way to maintain the freedoms of childhood is to avoid having children altogether.

That's an increasingly popular line of reasoning. U.S. Census figures show that the percentage of women without children has doubled over the last two decades and now hovers around 20 percent. All told, about one in five American women between forty and forty-four have never had a child; studies show that this number breaks down evenly between women who were unable to have children (because they never found a suitable mate or because of fertility problems) and women who made a conscious choice to forgo motherhood. Often the choice not to have children is based on professional concerns. But according to members of a burgeoning movement of "proudly childfree" adults, another concern plays a big part—a desire to keep on living as a kid, except with all the freedoms and fewer of the responsibilities of adulthood.

"Adult life has enough obligations and restrictions—why add more?" asks Jerry Steinberg, a sixty-year-old college English instructor who lives with his wife, two dogs, one cat, and no children in the suburbs of Vancouver. For Jerry, not having kids means having time to play pickup volleyball with guys half his age. It means having more money and time for vacations. It means maintaining what he calls his "natural joie de vivre." To Jerry, children and the responsibilities they demand would sap the energy and humor out of life.

Soon after deciding once and for all not to have children,

Jerry began hosting social events for like-minded adults. He dubbed the group No Kidding! and named himself "founding non-father." The group was established, he says, to provide a network for other adults who "could chat on the phone for half an hour without thirty interruptions." Often those conversations turned to common pet peeves (children in restaurants, friends who prattle on endlessly about their progeny, and the word *childless,* which to many members suggests deficiency). The group grew and spawned other chapters. Twenty years after he held his first meeting, Jerry says he now has ninety-six chapters in six countries around the world.

Many of those who've taken up the "childfree" banner are not the least bit rejuvenile. They are by all appearances respectable adults, lovers of fine wine and expensive cheese and classical music. They feel an aversion to anything relating to children or childhood. But for many others, being "childfree" is a license to be childlike, which explains why some of the best-attended No Kidding! events include activities like pumpkin carving, pajama parties, board games, and miniature golf.

The appeal of such activities to childfree adults like Rebecca is simple enough: They give them a chance to live out the perfect childhood they never had. "I hated my childhood," Rebecca says. "There was so much worry, pressure, and fear. So many people forget what it was actually like to be a child, and the reality is that it can be horrible. I much prefer being an adult."

It's clear that Rebecca has a very different conception of what it means to be an adult than, say, her own parents. She thinks of her own father, who worked as a truck driver to provide for his three kids and who seemed burdened his entire life. "He had this one phrase he said again and again, 'You do

217

what you have to do,'" she says. "His whole life was about providing and fitting a mold and marching on until it's over. It was really a death march. I never understood that."

That's a common story among adults who forgo parenthood. A week or so after talking to Rebecca, I heard an almost identical story from a thirty-six-year-old video game collector named Lance Beckstrom whose decision not to have kids is based in part, he says, on the example set by his own father. "I love my dad, but he has no hobbies or interests at all," he says. "His whole life revolves around work. I never understood how you could grow up and just abandon all the things you once loved."

Lance is the manager of a stained-glass factory in Portland, Oregon, where he puts in long hours and supervises sixteen employees. But when work is over and Lance's coworkers go home to their spouses and children, Lance turns his attention to one of several hobbies that relate to interests of his youth. He restores cars and owns three Ford Mustangs, including the 1977 Cobra that he bought when he was nineteen. His most recent obsession is classic coin-operated arcade games and specifically Spy Hunter, a driving game that was a mainstay of the roller rinks, minigolf courses, and arcades of the mid-eighties. Lance talks of Spy Hunter with the affection most people reserve for a spouse or child. He first played it at the age of thirteen, when his family made the trip from their remote cattle ranch into Great Falls, Montana, where he and his brother headed straight to the arcade. Soon he could play Spy Hunter for an hour on a single quarter.

He moved on to home systems like Nintendo and Sega Genesis in college and even learned to build computers from the motherboard up. But he never forgot Spy Hunter in its original cabinet, decked out with racing stripes and complete with a cheesy Casio-tone soundtrack. About a year ago Lance and his girlfriend moved into a new house and Lance set to work converting the garage into a play area. On the Internet he managed to track down an old Spy Hunter game, which he bought for $550 along with two other vintage coin-operated games. Between the hours spent attempting to beat his personal-high score and the time spent tinkering with his cars, there's simply not much time left for anything else.

Listening to Lance wax sentimental about Spy Hunter and his beloved Mustangs, it's clear that nostalgia plays a huge part not only in his hobbies but in his decision to remain child-less. He's doesn't need kids; he still is one. "I am merely a child in a grown-up body," he says. "The best part of being a grown-up is allowing yourself to do the things your parents never let you do."

Not all video gamers are so ambivalent about adulthood, even those so busy playing that they don't have time to start a family of their own. Dan Birlew grew up with video games, playing Space Invaders as a preteen, Missile Command as an adolescent, and Legend of Zelda as a young adult. After college, while working as an office technician for IBM, he'd often come home from work and stay up all night playing one game or another, then trading notes and strategy tips with other gamers online. Five years ago he gave up his day job and began publishing strategy guides filled with pointers and walk-throughs that many players use to advance through increasingly labyrinthine home video games. Nowadays, Dan routinely spends sixteen hours a day holed up in a room cluttered with consoles and his vast collection of action figures.

Given the long hours he spends working, kids are out of the question: "I'd just neglect them," he says. But even more important than his work schedule—which is not, after all, much different from those of workaholic parents—is his sense that kids would intrude upon the world he's created for himself. "If I had kids, I'd have to compete with them for all my toys."

Dan says he understands that some might say he has an acute case of arrested development. Still, he insists that he's one of the most grown-up people he knows. He's been married for more than fifteen years. He and his wife own a tract house outside Las Vegas. His neighbors are accountants and office managers. He pays taxes, has a small investment portfolio, and has more than forty published books under his belt. What's more, he's conscientious about keeping up adult appearances, which is not exactly a big priority among his peers in what he calls "the interactive entertainment industry."

"I'm a professional," he says. "I don't even really have much of a kid side. I have a side that's very imaginative, and that side of me is very hungry. Video games feed that. This isn't about my inner child. It's about my creative interest."

To Dan, then, the standards of adulthood are relics from an analog age. Still, it's hard to accept that a guy who plays video games sixteen hours a day has reached maturity—especially one who sounds as though he resists having kids because they'd usurp his standing as the favorite child in the house. But in the end, is that really so wrong? Self-absorbed, obsessive, not particularly nurturing personalities have always existed—perhaps we should be grateful that we live in an age when it's become more acceptable than ever for those people *not* to have children.

the rejuvenile
grown up

IN OUR INNERMOST SOUL
WE ARE CHILDREN AND REMAIN SO
FOR THE REST OF OUR LIVES.

— Sigmund Freud

Rejuveniles tend not to think much about the future. The joy of being a kid, after all, is mostly about being absorbed in the present, and there's nothing to yank you out of Now faster than mention of a Five-Year Plan. Sooner or later, however, all of us bump up against one inevitable question: What's next? At some point will we snap out of it and trade our motor scooters for lawn mowers? Or are we laying down new track on the developmental pathway? Any thinking rejuvenile can't help but wonder whether his or her dedication to play and love of kid stuff will at some point—if it hasn't already—morph from fun and free-spirited to just plain pathetic.

Undoubtedly, there are serious risks that all long-term rejuveniles face. And not just the obvious peril faced by brittle-boned skateboarders or the fashion faux pas tempted by soccer moms in sweatpants with the word *juicy* printed on the rear end. To my mind, the biggest inherent risk of rejuvenalia is philosophical. You rediscover a favorite book or record from childhood, marvel at the sophistication of a video game, or spend an hour watching kids in the park blow bubbles, and pretty soon you start thinking of youth and childhood as the fount of all that is good and right with the world. One moment you're cracking up at *SpongeBob SquarePants,* the next you're quoting William Wordsworth (for whom children "trailed clouds of glory") or even Robert Fulghum (for whom "wisdom was not at the top of the graduate school mountain, but there in the sand box at nursery school"). Before you know it you're rethinking the whole early-nineties inner-child therapy craze, which seemed hopelessly flaky in your cynical youth but seems worthy of a second look now that you're a bubble-admiring, cartoon-watching adult.

There is, however, a quick cure for the unqualified celebration of the child: a few hours with an actual kid. Children, of course, are not just wide-eyed and innocent and playful. They can also be stubborn, petulant, and shockingly mean. Care to gaze on cruelty in its pure, white-hot form? Watch an unmonitored bully have his way with someone he considers weak. Need a reminder of irrational rigidity? Explain to a groggy five-year-old that she can't have her soy milk in her favorite sippy cup. Wonder what's meant by the term "lack of emotional restraint"? Flip on MTV's *Total Request Live* and watch its preteen audience greet this week's pop star with the abandon of starved hyenas. Yes, some of these behaviors have more to do with personality than age; there are born bullies, born whiners, and born extroverts. But there's no getting around the fact that certain qualities and characteristics come naturally to kids—and not all of those qualities contribute to a healthy, happy adulthood.

Which brings us to a crucial distinction: the difference between childlike and childish. On the one hand, we rejuveniles are right to cultivate innocence, fantasy, and fun. On the other, there's no use romanticizing a lack of good sense or basic self-sufficiency. Childishness is no virtue. It means being egocentric and easily manipulated. It means forgetting your

223

considered goals when distracted by immediate impulses—
Look, a shiny thing! Wait, I want candy! It means shirking responsibility and leaving messes for others to deal with. It
means confusing the way things look with the way things are.
It means calling people names, throwing temper tantrums,
and clinging to petty resentments and wishful thinking. Knowing the difference between childlike and childish is not just
a matter of semantics. It's an essential distinction for long-
term rejuveniles who have an instinctive aversion to the old
model of adulthood but who'd also like to avoid becoming
self-centered, hot-tempered babies.

And here we run smack dab into a pileup of doubts I've
been accumulating since beginning this book. I worry that my
enjoyment of *Schoolhouse Rock!* and *H.R. Pufnstuf* is an exercise
in indulgent nostalgia (ah, to be ten, carefree, and splayed on
the shag carpet . . .). I worry that Gail Sheehy is right—that life
is arranged in sequential stages and that when you approach a
new one, you have a choice, either to advance or to regress.
"If you deny it or avoid the passage," Sheehy says, "you won't
advance and there will be penalties for it." You heard the
lady: penalties! I worry that my attraction to Etch A Sketch
art and weird old kids' music is an expression of insecurity
(or, as writer Choire Sicha said in a discussion of the Langley
Schools Project, a recording of Canadian schoolchildren that
became a rejuvenile hit in 2001, "I want people to love me because I suck in a cute way. Is that wrong? Is that self infanti-
lizing? Do I semi-like Langley Schools because, in my mind,
I'm still in junior high?").

Worst of all, I worry that the whole of the rejuvenile phenomenon is a diabolical plot cooked up by a black-ops marketing firm (subcontracted out by the Heritage Foundation in
association with Clear Channel) to keep citizens and con-

sumers in a tractable preadult state—that we're all too busy being amused by this pricey doodad or that youth-enhancing cosmetic procedure to recognize the debt piling up around us, the wars overseas, or the worsening poverty and pollution at home.

It's one thing to cherish Quisp cereal or snip paper dolls as an adult; it's another to embrace the total mind-set you had when you fell in love with those things. If that mind-set can be creative, comforting, and constructive, it can also be narcissistic, shallow, even delusional. It's not, as much as we might wish for it to be, a single-ingredient recipe for a new, better brand of maturity.

What's required of the rejuvenile, then, is a careful, deliberate, and yes, *mature* accounting of those qualities that come naturally to kids that can also contribute to rich and meaningful adult lives—and a weeding out of those qualities that are best consigned to childhood.

Herewith, then, a rejuvenile gut check.

The First Time, Again and Again

The quality in children rejuveniles most covet is the upside of their inexperience—the ability to see things fresh. Grown-ups might have the experience, but kids have a near-miraculous ability to appreciate the new and absorb the unfamiliar. Some kids, of course, appear born blasé, as if they've seen it all before they've had a chance to see much of anything. I'm thinking here of children I occasionally spot at the zoo, kids who stroll from enclosure to enclosure like world-weary cynics in a fog of Gitane smoke. "Ah, monkeys," they seem to say. *"Fascinating."* All around them, however, are the usual assortment of wide-eyed live-wires, who point and holler and simply stare, slack-jawed and intense, living reminders of how our early years are spent in a near-constant state of wonder, alternately amazed or terrified or confused by the newness of it all.

It doesn't take a nostalgic romantic to recognize this quality in children. Wonderment is a biological fact documented by neurologists, a reflection of how busy children's brains are. Neurologists call it synaptic interconnectivity, and by all objective measurements, children have it all over adults. It peaks at the age of three, when children outpace adults in key measurements of brain activity by a factor of ten. "Babies are just plain smarter than we are, at least if being smart means being able to learn something new," report Alison Gopnik, Andrew Meltzoff, and Patricia Kuhl in their book *The Scientist in the Crib*. "They think, draw conclusions, make predictions, look for explanations and even do experiments . . . In fact, scientists are successful precisely because they emulate what children do naturally." This natural receptivity accounts for kids' astonishing ability to learn new languages.

It also accounts for children's insatiable curiosity, for their constant questions: What is that? Where does it come from? How does it work? And the doozy, the single word with the power to elicit tremors of fear in the weary parent: Why? As in, why is that lady fat? Why do people die? Why can't I fly? Why do people shake hands? Why don't ladies wear ties? After a few rounds, many parents pull out the trump card, a statement that neatly sums up all that is to be despised about traditional maturity: "Just because." No matter that no child in history has ever been satisfied with "just because." And thank God they aren't—that's a huge part of why we admire them. We resent our psychosclerosis, the hardening of our minds. We wish our minds were still so open.

Some of the greatest minds in history have recognized the importance of this childlike capacity. Albert Einstein credited his theory of relativity to his talent for asking questions that wouldn't occur to a respectable adult: "The normal adult never stops to think about space and time," he wrote. "I, on the other hand, was so slow to develop that I only began thinking about space and time when I was already grown up." Then there's Isaac Newton, the great childless alchemist and mathematician, who famously remarked that "I do not know what I may appear to the world; but to myself I seem to have been only like a boy playing on the seashore."

Preserving the wonder of childhood is not easy. It's often, frankly, a nuisance. I feel no admiration at all for the lost paradise of curiosity when my six-year-old is crouched over a muddy puddle or colorful scrap of trash at eight in the morning when I'm trying to get him to school on time ("Move it— *now*! No, you cannot take that worm in the van! I'm counting to three!") or when my three-year-old goes hunting for gobs of old chewing gum stuck to the bottom of restaurant tables ("What's that in your mouth? Honey, what *is* that? Oh, God! *Not again!*"). Faced with such horrors, I most often turn to the reflexive parental responses: I holler, cajole, threaten, or bribe. But sometimes, when I've got time to kill or when I'm too worn out to fight, I slow down and let them wander and scatter, examine and sniff, ponder and question (but not, I should stress, chew). It's in these extended periods of dawdling that I can see, just for a moment, the world through their eyes. And it's a marvelous place indeed.

It takes about five minutes to walk my dog around the block where I live. That time is multiplied exponentially when the distance is covered with my two oldest kids. On a recent predinner walk, we stopped for a good twenty minutes when my son looked up at our house and noticed how our front door looks like a mouth, how the two windows above it look like eyes, and how, if you squint, the tiles on the roof look like hair. Ten minutes and a few steps later, my daughter discovered a loose plank of sidewalk that rocked back and forth when we jumped up and down on the ends. Next, there was a long lollygag near a patch of weeds, where they discovered an outcropping of dandelions. Before we'd turned the first corner, there were stops to look up at a police helicopter and an explanation of why a neighbor's dog pokes his frothing snout under the gate when we pass. It took more than an hour, but we returned home happy and oddly calm, as we always do when we walk at kid speed.

That's the thing about recapturing the immediacy of childhood: It takes *forever*. Indeed, there's a huge chasm between the languorous pace at which kids operate and the bustle of adulthood. Being goal-oriented is in fact synonymous for many with being mature—for what else is an adult but someone who keeps his or her focus on the future? Kids, by contrast, have to be socialized out of their present-mindedness and trained to wait, plan, and anticipate. (High on the list of phrases kids hear over and over again: Sit still, not now, wait your turn, stand in line, after dinner, when you're older.) No doubt these are important life lessons, but it seems to me we lose an essential part of ourselves when we finally learn to sit tight and wait. For one thing, when we set our sights so firmly on the future, we lose our grasp of the potential of each moment. We adults never quite get over losing this sense of immediacy; some of us try to recapture it by taking up meditation or skydiving, dodgeball or skateboarding. The primary appeal of these thrill-seeking, irrational acts is the way they force us to pay attention and react only to what's in front of us, just as we did as kids. And in that slowing down, we discover another, closely related quality of childhood that we covet as adults: their experience of time.

It's easy to forget as adults that time to a child is entirely different than it is to a grown-up. To kids, time stretches out like taffy, soft and expandable. Try telling a child under the age of six to wait an hour for this or that—you might as well tell a kid to wait sixteen years. Their minutes are our hours. Their hours are our days. Most of us still remember eons passing as we waited in class for the second hand to reach the spot signaling dismissal; we shake our heads in astonishment at the memory of never-ending summers that all happened in *three months*.

This is, I think, one of the more important, though rarely acknowledged, motivations for adults who reclaim childhood passions. We want to experience time the way we did as kids, to find some relief from the anxiety of the future *tense*. It's as if our lives are birthday cakes, with each year represented by one slice. When we're kids, the pieces are huge. But as we grow up and keep slicing, the pieces get smaller and smaller. We know there's no going back, that we're incapable of returning to the child's-eye perception of time (or birthday cake). We can't help it, though. We want the big piece.

The Downside of Now

It's nice to think of rejuveniles as freethinking romantics guided only by their own childlike spirits, but it's clear that outside forces also have a hand in shaping who they are. The media, for one. The hurricane of mass media, constantly churned and regenerated via television and the Internet, and even books like this one, encourages us to see maturity as irrelevance. From the wrinkle-free models on billboards to the savvy-kid/clueless-parent plotlines on TV, youth has become synonymous with what matters, with buzz, with sizzle, with what the writer Joseph Epstein calls "with-it-ry." In marketing circles the demographic of people aged eighteen through thirty-four is the most highly valued and is known as the "sweet spot." Pretty soon the underlying assumption—that the older you get, the more predictable and habitual you become—rubs off on us all.

This doesn't bother us while we're young, but it starts to rankle when we pass out of the prized demographic. And so we rebel, acting out in ways that prove to ourselves and the world that we are not done, that we still matter. We dye our hair, seek out clothes our kids might wear, take up extreme sports.

This acting-out is most obvious in consumer choices, contributing to a spike in the middle-age market for designer jeans, "combination dorm room/base camp" automobiles, and movies about princesses and superheroes. Marketers have a name for it: "downward aspiration," a phrase that typically describes Boomers' search for stuff made for younger consumers. "They're looking for brands that make them feel young and feel more vibrant," says Keith McVaney, director of planning at Arnold Worldwide in Boston. "When your job, your house and your family don't change, brands become the great variable in your life. You might be getting older but you can still get new sneakers, you can still hear new music. That's a way of keeping up the pace of your life and not drawing to a halt."

All this is great news for marketers like McVaney, since it expands the number of consumers who might be persuaded to buy the latest gadget or snack food or cartoon character. It's all part of what McVaney calls "the velocity philosophy," an individual mind-set that stresses above all the need to stay on top of whatever is presented as new—be it information, trends, or ideas. It's more than just good business, he insists; it's good for the soul. "We've democratized relevance," he proclaims. "It's now available to everyone, regardless of age."

There are other, less obvious but perhaps more significant ways that the media stokes our rejuvenile impulses. It inundates us with images, messages, and stories that try and too often fail to arouse the enchantment of childhood. It dulls our senses, inflames our prejudices, and fixes our preferences. In the face of this bombardment, some of us simply go limp and fall into a reactive cycle of desire and consumption, work and recreation. But many of us can't shake the memory of a time when we didn't feel so jaded, when self-consciousness didn't reign supreme, when we saw, as de Zengotita writes, "all things given for the first time." We long to feel that way again, to see how we once did, through the eyes of a child. The loss of childhood wonder and all that goes with it surely ranks among the worst casualties of maturity.

So we embrace the things we associate most vividly with childhood, the trinkets and toys and games. And this is fine up to a point. The trouble comes when we go too far, when we give ourselves over entirely to the raw id of our childish desire. As much as I enjoyed the company of Daniel Bowen, the thirty-eight-year-old Tinkerbell fanatic who visits Disneyland two or three times a month (most often with his parents, since he doesn't have a car), I found myself wondering if his health insurance plan had an allowance for therapy when he

231

described how he'd accumulated such an enormous collection of fairy memorabilia: "If my mom doesn't want to buy me something, I'll throw a temper tantrum," he explained. "I'll start whining, 'Mommy! Mommy! Give it to me!' I'll hang my head down and hold my hand out. She'll tell me to shut the hell up and walk out of the store. But then the older boy in me comes out. I'll run up and say, 'But I'll pay you back!'"

That's an example of what happens when the quest for the immediacy of childhood goes too far: It devolves into a childish need for immediate gratification. Think of it as an occupational hazard of going with the flow: the inability to see anything ahead, the conviction that all present needs and desires are best satisfied this very instant.

Tantrums like Bowen's may be extreme, but the need for instant gratification has become a common feature of the adult world. What else is our current obsession with speed, convenience, and efficiency but the impatience of childhood writ large? We fill up on fast foods and Instant Nutritional Meals, send our packages via FedEx, maintain friendships via instant messaging, and get our news in presweetened bites on twenty-four-hour satellite or cable (brought to you by Reuters, the wire service that sums up the ethos of its impatient readership with the slogan "Know, now"). We stay fit with twenty-minute workouts and miracle potions that promise to melt away pounds while we sleep, or else we say the hell with it and opt for liposuction. Then there's the Internet, born amid grand claims of community-building and togetherness, but since revealed for what it is: a magnificent tool of instantaneousness, empowering us to have whatever we want, when we want it. As our attention spans grow progressively shorter, we feel ourselves joining the chorus sung by Veruca Salt, the candy-chomping über-brat from the rejuvenile favorite *Willy Wonka and the Chocolate Factory*:

> *I want the world*
> *I want the whole world*
> *I want to lock it all up in my pocket*
> *It's my bar of chocolate*
> *Give it to me now*

This current of insatiability runs strongest in the world of business, where speed and satisfaction have become near-unassailable goods. One look at the business section at the local bookstore reveals how the sensible Industrial Age goal of economic efficiency has blossomed into a postmillennial spiritual quest. *Speed Is Life,* proclaims management guru Bob Davis. *It's Not the Big That Eat the Small . . . It's the Fast That Eat the Slow,* opine business writers Jason Jennings and Laurence Haughton. Perhaps the most significant contribution to the genre comes from Bill Gates, the embodiment of the twitchy high school A/V geek–turned–Master of the Universe. His 1999 book, *Business @ the Speed of Thought,* is a sort of über-nerd tutorial on the development of what Gates calls "a digital nervous system."

In a sort of parody of childhood, even our most intimate moments have become charged with impatience. Thus does the harried executive attempt to shave a few minutes off his kids' bedtime ritual by reaching for a copy of *Once Upon a Time, The End (Asleep in 60 Seconds),* a book of soundbite-sized summaries of the world's most enduring stories for children (no doubt express-delivered in the same package with Spencer Johnson's blockbuster *One-Minute Parenting,* which promises to make quick work of the business of parenthood).

233

The difficulty, of course, is that the quick-hit approach never quite pays off—the faster you go, the less time there seems to be. The more we get what we want, the less satisfied we are. Actress-cum-author Carrie Fisher knows a thing or two about indulging her childlike self, having lived in a "house filled with toys, a place that will one day make an ideal miniature golf course," as she described it in a 1997 essay. But somehow, all the childlike trinkets in the world never seemed to be enough. "Instant gratification takes too long," she wrote.

And when we don't get what we want, when our need for instant gratification is inevitably frustrated, we do what Veruca Salt did: We blow our tops. Today our tempers are nearly as short as our attention spans. The slightest setback or merest sign of slowness will often trigger a vein-popping outburst. Here we confront another characteristic of childhood that has become distressingly common among grown-ups. While social norms once dictated that adults stay in control of emotions that might upset others, today's adults tend to express themselves all too freely, in extreme cases resulting in restraining orders or court-ordered anger management training. Stories of road rage, air rage, and shopping rage are now a regular feature of the morning papers. As an addendum to her 2001 self-help book *Taming Your Inner Brat,* psychotherapist Pauline Wallin keeps an ongoing list of stories of such cases that appear in newspapers around the world. Among the highlights: In California, a relief pitcher for a pro baseball team was so riled by a heckling fan that he hurled a folding chair into the stands, breaking the nose of the heckler's wife. On a Canadian airline, a man upset by the slowness of service grabbed a stewardess by the neck and threatened passengers who tried to intervene. In Michigan, the father of a trick-or-treating son vandalized the house of a woman he felt was stingy with her candy. And in New Hampshire, the mother of a ten-year-old boy was arrested for assault after stabbing her son with a kitchen knife. Her motive: The boy had damaged her favorite stuffed animal.

In a World of Pure Imagination

Stabbing your son because he messed with your Pooh bear, I think we can all agree, qualifies as rejuvenalia carried too far. The moral for the self-aware rejuvenile? Never allow yourself to get *too* caught up in the immediacy of childhood (especially while in range of sharp objects).

The same sort of balancing act is required when it comes to fantasy, one of the creative abilities of children most admired by rejuveniles. Children spend much of their life on the threshold between fact and fantasy, as if on a beach between solid ground and the unfathomable ocean. They breathe life into toys. They have conversations with invisible playmates and set places at the dinner table for fantastical creatures. They hear voices in the wind and see shapes in the clouds. And while what developmental psychologists Dorothy and Jerome Singer call "the high season of imaginative play" ends for most kids around the age of seven, it lingers for the fortunate few. It's not uncommon, for instance, for kids as old as twelve to create make-believe societies called paracosms. Children, in short, are born aviators of flights of fancy, happy to be enchanted and desperate to be dazzled. Suspension of disbelief simply isn't an impediment to those with no disbelief to suspend.

Of course, there are exceptions—wonder-resistant kids who seem born with appointment books in hand; literal-minded children with little tolerance for make-believe. But in general, children are simply better than adults at summoning and interacting with the unreal. It doesn't take much imagination to see how this natural skill of childhood can benefit us as adults. Most obviously, it comes in handy in the arts. Musicians "play," actors pretend, and writers conjure, skills that may be refined and developed in adulthood but which are born in childhood. Examples of childlike artists abound in high culture and low. The Brontë siblings based some of their greatest works of fiction and poetry on a paracosm of toy soldiers they created as children. Italian screen actor Marcello Mastroianni famously remarked that "movies were the most beautiful set of toy trains I ever found." Mexican-American movie maverick Robert Rodriguez produced his *Spy Kids* trilogy at his home outside Austin, Texas, a stone castle complete with turrets and secret passageways to amuse his three sons, Rocket, Racer, and Rebel.

Many painters have famously drawn on imaginative powers that came naturally when they were little. Miró's energetic squiggles, Pollock's chaotic splatters, and Matisse's paper cutouts all owe more to the spirit of childhood than the skills honed in formal training. Not that recapturing that essence is easy. Said Picasso: "Every child is an artist. The problem is how to remain an artist once he grows up." More recently, contemporary artists have drawn even more explicitly from the culture of children and adolescents. Jeff Koons became a pop art star creating metal artworks in the shape of blow-up carnival bunnies; Maurizio Cattelan created a mechanical boy on a Big Wheel to pedal around museum floors;

Takahi Murakami has sparked a global art phenomenon by creating cartoon statuary and toy-size fine art.

Art is not the only adult arena in which a childlike capacity for make-believe can be richly rewarding. Computer technology would seem at first to be best suited to hyperlogical grown-ups who keep their heads high above the mists of make-believe. That was the stereotype when computer science took off in the early 1970s: "Information architects" were characterized as men in crisp white lab coats, hardheaded engineers who dreamed in sequences of 0s and 1s. But that picture was quickly made obsolete by the ascendancy of thrill-seeking teen hackers and moguls like Bill Gates and Steve Jobs—boy-men whose successes stemmed more from their vision of the not-yet-realized than their mastery of the literal.

The experience of using a computer turns out to be about as close as you can get to recapturing what it's like to play make-believe as a child. We check our "desktop" for "files" and "viruses" and visit online "marketplaces" and "chat rooms," quickly forgetting (if it ever occurs to us at all) that there is no actual desktop, no actual file, no walls or doors. We are completely immersed, convinced of the reality of the metaphor. Far from being instruments of cold rationality, computers encourage us to see the abstract as concrete—perhaps one reason why the ranks of the rejuvenile are so heavy with the navigators of digital space. Witness the overlap between Web designers and fans of anime; between software engineers and toy collectors; between IT geeks and Pac-Man champions. Spend time with computer coders and you'll hear schoolyard slang, see junior high fashions, and observe workspaces decorated with gel-filled ant farms, bobbleheaded dolls, and other kiddie knickknacks. Amanda Cohen, the thirty-five-year-old face painter and temp office worker whose story I related in chapter 5, says that when she's sent to a new assignment, she can always tell who is most likely to share her love of "Weird Al" Yankovic and science fiction. "It's the IT guys, always," she says. "And I can always tell who they are immediately—they're the ones with the Slinkies on their desks."

These adults are often dismissed as escapists who'd rather bury their heads in the sugary sands of make-believe than face the scary uncertainties of the real world. To which they might reasonably respond: *What* real world? Hardheaded literal-mindedness may have been a sound strategy for success a hundred years ago, but it isn't much use in an age of e-mail, digital cash, virtual sex, and chaos theory. This point is well argued by Douglas Rushkoff, whose 1999 book *Playing the Future: What We Can Learn from Digital Kids* pointed out that the children of the Information Age offer adults a model for how to best adapt to a world of rapid, nearly incomprehensible change. In this view, peer-to-peer file sharing, video games, and techno-leaning kids' TV programs like *Teletubbies* and *Power Rangers*—which commonly elicit a dismissive shrug from elders—aren't indulgent entertainments so much as training grounds for an uncertain future:

> Looking at the world of children is not looking backward at our own past—it's looking ahead. They are our evolutionary future . . . So please let us suspend, for the time being, our grown-up function as role models and educators of our nation's youth. Rather than focusing on how we, as adults, should shape our children's activities for their better development, let's appreciate the natural adaptive skills demonstrated by our kids and look to them for answers to some of our own problems. Kids are our advance scouts. They are, already, the thing that we must become.

Rushkoff has it right. Traditions and institutions we saw as everlasting a generation ago—nuclear families, career paths, community structures—are now rapidly shifting, sometimes imploding. In such unstable, anxious times, it's easy to regard the current outbreak of childishness as a fearful retreat into a never-never land of false comfort and predictability. Perhaps the rejuvenile impulse isn't so much an escape mechanism as an adaptive strategy. It might well be that in the twenty-first century the wisest and most efficient people are the most rejuvenile.

Through the Looking Glass

Not all adults who keep alive a sense of make-believe are better off for it. Part of the process of growing up is shedding the comforting illusions and irrational fears of childhood. We stop worrying about the slithering beasts under the bed, grow suspicious of Dad's story about the stork and the new baby, and finally figure out why Santa's handwriting looks so similar to Mom's. As our rationality develops, we sour on the tooth fairy, reject the Easter Bunny, and stop dreaming of superheroes.

Shedding those illusions can be intensely bittersweet. As much as we understand the value of skepticism and crave objective answers, none of us wants to become chilly and soulless adults. We feel bad about rejecting the fantasies that so completely enchanted us as kids. And so we tear up when Peter Pan leads the world in a chant of "I do believe in fairies." We root for the warmhearted Kris Kringle over the cynical prosecutor in *Miracle on 34th Street*. And many of us simply clothe our childish fantasies in new, less overtly childish garb.

rejuvenile

We seek guidance from phone psychics, scour the heavens for UFOs, or pore over grainy photographs of the Loch Ness Monster. We devour books on Bible codes and the predictions of Nostradamus. We accept that Ronald Reagan consulted with astrologists, that Hillary Clinton had conversations with the ghost of Eleanor Roosevelt, that Mel Gibson was divinely instructed to make his proto-Catholic snuff film, *The Passion*.

Meanwhile true rationality is rarer than ever, cultivated by an elite of engineers and academics while the rest of us splash around in an ever-widening pool of mumbo-jumbo.

It all adds up to what British journalist Francis Wheen calls the "the counter-Enlightenment" and social critic Wendy Kaminer calls "the rise of irrationalism." Both authors identify religious and commercial forces as the source of this drift away from logic. But there's another, far more personal, force at work: our reluctance to give up the magical thinking of childhood.

This is most obviously seen in the arena of pop spirituality, which downplays the devotional demands of traditional religion in favor of simple wish fulfillment. Thus do the contemplative mysteries of the Christian tradition take wing as guardian angels, whose presence on earth is professed by 78 percent of Americans, according to a 2004 Gallup poll. Angels have the power to care for the sick, repel criminals, and even make automotive repairs, writes Billy Graham in his best-selling contribution to angel folklore, *Angels: God's Secret Agents*. In counterculture circles, so-called eco-pagans have embraced the existence of gnomes, trolls, and fairies, otherworldly creatures said to possess magical powers. "They were really sparkly inside," an English believer told the folklorist Andy Letcher about his encounter with a tribe of trolls. "They were just infinite space inside them and sparkling, but they were definitely totally loving, and totally dudes."

Believing in angels, fairies, or trolls in the face of all rational evidence might be crazy, but it's easy to understand—we want to be protected and guided, just as we were as kids. We want our wishes granted. The most successful pop mystics cater specifically to that desire, from pop medium James Van Praagh, who promises to deliver messages of reassurance from dead loved ones, to Deepak Chopra, whose *Seven Spiritual Laws of Success* promises to teach "the ability to create unlimited wealth with effortless ease." More benignly, there's "The Hugging Saint," a fifty-two-year-old mystic who travels to suburban hotels and meeting halls around the world, offering free hugs to all comers. A single embrace from this small, hirsute Indian is said to transmit love, understanding, and healing. It's everything a rejuvenile could hope for in a spiritual authority: echoes of maternal comfort, promises of instant improvement, and a complete lack of specifics.

More recently an even more overtly rejuvenile strain of magical thinking has produced a mystical presence known as the Indigo Child. Having previously written books on angels, channeling, and a magnetic energy force known as Kyron, authors Lee Carroll and Jan Tober turned their attention to children. In their 1999 book *The Indigo Children: The New Kids Have Arrived,* they proclaimed that 90 percent of all children now being born represent a more evolved, spiritual breed of human. These children are imbued with psychic and supernatural powers—evident by their eyes, which are said to be "large, penetrating and wise beyond their years." The discovery was soon followed by the announcement that another, even more enlightened breed of child had arrived on the earth: the Crystal Child. Parents who believe their kids qualify as Indigos or Crystals have happily embraced the dozens of books and websites that have since appeared on the phenomenon. They send their kids to special schools and camps and regale each other with tales of their child's divinity. Many of the Indigo kids themselves are only too happy to be cast as divine beings of the household. "I'm a sacred warrior," nine-year-old Elias Day Lavelle told a reporter in St. Catherines, Ontario. "I have the most powerful weapon in the world—love."

Believers in Indigo and Crystal Children fall into the same broad category as another constituency of fantasy-prone adults. I'm thinking here of the fantasy and sci-fi fans whose kidcentric fantasies have come to consume their adult lives. Most of these adults are harmless, intelligent sorts who maintain productive and meaningful lives outside their hobby. Others are just plain creepy.

Every summer, the far-out faithful flock to Comic-Con, a "pop culture media fan fest" that started as a trade show for the comic industry but has since became a sort of Super Bowl for extreme rejuveniles. There is nothing quite like the sight of eighty thousand über-nerds gathered in one place. Gray-haired autograph hounds slouch in T-shirts that announce "All I Need to Know I Learned from *Star Wars*." Pudgy women prance around in tutus and silver lamé wings. A division of storm troopers occupies a booth next to a club of Jedi warriors. Goths in pancake makeup and saucer-sized earlobe stretchers mill around booths selling black onesies printed with the slogan "My Mom Kicks Ass!" At a booth specializing in cutesy kid toys, a twenty-seven-year-old with bleached hair and chunky eyeglasses opens her shopping bag to reveal an assortment of My Little Pony dolls. "I used to have these as a girl," she says, stroking a rainbow-colored mane. "Collecting them makes me feel like I'm *still* a girl."

In line to meet the animators of a cartoon called *Teen Titans,* I meet a fifty-two-year-old self-described "superfan" lugging a rolling suitcase filled with camera equipment, toys, and photos. Charles Dunn is a seasoned veteran of events like this; he spends all his vacation time traveling to conventions devoted to comic books, *Star Trek,* and *Star Wars.* Despite his rich fantasy life, he says he fully understands the difference between make-believe and reality. The distinction is simple enough: Make-believe is what happens when he's off work, when he has time to look after his collection of action figures or work on his fan club newsletter. Reality kicks in on the job. And a stark reality it is, too: Dunn is a respiratory care practitioner. It's his job to maintain the life support systems at a county hospital. "The doctors and nurses think I'm crazy, but it doesn't bother me. I just do what I do," he says.

Scrunched against a wall of the arena-sized convention floor, I watch the parade go by with Mark Todd, a comic book artist who made the trip to San Diego with his mom and toddler daughter to sell a collection of his "minis," notepad-sized doodles of anguished teens, Pac-Man characters, and algebraic formulas. His work looks less like a typical comic book than the sketchpad of a kid from junior high. It's nonfiction in a world of deep fantasy, and it makes Todd feel alienated from most other convention-goers. "Being here mostly just makes me sad," he said. "You know that for a lot of people here, this is the only day of the year they can be themselves. People are so messed up that idolizing superheroes isn't enough—they have to *be* superheroes."

He's not kidding. Fifty feet away from us at the snack bar

there's a Captain America eating a turkey sandwich. But superheroes are actually a minority; much more with-it are the so-called Cosplayers, fans of Japanese anime, manga, and video games who dress up in elaborate homemade costumes of their favorite characters. They parade through the aisles in bright green wigs and platform shoes, posing for pictures and occasionally stopping for what's called a "glomp"—a tight hug in the style of a toddler grasping her mom's leg. Then there are the foxes and bunnies and pandas known as Furries, men and women whose fondness for a particular animal or animated character has evolved into a love of dressing up in (and occasionally have sex wearing) cartoon animal costumes.

As much as I'd like to leave the above parenthetical alone, I have a hard time casually glossing over mention of a subculture of people who enjoy having sex dressed as cartoon animals. And once I've mentioned Furries, I'm pretty much obligated to move on to the topic of Plushies, people whose intense-bordering-on-impure attachment to stuffed animals sometimes results in the creation of "strategically-placed-holes" or "strategically-placed-appendages" (known in Plushies circles by the helpful acronyms SPHs and SPAs). And once I've covered Plushies, it's only natural to discuss Adult Babies, those grown-ups who derive sexual pleasure from being swaddled in jumbo-sized diapers.

Here we've reached the furthest points of the rejuvenile universe, a place so far removed from a traditional understanding of adulthood that it is hard to know how any of it relates to the larger rejuvenile phenomenon. While they certainly meet the basic definition of the rejuvenile—that is, their tastes are traditionally associated with those younger than themselves—it's obvious that these proclivities aren't essentially kidcentric. Many Furries, for instance, believe that they are in fact animals trapped in the bodies of humans. Dressing up becomes a way to summon their animal natures. "A Furry typically thinks of himself (and let's face it, he's typically male) as though his 'real' self is an ocelot-centaur, or a silver-furred wolf, or what have you," says a software designer from Oregon who keeps tabs on the Furry community. "Some Furries talk about totem animals, or animal spirit guides, or being gazelles in previous lives. Some just sit around and wish with all their might that they had paws and a tail."

From this vantage point on the outer reaches of adult appreciation for children's playthings, it's easy to see sinister sexual subtext in all sorts of kiddie culture. Some of that subtext is right out in the open—from the tarting up of prepubescent girls in junior beauty pageants to the coquettish poses adopted by child stars as recent as the Olsen twins and as distant as Shirley Temple (of whom Graham Greene once remarked, "A fancy little piece . . . a complete totsy with a well-developed rump"). But while I'm as bothered as the next dad by the increasingly sexualized content of kid culture, it's clear that sex doesn't play much of a role in the motivations of the vast majority of rejuveniles. Yes, there are those who derive sexual pleasure from cartoon characters and stuffed animals—just as there are those aroused by shoes, chickens, and coughing.

So while the kinkily inclined have their fun, the rest of us rejuveniles are happy getting our kicks from cupcakes, circuses, and all our other mostly innocent enthusiasms. Sometimes a lollipop is just a lollipop.

rejuvenile

Into a Rejuvenile Future

But what, then, *are* our true motivations? What, in the deepest recesses of our hearts, has driven us to turn our backs on age norms that go back generations? The rejuveniles I've met in these pages have offered all sorts of answers—some are in it for the nostalgia, some for the kitsch, some for the therapeutic value, some to rebel against the perceived seriousness of tradition.

In the end, though, I don't think the rejuvenile impulse is ultimately rooted in any of those things. When you boil it down, I think we rejuveniles are attempting to hang on to the part of ourselves that feels most genuinely human. We believe that there is more value in what we came in with than what we are taught. We believe in play, in make-believe, in learning, in naps. And in a time of deep uncertainty, we trust that this deeper, more adaptable part of ourselves is our best tool of survival. This notion was nicely summed up by Diana Klitsch-Polansky, a twenty-five-year-old New Yorker who attends an "inner child playgroup" that meets for arts-and-crafts nights and outings to the circus and Chuck E. Cheese. She insists her pigtails, coloring books, and stuffed animals are signs of a basic philosophy: "No matter what the world throws at me and how many times people disappoint me, I continue to believe that people are good and reliable until they prove otherwise. Maybe that makes me gullible; maybe that makes me an optimist; or maybe it just makes me happy."

That basic notion is held by more than urban hipsters looking to justify their love of juvenile leisure. British child psychologist Oliver James argues that whole societies should join the rejuvenile quest to maintain the spontaneity and inventiveness of children. "I believe that creating the context in which these childlike attributes can flourish in adults should be the principal goal of politics; they are the cornerstone of well-being."

For all our posturing and consumerism, we rejuveniles are capital-R Romantics, the natural descendants of Rousseau and the nobleman described at the beginning of his *Émile,* who when asked by Louis XV whether he preferred the eighteenth century over the seventeenth, answered, "Sire, I spent my youth in reverence towards the old. I find myself compelled to spend my old age in reverence to the young."

All of which suggests that the answer to the question of whether rejuveniles represent a healthy step forward or a pitiful regression depends entirely on how we view human nature: On balance, are we born good or bad? This is of course a ridiculously reductive question, but that hasn't stopped people from aligning themselves on either side for centuries. Those who take the latter view include fundamentalist preachers, "parent-centered" childrearing experts, and the creators of *South Park*. Followers of this classically Protestant view hold that we are all problem children at birth; our only hope for civility and progress is through the careful, disciplined ministrations of adults.

Rejuveniles act out an opposite view, siding with Romantic poets, humanistic educators, and Disney myth-makers. For them, children are born with a capacity for wonder, curiosity, and understanding that is too often stripped away in the process commonly known as "growing up." In this view, the spirit of the child represents the best of humanity, an unquenchable optimism and energy that deserves respect and protection from adults.

This basic understanding has been shared by some of the great innovators and artists of our time. It's fun to imagine a

Rejuvenile Hall of Fame, with headquarters in Coney Island and exhibits honoring luminaries like Edward Lear, J. M. Barrie, Walt Disney, Ruth Handler, Theodore Geisel, and Albert Einstein. Every year the Hall might host an annual playdate-cum–award banquet in which honorees would be presented with a gilded spaldeen or a jewel-encrusted Magic Eight Ball. I herewith nominate the following for induction: physicist Richard Feynmann, the bongo-playing Nobel Prize winner who credited his most significant discoveries to a childlike impulse to question and play; comics Harpo Marx and Peter Sellers, who elevated childlike antics into high art; Apple founder Steve Jobs and master hacker Pekka Himanen, whose playful innovations revolutionized high tech; artists Takahi Murakami and Hayao Miyazaki, creators of museum-quality playthings and groundbreaking animated features; and anthropologist Ashley Montagu, whose study of the biological process of neotony led him to celebrate "the bountiful promise of the child."

The example of every one of these individuals has the power to radically alter our conception of maturity. They offer proof that an adult life can be both productive and spontaneous, effective and serendipitous, smart and silly. They pulled off the ultimate rejuvenile trick: They grew up without getting old.

This seems as good a goal as any to me. Not that I've resolved all those doubts of mine. I still get twitchy pondering the commercial forces at work in encouraging adults to think (and buy) like kids. I still feel vaguely guilty reading a graphic novel instead of a proper book. I still worry that I've missed out by never really learning about lawn care, fine wine, or mutual funds.

Still, I'm not about to renounce my rejuvenile tendencies. Not for me that secure, mahogany-paneled, adults-only comfort zone to which so many eighty-year-olds find themselves exiled. With luck, I'll be tooling around on a jet-powered scooter, sneaking comic books from my grandkids, and playing kickball and Frisbee Golf with a gang of rejuvenile cronies. To be sure, I hope I will have gained some wisdom and serenity along the way. But I can't help but conclude that the benefits promised by traditional adulthood pale in comparison to the pure energy and imaginative powers possessed by children. Their exuberant spirit is not something to outgrow—it's the best thing we have going.

notes

INTRODUCTION

page 3: Information about adult viewership of the Cartoon Network compared with ratings for cable news channels was provided by parent company Turner Broadcasting in interviews with author, August 2004.

page 3: The Walt Disney Company declined to discuss the age makeup of its park guests; I relied on Rita Aero's *Walt Disney World for Adults* (Fodor's Travel Publications, 1996) for attendance figures.

page 3: Demographic data on the age of first childbirth and average life spans is drawn from reports published by the U.S. Census Bureau, particularly "Statistical Abstract of the United States, 2004–2005." For data on changing divorce rates, see "Recent Trends: Population of Statistical Abstract of the United States," 1979, 1982, and 2004 editions.

page 5: Frank Furedi's diagnosis of "self-conscious regression" among rejuveniles is from his essay "The Children Who Won't

Grow Up," published in the online magazine Spiked (at spiked-online.com), July 2003. Furedi, a professor of sociology at the University of Kent, has become a go-to guy for journalists writing about immature adults; he's played the part of scholarly authority in stories published by the *Mirror* and the *Guardian* in the U.K. and the *Washington Times* and the *New York Times* in the U.S.

page 5: For more on kidcentric culture in Japan, I highly recommend British researcher Sharon Kinsella, who has written extensively on "kawaii," which roughly translates as "cute" or "adorable" and is used to explain the ubiquity of Hello Kitty, kiddie fashions, and childlike handwriting. For a list of publications, see her website www.kinsellaresearch.com.

page 6: The erosion of childhood has long been a favorite topic of social critics. Among the more popular works include Neil Postman's *The Disappearance of Childhood* (Delacorte Press, 1982) and David Elkin's *The Hurried Child* (Perseus Publishing, 1981). For a photographic treatment, see Lauren Greenfield's book *Fast Forward* (Alfred A. Knopf, 1997).

page 11: Art Spiegelman's comment about comics appealing to our "lizard brains" was made at a lecture entitled Comix 101 given at the University of California at Los Angeles.

page 11: Jake Austen's exhaustive appreciation of "rodent rock" and Alvin and the Chipmunks creator Ross Bagdasarian, "Mondo Chipmuk-o," was published in *Roctober* magazine, summer/fall 2001.

page 13: In addition to Frank Pittman's *Grow Up!: How Taking Responsibility Can Make You a Happy Adult* (Golden Books, 1998), other prescriptive manuals from the Harrumphing Codger school include Helen Kramer's *Liberating the Adult Within: Moving from Childish Responses to Authentic Adulthood* (Simon & Schuster, 1994), and Dan Kiley's *The Peter Pan Syndrome: Men Who Have Never Grown Up* (Dodd, Mead and Company, 1983).

ONE: ROOTS OF THE REJUVENILE

page 18: The story of J. M. Barrie and his ties to the Davies family is told through diary entries and correspondence in Andrew Birkin's book *J. M. Barrie and the Lost Boys: The Love Story That Gave Birth to*

Peter Pan (Clarkson N. Potter, 1979). See also Bruce Hanson's *The Peter Pan Chronicles* (Birch Lane Press, 1993). The 2004 film *Finding Neverland,* which starred Johnny Depp as Barrie, is a particularly unhelpful retelling, reshuffling and sanitizing some of the more unsympathetic aspects of Barrie's biography.

page 21: For more of Joseph Epstein's tirade against childish adults, see "The Perpetual Adolescent and the Triumph of Youth Culture," in the *Weekly Standard,* March 15, 2004.

page 21: My survey of the role of children in premodern history is based on Colin Heywood's *History of Childhood: Children and Childhood in the West from Medieval to Modern Times* (Pollity Press, 2001), Neil Postman's *The Disappearance of Childhood* (Delacorte Press, 1982), *Growing Up in Medieval London* by Barbara Hanawalt (Oxford University Press, 1993), and *A History of Young People in the West, Vol. 2: Stormy Evolution to Modern Times,* edited by Giovanni Levi and Jean-Claude Schmitt (Belknap Press of Harvard University Press, 1997).

page 24: For more on the connection between age norms and the Industrial Revolution, see Howard Chudacoff's brilliant survey *How Old Are You? Age Consciousness in American Culture* (Princeton University Press, 1989).

page 25: My detour into turn-of-the-century etiquette guides was inspired by my wife's collection of historic how-to manuals. Favorite titles include *Manners, Etiquette and Deportment* by John Young (The Lyons Press, reprint of original 1879 edition), *Book of Etiquette* by Lillian Eichler (Nelson Doubleday, 1921), and *What a Father Should Tell His Little Boy* by Isabelle Thompson Smart (The Bodmer Company, 1911). More highly amusing advice is retold in *Rudeness and Civility: Manners in Nineteenth Century Urban America* by John F. Kasson (Hill and Wang, 1990) and doled out in the amusing reprint of *Never Give a Lady a Restive Horse: A 19th Century Handbook of Etiquette* by Professor Thomas E. Hill (Diablo Press, 1967).

page 28: For more on Edward Lear, his biography and artwork, both silly and serious, see *Edward Lear: A Biography* by Peter Levi (Macmillan, 1995) and *Edward Lear: 1812–1888,* by Vivian Noakes (Royal Academy of Arts, 1985).

page 29: My take on Victorian-era children's authors was shaped by the following titles: *Three Centuries of Children's Books in Europe* by Bettina Hurlimann (World Publishing Company, 1968), *The Poetics of Childhood* by Roni Natov (Garland, 2002), *Through the Eyes of a Child: An Introduction to Children's Literature* by Donna E. Norton (Macmillan Publishing Company, 1991). Of particular help was Kenneth S. Lynn's blistering essay "Adulthood in American Literature," which appeared in the book *Adulthood*, edited by Erik Erikson (WW Norton & Company, 1978).

page 34: Two books were particularly helpful in tracing the emerging market for products created specifically for kids: Stephen Kline's *Out of the Garden: Toys, TV, and Children's Culture in the Age of Marketing* (Verso, 1995), and *Panati's Parade of Fads, Follies and Manias*, by Charles Panati (HarperCollins, 1991).

page 37: Many books have been written about the history of comics; I relied on *The Comics: An Illustrated History of Comic Strip Art* by Jerry Robinson (G.P. Putnam's Sons, 1974) and *Children of the Yellow Kid: The Evolution of the American Comic Strip*, by Robert C. Harvey (Frye Art Museum, 1998).

page 38: The extraordinary biography of amusement entrepreneur Fred Thompson is told in *The Kid of Coney Island: Fred Thompson and the Rise of American Amusements* by Woody Register (Oxford University Press, 2001). On Coney Island and the early evolution of amusement parks, see *Amusing the Million: Coney Island at the Turn of the Century* by John F. Kasson (Collins Publishers, 1978).

page 39: For more on the 1893 Columbian International Exposition, see Robert Muccigrosso's *Celebrating the New World: Chicago's Columbian Exposition of 1893* (Ivan R. Dee Publisher, 1993), Norman Bolotin and Christine Laing's *The World's Columbian Exposition: The Chicago World's Fair of 1893* (University of Illinois Press, 2002), and Erik Larson's *The Devil in the White City: Murder Magic and Madness at the Fair That Changed America* (Crown, 2003).

page 42: For more on Jane Addams, Joseph Lee, and other turn-of-the-century advocates for children, see James Weber Linn and Anne Firor Scott's *Jane Addams: A Biography* (University of Illinois Press, 2000), Gioia Dilberto's *A Useful Woman: The Early Life of Jane Addams* (Scribner, 1999), Tim Jeal's *The Boy-Man: The Life of Lord*

Baden Powell (William Morrow, 1990), Joseph Lee's *Play in Education* (Macmillan, 1916), and Catherine Reef's *Childhood in America: An Eyewitness History* (Facts on File, 2002).

TWO: THE REJUVENILE AT PLAY

page 50: The sampling of childhood games enjoying a resurgence among adults is drawn from several newspaper and magazine accounts, among them: James A. Fussell, "Adults Rediscover Playful Pasts with Retro Games," Knight Ridder Newspapers, December 7, 2003; Alison Ross, "Carolina Four Square Brings Back Good, Old-Fashioned Fun," *Daily Tar Heel,* University of North Carolina, February 5, 2003; Warren St. John, "Quick, After Him: Pac-Man Went Thataway," *New York Times,* May 9, 2004; Janelle Brown, "Wham! Dodgeball Grows Up, Sort Of," *New York Times,* March 12, 2004; and Lauren Lipton, "Nightlife, with Nighties," *Wall Street Journal,* January 9, 2004. The extraordinary story of how Japanese executives used Rock Paper Scissors to decide which rival auction house would sell its art collection is told in Carol Vogel's "Rock, Paper, Payoff: Child's Play Wins Auction House in Art Sale," *New York Times,* April 29, 2005.

page 59: The meaning and function of play is explored in Brian Sutton-Smith's wonderful *The Ambiguity of Play* (Harvard University Press, 1997). See also Erik Erikson's *Toys and Reasons: Stages in the Ritualization of Experience* (WW Norton & Company, 1977) and, most famously, J. Huizinga's *Homo Ludens: A Study of the Play-Element in Culture* (The Beacon Press, 1944). See also Paul Robert, "Goofing Off," *Psychology Today,* July–August 1995.

page 66: For more on the playful work ethic of the dot-com era, see Amanda Paulson, "Fun at the Firm: The Role of Play at Work," *Christian Science Monitor,* December 17, 2001; Cheryl Dahle, "Mind Games," *Fast Company,* January 2000. *Inc* magazine profiled Richard Tuck in October 1998.

page 70: The essay on the glories of Pop-A-Shot appears in Sarah Vowell's *The Partly Cloudy Patriot* (Simon & Schuster, 2002).

page 71: Bernie DeKoven has written several terrific books on the value of playfulness, notably *The Well-Played Game: A Playful Path to Wholeness* (Writers Club Press, 2002). He also regularly updates a weblog on the topic: www.deepfun.com.

page 80: Essays by Rob Reiner and Hillary Clinton on the joys of childhood play appear in *The Games We Played: A Celebration of Childhood and Imagination* (Simon & Schuster, 2001).

page 91: Assessments of financial expenditures on recreation and leisure are reported by the Bureau of Economic Analysis, a division of the U.S. Department of Commerce. See also Barbara Wexler's *Recreation: Having a Good Time in America* (Information Plus, June 2003).

page 91: On the division between time spent at leisure and work, see Juliet Schor's *The Overworked American: The Unexpected Decline of Leisure* (Harvard University Press, 1991); Edward Vacek, "Never on Sundays: Whatever Happened to Leisure?" *Commonweal,* February 11, 1994; Gwen Gordon, "Letting Leisure Get Away," Knight Ridder Newspapers, July 21, 1995. For an excellent overview of how leisure time has changed over the past century, see Witold Rybczynski's *Waiting for the Weekend* (Penguin Books, 1991).

THREE: THE LURE OF THE TOY

page 96: On John Darcy Noble, see his *Selected Writings of John Darcy Noble: Favorite Articles from Dolls Magazine* (Portfolio Press, 1999) and *Rare and Lovely Dolls: Two Centuries of Beautiful Dolls* (Holby House Press, 2000).

page 100: The anecdote about K'Nex enthusiast David Brooks is by Stephanie K. Taylor, "Delaying Adulthood," the *Washington Times,* August 15, 2003.

page 101: Data on toy sales is from the NPD Group, a privately operated market and sales information agency. Statistic on toy sales in America relative to population comes from Katy Kelly and Linda Kulman, "Kid Power," *U.S. News & World Report,* September 13, 2004.

page 101: For more on the "age compression" phenomenon in the toy industry, see Michael Marriott, "Gadget or Plaything? Let a Child Decide," *New York Times,* February 17, 2005; Fern Shen,

"Barbie, Bratz and Age Compression," the *Washington Post,* February 17, 2002; and Juliet Schor's *The Commercialized Child and the New Consumer Culture* (Scribner, 2004).

page 101: Examples of toys sold in nontraditional outlets taken from Pamela Brill, "No Stone Unturned: Toys Expanding Into New Retail Terrain," *Playthings* magazine, March 1, 2004.

page 103: The Internet abounds with resources for AFOL; a good place to start is www.lugnet.com, a fan-run site that includes links to convention information, parts databases, and links to sites dedicated to Lego space stations, trains, and castles. Also see the website www.brickfilms.com, a gathering place for fans who make Lego stop-motion movies.

page 104: The synopsis of the history of toys was drawn from Gary Cross's engrossing *Kids' Stuff: Toys and the Changing World of American Childhood* (Harvard University Press, 1997) and Antonia Fraser's *A History of Toys* (Delacorte Press, 1966). See also Marvin Kaye's *A Toy Is Born* (Stein and Day, 1973).

page 108: On paper dolls and their use among nineteenth-century adults, see Miriam Formanek-Brunell's *Made to Play House: Dolls and Commercialization of American Girlhood 1830–1930* (Johns Hopkins University Press, 1993).

page 109: Columns by Doll Lady doyenne Denise Van Patten are archived at www.dollymaker.com. Her column on misconceptions about doll collectors appeared on the website www.about.com.

page 111: On the success of the Disney princess line, see Laura M. Holson, "A Finishing School for All, Disney Style," *New York Times,* October 4, 2004; Christopher Healy, "A Nation of Little Princesses," Salon.com, November 24, 2004; Mary McNamara, "A Royal Gain," *Los Angeles Times,* August 17, 2004.

page 112: The origin and ascendance of Barbie is told in *Dream Doll: The Ruth Handler Story* by Ruth Handler and Jacqueline Shannon (Longmeadow Press, 1995). Another perspective is offered by M. G. Lord in *Forever Barbie: The Unauthorized Biography of a Real Doll* (William & Morrow Company, 1994). For more on Barbie's popularity among adult collectors, see Elizabeth Stephenson, "Mattel Dolls Up Barbie for Adult Collectors," *Advertising Age,* October 9, 1995.

page 115: On the sale of the $70,000 Beach Bomb and the adult market for Hot Wheels, see John O'Dell, "Toy Cars for Adult Budgets," *Los Angeles Times,* December 18, 2003. For more on action-figure superstar Todd McFarlane, see Bruce Handy, "Small Is Beautiful," *Vanity Fair,* December 2003.

page 118: My account of the popularity of characters like the Care Bears, Teenage Mutant Ninja Turtles, and Strawberry Shortcake among Gen X parents is based on interviews with Holli Hoffman, marketing manager at Bandai America; Sara Rosales, vice president of public relations at Mattel Brands; and Debra Joester, president of the Joester/Loria Group.

page 123: On the aesthetics of mass market design, see Virginia Postrel's *The Substance of Style: How the Rise of Aesthetic Value Is Remaking Commerce, Culture, and Consciousness* (HarperCollins, 2003).

page 125: Among the automotive writers who have extolled the childlike nature of the Hummer are Glen Woodcock, "The Biggest Toy in the Sandbox: 2005 Hummer H2," *Toronto Sun,* November 21, 2004; and Tom Teepen, "SUV Lunacy Continues to Hum Along on Nation's Roads," *Ventura County Star,* December 23, 2002.

page 128: On Apple's role in creating the graphical user interface, see Bruce Horn's "On Xerox, Apple and Progress," published on Apple History website, www.applehistory.glen.nu/?page=gui_horn1.

FOUR: UNCLE WALT AND THE ADULT PLAYGROUND

page 132: Statistics on travel to Orlando are drawn from Carl Hiassen's *Team Rodent: How Disney Devours the World* (Ballantine, 1998). Data also available in annual American Society of Travel Agent/Fodor's Summer/Winter Hot Spots Surveys, 2003/2004.

page 133: Disney's 1948 memo on "Mickey Mouse Park" is excerpted in Michael Broggie's *Walt Disney's Railroad Story: The Small-Scale Fascination That Led to a Full-Scale Kingdom* (Pentrex, 1997). On Disney's Griffith Park Credo, see Kevin Yee and Jason Schultz, *101 Things You Never Knew About Disneyland: An Unauthorized Look at the Little Touches and Inside Jokes* (Zauberreich, 2005).

page 134: On attendance at U.S. amusement parks, see projections by Christine Blank, "Parking It for Fun," *American Demographics,*

April 1998; Paula Szuchman, "Theme Parks Lower the Thrill Factor," *Wall Street Journal,* August 15, 2003.

page 134: The Disney World guidebooks for adults are Rita Aero's *Walt Disney World for Adults: The Original Guide for Grown-Ups* (Fodor's Travel Publications, 1996) and *Birnbaum's Walt Disney World Without Kids 2005: Expert Advice for Fun-Loving Adults* (Birnbaum, 2005).

page 135: Six Flags's "brand character" Mr. Six was unveiled in a March 19, 2004, press release distributed by PR Newswire.

page 135: American Coaster Enthusiasts maintains a comprehensive website at www.aceonline.org.

page 136: Gary and Anita Schaengold are officers in the National Fantasy Fan Club (NFFC), a nonprofit organization "committed to preserving and sharing the rich legacy of Walt Disney." Their website is www.nffc.org.

page 141: For more on Disnoids, see fascinating account by Adam Davidson, "Keepers of the Magic Kingdom," *L.A. Weekly,* September 5, 2003. For an astounding collection of Disney "paper ephemera," see the Disney Paper Resource center at www.mattlori.ca/themepark/index.htm.

page 144: My summary of Walt Disney's biography is drawn from several sources: Richard Schickel, *The Disney Version* (Simon & Schuster, 1968); Leonard Mosley, *Disney's World* (Stein and Day, 1985); Katherine and Richard Greene, *The Man Behind the Magic* (Viking Books, 1998); David Koenig, *Mouse Tales: A Behind-the-Ears Look at Disneyland* (Bona Venture Press, 1995); and Marc Eliot, *Walt Disney: Hollywood's Dark Prince* (Birch Lane Press, 1993).

page 146: Observations of Margaret King were drawn from interviews and "The Theme Park: Aspects of Experience in a Four-Dimensional Landscape," *Journal of the Pioneer America Society,* Fall 2002.

page 147: For more on Neverland Ranch and Michael Jackson, see Dan Glaister, "A Surreal World: Behind the Façade of Neverland," *Guardian* (U.K.), June 14, 2005; Paul Farhi, "Kingdom of Pop: At Neverland Ranch, Light and Shadow Play All Day," *Washington Post,* May 22, 2005. Filmmaker Brett Ratner's Q&A with Michael Jackson appeared in the February 1, 2004, issue of *Interview.*

page 150: On Disney's role in the invention of the "high-end Saturday matinee for grown ups," see Kurt Andersen, "Kids Are Us: These Days Behaving Like a Grown Up Is Child's Play," *New Yorker,* December 15, 1997.

page 151: On faltering attendance and changes at Disney's California Adventure, see Kimi Yoshino, "Disney Pins Theme Park Hopes on Tower of Terror," *Los Angeles Times,* May 2, 2004.

page 153: For an updated list of the top-grossing movies of all time, see the website Box Office Guru, www.boxofficeguru.com/blockbusters.htm.

page 153: On Bart Simpson's place on a list of twentieth-century icons, see Andrew Pulver, "What's All The Fuss About Bart Simpson," the *Guardian* (U.K.), March 31, 2000.

FIVE: BOOMERANGERS, TWIXTERS, AND PANIC OVER GROWN-UP KIDS

page 156: Data on average age of marriage and average age of first childbirth is drawn from the U.S. Census. Higher-than-average age of marriage and childbirth among New Yorkers reported by Vanessa Grigoriadis, "Smiling Through the 30s, a Birthday Once Apocalyptic," *New York Times,* July 20, 2003.

page 157: Comparative data on average life spans is drawn from the U.S. Census—which reports that the average U.S. life span in 1850 was 40 years of age. See also "Ten Great Public Health Achievements, United States, 1900–1999," *Morbidity and Mortality Weekly Report,* Centers for Disease Control, April 2, 1999.

page 157: On increased mobility of Americans, see U.S. Census report "Journey-to-Work and Migration Statistics," January 2001.

page 157: On fluctuations in the roles of young adults, see Jeffrey Arnett and Susan Taber, "Adolescence Terminable and Interminable: When Does Adolescence End?" *Journal of Youth and Adolescence,* vol. 23, no. 5, 1994.

page 158: For more on movement against "the tyranny of coupledom," see Sasha Cagen's *Quirkyalone: A Manifesto for Uncompromising Romantics* (HarperSanFrancisco, 2004).

page 159: Gail Sheehy coined the term "provisional adulthood" in

New Passages: Mapping Your Life Across Time (Random House, 1995); Jeffrey Arnett proposed "emerging adulthood" in *Emerging Adulthood: The Winding Road from the Late Teens Through the Twenties* (Oxford University Press, 2004); "back-to-bedroom" and other Faith Popcorn buzzwords are collected in *Dictionary of the Future: The Words, Terms and Trends That Define the Way We'll Live, Work and Talk* (Hyperion, 2001).

page 159: Susan Littwin was among the first to tackle the topic of adults drifting home in *The Postponed Generation: Why America's Grown-Up Kids Are Growing Up Later* (William Morrow and Company, 1986).

page 160: For more on the Twixter phenomenon and response among conservative critics, see Lev Grossman, "Grow Up? Not So Fast," *Time,* January 24, 2005; Betsy Hart, "Forever Teens," Scripps Howard News Service, May 21, 2004; Kay R. Daly, "It's a Matter of Parenting: The Twixters," www.gopusa.com, January 18, 2005.

page 166: The study on adult children living at home is from Barbara Mitchell and Ellen Gee, " 'Boomerang Kids' and Midlife Parental Marital Satisfaction," *Family Relations,* 1996. Similar results were reported by University at Albany, State University of New York sociologists Russell Ward and Glenna Spitze, "Marital Implications of Parent-Adult Child Coresidence: A Longitudinal View," *Journal of Marriage and the Family,* 1996. They concluded that "there are no effects of moves in or out on the marital happiness of parents or the number of marital disagreements they have."

page 171: Among the most comprehensive studies on adulthood is John Modell's *Into One's Own: From Youth to Adulthood in the United States 1920–1975* (University of California Press, 1989).

page 173: For more on transitions to adulthood in non-Western societies, see Frank Furstenberg (editor), "Early Adulthood in Cross-National Perspective," *The Annals of the American Academy of Political and Social Science,* Sage Publications, March 2002.

SIX: PLAYALONG PARENTS AND THE PROUDLY CHILDFREE

page 187: Passages from advice manuals written for young people considering family life were drawn from Michael Pennetti's *Coping with School Age Fatherhood* (The Rosen Publishing Group, 1987) and Dick Clark's *Your Happiest Years* (Rosho Corporation, 1959).

page 190: For more on the spiritual benefits of parent-child play, see Cary Thomas's *Sacred Parenting: How Raising Children Shapes Our Souls* (Zondervan, 2004) and Myla Kabat-Zinn and Jon Kabat-Zinn's *Everyday Blessings: The Inner Work of Mindful Parenting* (Hyperion, 1997).

page 191: Pat Kane has written widely on the value of play, most thoroughly in his wonderful book *The Play Ethic: A Manifesto for a Different Way of Living* (Macmillan, 2004). He also maintains a weblog devoted to the topic at www.theplayethic.typepad.com/play_journal.

page 192: For a complete guide to Gymboree games and activities, see Wendy S. Masi, Roni Leiderman (editors), *Baby Play* (Weldon Owen Publishing, 2001). Journalist Andrew Santella contributed a highly amusing account of his own Playalong Parent tendencies in "Game Dad," *GQ*, July 2004.

page 194: Adam Gopnik's account of his family's resistance to (and eventual acceptance of) the purple dinosaur Barney is included in *From Paris to the Moon* (Random House, 2000).

page 195: For an excellent overview of the conflict between "hard" and "soft" childrearing advisors, see Ann Hulbert's *Raising America: Experts, Parents and a Century of Advice About Children* (Alfred A. Knopf, 2003).

page 195: My sampling of "hard" childrearing manuals included Perry Buffington's *Cheap Psychological Tricks for Parents: 62 Sure-Fire Secrets and Solutions for Successful Parenting* (Peachtree Publishers, 2003), H. Jackson Brown's *A Father's Book of Wisdom* (Rutledge Hill Press, 1991), John and Linda Friel's *The Seven Worst Things Parents Do* (Health Communications, 1999). For more on John Rosemond's Affirmative Parenting and *Traditional Family* magazine, see his website at www.rosemond.com.

page 197: My sampling of "soft" childrearing manuals included Martha Sears and William Sears's *The Successful Child: What Parents Can Do to Help Kids Turn Out Well* (Little, Brown and Company, 2002), Stanley Greenspan and Jacqueline Salmon's *Playground Politics: Understanding the Emotional Life of Your School-Age Child* (Perseus

Books, 1993), and William Crain's *Reclaiming Childhood: Letting Children Be Children in Our Achievement-Oriented Society* (Times Books, 2003).

page 199: Barbara Odanaka maintains a website for the International Society of Skateboard Moms at www.skateboardmom.homestead.com/skateboardmomsclub.html.

page 205: On differences between Gen X and Boomer parents, including a discussion of the Reach Advisors study on time spent with kids, see Ann Hulbert, "Look Who's Parenting," *New York Times Magazine,* July 4, 2004.

page 207: *South Park* creators Trey Parker and Matt Stone made their comments about the "philosophical underpinnings" of the program on the Oct. 13, 2004, edition of *60 Minutes.*

page 211: On the "blizzard" of modern media and how it influences our ideas about childhood and adulthood, I am indebted to Thomas de Zengotita's dazzling *Mediated: How the Media Shapes Your World and the Way You Live in It* (Bloomsbury, 2005).

page 212: For more on Belinda Miller and Hova Najarian's fantastic radio program, *Greasy Kid Stuff,* see www.wfmu.org/gks.

page 213: Jake Austen's various projects, including his local-access TV program *Chic-a-Go-Go,* his magazine *Roctober,* and his band the Goblins are detailed on his website, www.roctober.com.

page 216: Figures on the percentage of women without children were drawn from U.S. Census Bureau and Amara Bachu, "Fertility of American Women," *Current Population Reports,* June 1995.

page 216: For more on the childfree movement, see Patricia Lunneborg's *The Chosen Lives of Childfree Men* (Bergin & Garvey, 1999), Madelyn Cain's *The Childless Revolution: What It Means to Be Childless Today* (Perseus Books Group, 2002). Many childfree adults gather on the newsgroup alt.support.childfree.

page 218: Enthusiasm for classic arcade games is playfully and graphically covered in John Sellers's *Arcade Fever: The Fan's Guide to the Golden Age of Video Games* (Running Press, 2001).

263

SEVEN: THE REJUVENILE GROWN UP

page 223: Children "trail clouds of glory" in William Wordsworth's poem "Intimations of Immortality from Recollections of Early Childhood." Wisdom is found "in the sand box" in Robert Fulghum's *All I Really Need To Know I Learned In Kindergarten* (Ballantine Books, 1988).

page 224: Gail Sheehy made her remarks about "penalties" for avoiding milestones of maturity in "Are You a Grown Up Yet? Do You Know Anyone Who Is?" *Utne Reader,* July–August, 2004.

page 224: Culture writer Choire Sicha's commentary on The Langley School Music Project appeared as part of a discussion of children's music published in the online magazine www.themorningnews.org on March 3, 2004.

page 226: For more on brain activities in babies, see Alison Gopnik, Andrew Meltzoff, Patricia Kuhl, *The Scientist in the Crib: Minds, Brains and How Children Learn* (William Morrow & Company, 1999). Steve Jurvetson extrapolated on those findings on his weblog at www.jurvetson.blogspot.com.

page 227: The Albert Einstein quote about "the normal adult" appeared in his obituary, *New York Times,* April 19, 1955. Isaac Newton's oft-quoted characterization of himself as a "boy playing on the seashore" was published in David Brewster's *Memoirs of the Life, Writings and Discoveries of Sir Isaac Newton* (Thomas Constable, 1855).

page 230: For more on "downward aspiration" among Boomer consumers, see "Love Those Boomers," *BusinessWeek,* October 14, 2005. Among the first marketers to describe what they called "Peterpandemonium" were Becky Ebenkamp at *Brandweek* magazine and Jeff Odiorne, then a partner at the San Francisco agency Odiorne Wilde Narraway & Partners.

page 232: My sampling of business books that emphasize the importance of immediate gratification included Bob Davis's *Speed Is Life: Street-Smart Lessons from the Front Lines of Business* (Currency, 2001), Jason Jennings and Laurence Haughton's *It's Not the Big That Eat the Small . . . It's the Fast That Eat the Slow: How to Use Speed as a Competitive Tool in Business* (Diane Pub Co, 2000), and Bill Gates's *Busi-*

ness @ the Speed of Thought: Using a Digital Nervous System (Warner Books, 1999).

page 233: On books that promise to make quick work of parenting, see Geoffrey Kloske's *Once Upon a Time, The End (Asleep in 60 Seconds)* (Atheneum/Anne Schwartz Books, 2005) and Spencer Johnson's *One Minute Parenting* (Wings Books, 1993).

page 234: For more on childish adults, see Pauline Wallin's *Taming Your Inner Brat* (Beyond Words Publishing, 2001). Her compendium of "brats in the news" is updated online at www.drwallin.com/news.shtml.

page 235: Dorothy and Jerome Singer have written extensively on the imaginative capacities of children, notably in *The House of Make-Believe: Children's Play and the Developing Imagination* (Harvard University Press, 1990).

page 238: The excerpt from Douglas Rushkoff was taken from *Playing the Future: What We Can Learn from Digital Kids* (Riverhead, 1999). Rushkoff goes into more detail on how high technology has shaped our perceptions and imaginations in *Media Virus!* (Ballantine Books, 1996). He also keeps a terrific weblog at www.rushkoff.com/blog.html.

page 240: For more on angels, see Billy Graham's *Angels: God's Secret Agents* (Pocket, 1978) and a January 2002 poll conducted by Scripps Howard News Service and the E. W. Scripps School of Journalism at Ohio State University, which found that belief in angels "cuts across almost all ranges of education, income and lifestyle."

page 241: On belief in fairies among so-called eco-pagans, see "The Scouring of the Shire: Fairies, Trolls and Pixies in Eco-Protest Culture," *Folklore,* October 2001.

page 241: On Amma, "the hugging Saint," see Charles Haviland, "Embraced by India's Hugging Saint," BBC News, September 26, 2003.

page 241: For more on Indigo and Crystal Children, see Lee Carroll and Jan Tober's *The Indigo Children: The New Kids Have Arrived* (Hay House, 1999), Doreen Virtue's *The Care and Feeding of Indigo Children* (Hay House, 2001), and Dylan Otto Krider, "Alien-ated Youth," *Houston Press,* December 19, 2002. The Rainbow Kids

School in San Diego, California, offers a program specifically designed for Indigo Children; as does the summer camp Camp Indigo in Coeur d'Alene, Idaho.

page 244: For more on Plushies, Furries, and Adult Babies, see
George Gurley, "Pleasures of the Fur," *Vanity Fair,* March 2001,
and Peter Gilstrap, "The Diapers, They Are A-Changin'," *New
Times Los Angeles,* March 7–11, 1999. For a (deeply disturbing)
look at the Adult Baby subculture, see the Diaper Pail Friends website, www.dpf.com.

page 246: Diana Klitsch-Polansky is a member of the New York City
Inner Child Playgroup, which maintains a schedule of upcoming
activities at www.innerchildplaygroup.tripod.com.

page 246: Oliver James's comments about childlike attributes being
the "cornerstone of well-being" appeared in "Directions Home,"
the *Observer* (U.K.), October 16, 2005.

page 248: Ashley Montagu's *Growing Young* (McGraw-Hill Book
Company, 1981) might be as close to a rejuvenile Bible as one is
likely to find. In his survey of the evolutionary process known as
neotony, Montagu makes a convincing case that "the truth about
the human species is that in body, spirit, feeling, and conduct we are
designed to grow and develop in ways that maximize childlike
traits."

acknowledgments

I blame the minivan. Three years ago, after the birth of my second child, it became clear that the time had come to trade my single-guy car—an aerodynamic, two-door Saab 900—for a boxy minivan with dual-side airbags and about three dozen cup holders. As I took a long hard look at my new family wagon, it dawned on me that what the dealer called granite green looked an awful lot like tombstone gray.

Life as I knew it was over. I had only the vaguest notion of what came next, but I feared it involved a lot more History Channel, Home Depot, and Ben-Gay. I felt myself getting crankier and more ossified by the day.

There was just one problem: I wasn't ready to ossify. I

spent the next few weeks searching for a custom shop that would paint yellow and turquoise racing stripes from one bumper to the other. I knew it was silly, but I didn't care—all my anxiety vanished the moment I imagined a stranger mistaking my minivan for a Hot Wheel that had been miraculously enlarged to life size.

So I suppose my first thanks should go to the makers of the Honda Odyssey, an automobile with the power to prompt a rejuvenile reckoning. More sincere thanks go to my loved ones for being so tolerant of my foolishness. First and foremost, thanks go to my wife, Jenji, for indulging my odd enthusiasms and sharing so many of her own (among them Victorian etiquette guides, Golden Books, and sad-clown paintings). I am also deeply indebted to my father, Nicolas Noxon, for acting as an unpaid research assistant, strike-force fact finder, and all-around devil's advocate. I count it as an act of God that his retirement from National Geographic Television miraculously coincided with my beginning this book. My mother, Mary Worthington, also contributed invaluable guidance and encouraging words in my most despairing moments. Thanks also go to my sister Marti for all the love and cheerleading and to my brother-in-law Frank Still for sharing inside dope on old-school skateboarding. Thanks also to my other parents, Pam Gruber and Nicky Noxon, Buz Kohan and Rhea Kohan, and my extended circle of siblings: David and Jono Kohan, Megan and Rob Duncan, Traci Still and Jeff Bynum.

My friend Liza Cardinale deserves credit for leading me to crack research assistant Karen Ahn, who acted as gumshoe guardian angel to plug holes, confirm statistics, and untangle knotty bits of prose. She was helped in statistical duties by Allan Schenkel, reference librarian with the U.S. Census Bureau. A long list of other friends and family gave thoughtful and thorough notes—Morgan Neville, Bob Schmidt, Sue Carpenter, Doug Wilson, Gideon Brower, Natalie Kurlander, John Straley, Mitch Kamin, Matthew Cavanaugh, Arthur Spiegelman, and, perhaps most of all, Michele Raphael, whose meticulous edit saved me from many an error. I turned to the work of Pat Kane, Bernie DeKoven, William Crain, Douglas Rushkoff, and Thomas De Zengotita for doses of inspiration. Thanks to Danielle Mattoon and Trip Gabriel at the *New York Times,* who commissioned and edited my first story on rejuveniles; thanks also to the *Times*'s Ariel Kaminer, Jodi Kantor, Paul Tough, and Frank Rich. Special mention must also be made of Michael Cieply, who for no reason I have yet managed to fathom has acted as mentor and trusted advisor in my adventures as a freelancer.

My most heartfelt thanks go to my agent and editor. Betsy Amster helped shape my original idea, brought focus to early drafts, and acted as faithful reader and taskmaster during the long slog of composition. My editor at Crown, Rachel Klayman, went above and beyond in challenging assumptions, strengthening arguments, and helping me to avoid embarrassing affronts to grammar and style. All first-time authors should be so blessed to have such a brilliant pair in their corner. Thank you.

index

about the author

CHRISTOPHER NOXON has worked as a costumed character at Universal Studios, a speechwriter for Michael Milken, and a music supervisor for the television series *Weeds*. He has also written for *The New York Times Magazine, Los Angeles Magazine,* and *Salon*. He lives with his wife and three children in Los Angeles.